# HERITAGE

## Civilization and the Jews

*Study Guide*

# HERITAGE

## Civilization and the Jews

## *Study Guide*

### William W. Hallo
### David B. Ruderman
### Michael Stanislawski

edited by
**Benjamin R. Gampel**

Heritage Academic Development Team
Timothy Gunn, Project Director
Robert A. Miller, Project Coordinator

PRAEGER SPECIAL STUDIES • PRAEGER SCIENTIFIC

New York • Philadelphia • Eastbourne, UK
Toronto • Hong Kong • Tokyo • Sydney

Library of Congress Cataloging in Publication Data

Hallo, William W.
    Heritage : civilization and the Jews : study guide.

    Text element for a telecourse assembled by the
Public Broadcasting Service (PBS).
    Bibliography: p.
    Includes index.
    1. Jews—History.    2. Judaism—History.
I. Ruderman, David B.    II. Stanislawski, Michael,
1952–        III. Gampel, Benjamin R.    IV. Title.
DS118.H26  1984      909'.04924      84-15013
ISBN 0-03-000484-5 (alk. paper)
ISBN 0-03-000483-7 (pbk. : alk. paper)
ISBN 0-03-01472-7 (faculty manual)

All maps in this book have been reprinted with permission of
Macmillan Publishing Company from *Jewish People, Jewish Thought*
by Robert M. Selzer. Copyright © 1980 by Macmillan Publishing Co., Inc.

Chart 1 and 2 have been reprinted from *Encyclopaedia Judaica*, Vol. 5, p. 1501;
Vol. 13, pp. 889–92, 894–96. With permission from Keter Publishing House
Jerusalem Ltd.

Published in 1984 by Praeger Publishers
CBS Educational and Professional Publishing
a Division of CBS Inc.
521 Fifth Avenue, New York, NY 10175 USA

456789 052 987654321

Printed in the United States of America
on acid-free paper

# To the Student

## Benjamin R. Gampel

Welcome to *Heritage: Civilization and the Jews*, one of the most ambitious telecourses ever developed in the field of the humanities. Public Broadcasting Service is gratified to present this multi-media introduction to the glories of Jewish history and culture.

The Jews are an ancient people, having lived over three thousand years in many countries and among myriad civilizations. The expertise necessary to recount their story, and quite a story it is, requires the efforts of great thinkers and scholars.

These PBS has assembled in a telecourse containing three integral elements: the television series, *Study Guide*, and *Source Reader*. The course is divided into nine units and the *Study Guide* will serve to coordinate all the component parts. To gain the maximum benefit from the telecourse, you should proceed as follows.

Before viewing each television program, turn to the correspondingly numbered chapter in the *Study Guide*. Read the section "Before Viewing the Show." It contains a helpful overview of the program and notes the items you should look for while watching the show. After viewing, read "While Reading the *Study Guide* and *Source Reader*" also in the *Study Guide*. The issues presented there will help focus your attention on the most important points to be learned from the two books. Each *Study Guide* chapter contains references to the relevant *Source Reader* selections. You can choose to read the two books together or you might read the *Study Guide* chapter and then look through the *Source Reader* using the *Study Guide* for points of reference.

After you have seen the program and read the related chapters, make sure you can answer the questions in the "After Viewing and Reading" section at the end of the *Study Guide* chapter. If you can, you may be confident that you have been successful in digesting all the materials contained in this unit. You will repeat the same procedures for the other units.

You are now embarking on an exciting overview of the interrelationship of Jewish history and world civilization. When you have finished the course, you will have gained important insights into the development of Jewish culture throughout the ages.

# Contents

TO THE STUDENT    by *Benjamin R. Gampel*      v
MAPS AND CHARTS      xi
PREFACE    by *William W. Hallo*      xiii

**1   A People Is Born**      1
by *William W. Hallo*

    Before Viewing the Show   1
    While Reading the *Study Guide* and *Source Reader*   3
    The Protohistory of Israel   4
    Primeval History   6
    The Patriarchal Period   10
    Joseph in Egypt   12
    Oppression and Exodus   14
    In the Desert   17
    When the Judges Ruled   20
    The Emergence of Kingship   22
    The Solomonic Empire   25
    The Kingdom of Israel   27
    The Kingdom of Judah   29
    The Prophetic Role   31
    After Viewing and Reading   32
    Suggested Readings   33

**2   The Power of the Word**      35
by *William W. Hallo*

    Before Viewing the Show   35
    While Reading the *Study Guide* and *Source Reader*   36
    The Babylonian Exile   37
    The Judaean Restoration   38
    The Emerging Diaspora   39
    The Second Temple   41
    The Promise of Greece   43

by *Shaye J. D. Cohen*
    The Hasmoneans   45
    The Threat of Rome   48
    Religious Ferment   50

The Expanding Diaspora   52
After Viewing and Reading   55
Suggested Readings   56

3   **The Shaping of Traditions (First to Ninth Centuries)**          57
    by *David B. Ruderman*

Before Viewing the Show   57
While Reading the *Study Guide* and *Source Reader*   58
In the Aftermath of the Temple's Destruction   59
The Growing Estrangement Between Christians and the
    Jews   64
The Emergence of Rabbinic Law and Culture   73
Judaism and the Rise of Islam   81
The Beginning of Jewish Settlement in
    Northern Europe   89
After Viewing and Reading   91
Suggested Readings   92

4   **The Crucible of Europe (Ninth to Fifteenth Centuries)**          93
    by *David B. Ruderman*

Before Viewing the Show   93
While Reading the *Study Guide* and *Source Reader*   94
The Flowering of Jewish Civilization in Muslim
    Spain   94
The Rise of Medieval Anti-Judaism in Northern
    Europe   103
Patterns of Jewish Culture in Medieval Europe   113
The Decline and Expulsion of Spanish Jewry   118
After Viewing and Reading   122
Suggested Readings   123

5   **The Search for Deliverance (1492 to 1789)**          125
    by *David B. Ruderman*

Before Viewing the Show   125
While Reading the *Study Guide* and *Source Reader*   126
In the Wake of the Spanish Expulsion   127
Christian-Jewish Dialogue in the Setting of Renaissance
    Italy   130
The Deterioration of Jewish Life in the Late Sixteenth
    Century   136
Jewish Cultural Developments in the Ottoman
    Empire   140

The Jewish Experience in Eastern Europe    148
The *Converso* Diaspora in Amsterdam    153
The Road to Emancipation    156
After Viewing and Reading    159
Suggested Readings    159

6    **Roads from the Ghetto (1789 to 1914)**    161
     by *Michael Stanislawski*

     Before Viewing the Show    161
     While Reading the *Study Guide* and *Source Reader*    163
     The Challenges of Modernity    163
     The French Revolution and the Emancipation of the
          Jews    166
     The Fate of Emancipation, 1815–1858    171
     Social and Intellectual Changes    173
     Culmination of Emancipation in the West    178
     Eastern Europe    179
     Anti-Semitism, Emigration, and New Political
          Parties    183
     After Viewing and Reading    191
     Suggested Readings    191

7    **The Golden Land (1654 to 1932)**    193
     by *Michael Stanislawski*

     Before Viewing the Show    193
     While Reading the *Study Guide* and *Source Reader*    195
     The Beginnings of American Jewry    195
     The German Immigration    200
     Mass Migration from Eastern Europe    203
     A United Community    209
     After Viewing and Reading    212
     Suggested Readings    212

8    **Out of the Ashes (1914 to 1945)**    213
     by *Michael Stanislawski*

     Before Viewing the Show    213
     While Reading the *Study Guide* and *Source Reader*    215
     War and Revolution    215
     The Jews of East Central Europe    221
     Western Europe    222
     Nazi Germany    225
     Destruction    230

After Viewing and Reading    238
Suggested Readings    238

9   **Into the Future (1945 to 1967)**                                239
    by *Michael Stanislawski*

Before Viewing the Show    239
While Reading the *Study Guide* and *Source Reader*    240
The State of Israel    241
Jews in the Soviet Union    247
The Soviet Bloc    250
Integration in Western Europe and the United
    States    251
The Six Day War    254
After Viewing and Reading    256
Suggested Readings    257

GLOSSARY                                                            259
INDEX                                                              263
PROJECT FUNDERS                                                    283
ABOUT THE AUTHORS                                                  285

# Maps and Charts

Map 1   The Ancient Near East    5

Map 2   The United Israelite Monarchy Under David and Solomon    24

Map 3   The Hasmonean State    46

Map 4   Jewish Population Centers, First to Fifth Centuries C.E.    53

Map 5   Jewish Population Centers, Seventh to Eleventh Centuries    85

Map 6   Jewish Population Centers, Eleventh to Mid-Fifteenth Centuries    104

Map 7   Jewish Population Centers, 1500–1780    131

Map 8   Jewish Population Centers at the Beginning of the Twentieth Century    216

Chart 1   Jewish Population of the United States, 1776–1967    199

Chart 2   World Jewish Population, 1939, 1948, and 1967    236

# Preface

## William W. Hallo

The history of the Jews is a history of involvement: with Near Eastern and classical civilization in the biblical period, with Christendom and Islam in the Middle Ages, with the nations of all the earth in modern times. It is a history as old as civilization itself—of one people and civilization. The involvement was total, complex, and reciprocal. It was total in the sense that the Jewish people never enjoyed the luxury of detachment; even when masters in their own land, a land that was in the vortex of all the surrounding powers, it shared their fates. It was complex in that the Jewish people, before and above any other people, experienced the tension of Diaspora and homeland, a tension ever shifting but never resolved. It was reciprocal in that Judaism took, learned and borrowed from the civilizations of other peoples while continuously contributing in essential respects to civilization in many different places.

The interaction of Jewish history and Western civilization successively assumed different forms, each characteristic of a major phase of Jewish history. Three phases are distinguished here. In the first or biblical phase Israel was an integral part of the Near Eastern and classical world which gave birth to western civilization. It shared the traditions of ancient Mesopotamia and the rest of that world with regard to its own beginnings; it benefited from the decline of Egypt and the other great Near Eastern empires, emerging as a nation in its own right; it asserted its claim to the divinely promised land of Israel and struggled to maintain a precarious independence there for a thousand years, until forced to yield to the greater power of Greeks and Romans.

This first phase of Jewish history is largely contained in the Hebrew Bible, with important additional illumination provided by the discoveries of archaeology including inscriptions from all over the Near East. Comparison of the archaeological evidence with the Bible shows many similarities as well as contrasts between biblical Judaism and the high civilization of the ancient world. Biblical Judaism provided a channel by which ancient Near Eastern traditions and institutions reached the Western world, for example, the story of a great flood and the concept of solicitude for widows and orphans. But it also contributed some significant innovations unknown to any of the other Near Eastern peoples, for example, the institution of a weekly day of rest from labor and the moral exhortations associated with literary prophecy.

The second phase of Jewish history took place on a larger stage, including all of Europe and the Mediterranean world. Fewer and fewer Jews were able to remain in the Holy Land itself. For more and more of them, it became the object of a prayerful longing even as they left seeking refuge in the lands of the dispersion. Gradually the pious hope of an eventual return to the true homeland gave way to the more practical desire to participate in the life of their new surroundings. But no matter how deeply the Jews became involved in the various lands of the dispersion, they were faced with being uprooted again and again. They became the classical examples of a diaspora population: confined or committed to intellectual and commercial pursuits whose fruits could readily be exported; linked to their coreligionists in other lands through the bond of a common faith as interpreted by rabbinic authority; and ever yearning to live, or at least to die, in the Holy Land.

For all the shared characteristics common to the widely separated groups, Jewish life in its rabbinic phase nevertheless displayed many local variations depending on the host environment. In particular, it differed markedly in the spheres of influence of Christianity and of Islam after the seventh century. In Christian Europe, the Jews were often no more than tolerated, and their most notable achievements tended to be concentrated in the religious sphere, where their rabbinic leadership could minister to their own needs. In the Islamic world, the Jews enjoyed, at least at first, a warmer welcome. Here they contributed broadly to the emerging Mediterranean society and culture, actively engaging in international commerce, in the arts, the sciences, and in the professions. The contrast is epitomized by the figures of Rashi and Maimonides. The former was the great eleventh-century scholar whose commentaries on the Bible and the *Talmud* remain to this day monuments of rabbinic pedagogy and erudition. Maimonides was the illustrious twelfth-century sage who was as well versed in philosophy, astronomy, and medicine as he was in rabbinic lore. Rashi lived in France and Germany, Maimonides in Spain, North Africa, and Egypt.

The modern age enlarged the areas of Jewish contact with the wider world, both for good and for evil. In a geographical sense the age of exploration and mass migration opened whole new continents: North and South America, Australia, and South Africa became centers of increasingly important and sizeable Jewish settlements. In an intellectual sense, the Age of Enlightenment opened whole new vistas to Jewish participation: the energies concentrated for more than a millennium on religious issues were now released on the entire spectrum of human inquiry with spectacular Jewish contributions to the new quests for scientific and humanistic insights. The names of Sigmund Freud and Karl Marx, of Albert Einstein and scores of other Nobel laureates in physics, chemistry, medicine, and literature testify to the breadth and depth of these contributions. In a political sense the age of nationalism—that explosive political force—opened the Jews to dangers and possibilities: both the violent anti-Semitism that culminated in the destruction of European Jewry and the establishment of the State of Israel.

The contemporary pattern of Jewish life thus presents a third model for its interaction with civilization. Where previously that life had been concentrated successively in Israel and the Diaspora, it is now balanced between the two. Israel is once again politically sovereign, and it commands a central position within Judaism, both culturally and emotionally. But equally significant centers of Jewish population and hence of Jewish cultural, religious, and political activity exist in the United States, the Soviet Union, and other parts of the Diaspora. World Jewry, as always, continues to gravitate toward the rising centers of world power, and hence to play a part in the shaping of world events. At the same time it lives in a creative tension with the state of Israel. The interdependence of Diaspora Jewry with Israel on the one hand and with world civilization on the other characterizes the present scene and will no doubt influence yet other patterns, whatever precise shape they may take in the future.

# 1

## A People Is Born

### William W. Hallo

*Editor's Suggestions*
**BEFORE VIEWING THE SHOW**

Examine Map 1 in this *Study Guide* for a view of the ancient Near East, especially the three civilizations of Egypt, Canaan, and Mesopotamia (between the Tigris and Euphrates rivers).

Check Map 2 for an outline of David and Solomon's kingdom in the area that was formerly Canaan.

*Overview of the TV Program*

The first show opens with a description of contemporary Jewry and then asks when and where this people and their glorious civilization began.

For the answer we travel back to ancient times to the second millennium B.C.E. (before the common era; C.E. is the common era), and note that the Near Eastern world was divided among three cultures: Egyptian, Canaanite, and Mesopotamian. Mesopotamian culture is observed through its buildings, cuneiform writings, and its abundant artifacts. In this civilization, we recognize elements familiar from the Bible, such as the creation myth, the flood story, and certain laws.

In Egypt we not only glimpse the ruins of an ancient culture, but we also view a location where the Exodus from Egypt might have occurred. We follow the Israelites who originated in Mesopotamia, sojourned in Egypt, and left with the cultural baggage of two civilizations. The Israelites incubated a new idea: that one God alone controlled the world. This concept was given its full expression in the biblical story of the revelation at Mount Sinai.

The Israelites, after leaving Egypt, crossed the Sinai desert and took control of Canaan through military conquest and gradual infiltration. There they probably joined other Israelite tribes who had not been with them in Egypt. They worshipped at a portable shrine that contained a record of the covenant they had made with their

1

God. They were led by "judges," who responded to the external threats by rallying a few of the tribes to fight off their common enemies.

Tired of temporary rulers, the people demanded that the prophet Samuel give them a king; grudgingly he acceded to their wishes. Saul was chosen, but he and his children died in a battle with the Philistines, Israel's most ferocious enemy. Emerging as the next king, David subdued the Philistines and other peoples and greatly expanded the Israelite kingdom. His son Solomon, noted in the Bible for his wisdom, maintained David's kingdom and built a beautiful royal palace and a permanent temple in Jerusalem where the Israelites could worship.

But Solomon antagonized the people by overtaxing them and drafting them as laborers for his building projects. The country split in two: ten northern tribes formed the kingdom of Israel, the two southern tribes joined to make the kingdom of Judah.

Throughout the following years, Israelite prophets exhorted all the Israelites to be just and merciful, warning them against the idolatrous ways of the surrounding nations. Although it had an unstable government, the northern kingdom enjoyed periods of prosperity. Eventually it was overwhelmed by a new power in the Near East, the kingdom of Assyria. The Assyrians crushed Israel's capital, Samaria, and the kingdom fell in 722 B.C.E.

In the south the kingdom of Judah continued under the strong leadership of King Hezekiah, but it too was destroyed by another new power—Babylonia. The conquerors exiled many of the Israelites, transporting them to Babylon. Fortified by the messages of their prophets, the exiles continued their traditions on foreign soil.

*Watch for . . . and Think about*

Note the glories of the Mesopotamian, Egyptian, and Canaanite cultures. These were the civilizations from which the ancient Israelites emerged. What ideas did the Israelites take from these peoples and what did they discard? •

Observe the geography of Egypt, the Sinai desert, and Canaan. How did the Bible describe the Israelites' Exodus from Egypt and their entry into Canaan?

Note the Philistine artifacts. Why were the Philistines formidable enemies of the Israelites?

Look for the archaeological remains of David and Solomon's reign. What do they tell about the kings' political power and religious commitments?

The program shows much footage of Assyrian and Babylonian ruins and artifacts. Why couldn't the Israelites withstand their attacks?

WHILE READING THE *STUDY GUIDE* AND *SOURCE READER*

Look for the following:

- The differences between history and protohistory and how that affects our understanding of ancient Israel.
- The Bible's attempt to explain the origins of humanity.
- The similarities and differences in the many extant myths of the flood story.
- The parallels that exist between the biblical stories told of Abraham, Isaac, and Jacob and the realities of Near Eastern culture.
- How the scriptural account of Joseph accords well with known Egyptian documents.
- The biblical narratives of the Israelite Exodus from Egypt, the journey through the desert, and the arrival at Mount Sinai. What do historians use today to buttress the scriptural narratives? Is the attempt successful?
- The problems faced by the Israelites as they entered Canaan and attempted to establish their rule. Identify Joshua and the judges.
- The introduction of kingship into Israel. Who demanded it? Identify Saul, David, and Solomon.
- The accomplishments of King Solomon. Why was he so successful?
- The rise and fall of the two kingdoms, Israel and Judah. Why did the Israelites have two kingdoms? How did they eventually fall?
- The term "prophets." How did their messages spiritually and morally uplift the people in Israel and Judah? Did their beliefs provide comfort to the Israelites who were forced into exile?

## THE PROTOHISTORY OF ISRAEL

How does the history of a people begin? When does it begin? Where does it begin? If we ask these questions of the history of the American people, most of us would tend to answer with a nod at our European past. We might begin our history with Leif Ericsson and other Norsemen said to have reached North America from Scandinavia in the eleventh century; or with Columbus, setting sail for the New World from Spain in 1492; or with the Pilgrims, fleeing England via Holland in 1620 to settle New England and set the emerging thirteen colonies on a course destined to free them, eventually, from English rule but to bind them forever to the English language and culture.

But not all Americans will thus trace their origins to a European past. Black Americans can with equal validity look to Africa, Hispanic Americans to Latin America, and Oriental Americans to Asia. And Native Americans need look only to their own continent—though much further back in time—for the beginnings of history from their perspective.

Just so, when we ask these same questions of the history of the Jewish people, we may receive a variety of answers. Some of these are furnished by the Bible, some by archaeological discoveries, some by the insights of scholarly reconstruction. But the choice among them is ultimately a personal one, dictated by religious conviction and intellectual persuasion. There can be no certainty, only an awareness of the degree to which various reconstructions can be tested against the available evidence—be that evidence in the form of biblical passages, or ancient texts and objects recovered by the spade, or deductions drawn from the observation of geography, climate, human nature, or other permanent patterns of environment and culture.

The different scholarly reconstructions of the beginnings of Jewish history, or what can better be called Israelite origins, agree on one point: these origins lie somewhere in the ancient Near East, that part of the Old World in which civilization began some 5,000 years ago. This cradle of civilization, or Fertile Crescent as it is sometimes called, stretched in a broad arc or crescent from the Valley of the Two Rivers ("Mesopotamia") in the east (modern Iraq) to the valley of the Nile in the southwest. It thus included parts of two continents—the southwestern portion of Asia and the northeastern corner of Africa.

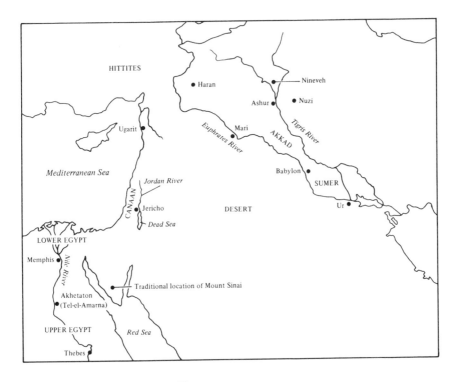

**Map 1 The Ancient Near East**

But beyond this, modern theories of Israelite origins diverge widely. Some would trace them to Mesopotamia, about 2000 B.C.E., when the first ancestors of the later Israelites moved westward to their ultimate destination in the Holy Land. Others derive them from Egypt, whence the Israelites moved eastward to launch the conquest of the Promised Land about 1200 B.C.E. Still others reject both these theories and insist that nothing can be said about Israelite origins before 1200 B.C.E., and that the ancestors of the Israelites could have been native Canaanites as well as arrivals from abroad.

The position taken here is not to choose between these and other widely divergent alternatives but to distinguish between two kinds of reconstructions of the entire Israelite past. Only one of these can claim to be history in the usual sense of the word, that is, a reconstruction based on all available evidence. The other is protohistory, that is, a hypothesis that accepts the biblical version about Israelite origins as a point of departure and relates it to the extra-biblical evidence wherever possible. The biblical record is largely contained in Genesis, the first book of the Bible; most of the extra-biblical records have been found among the ancient inscriptions of Mesopotamia and Egypt. The Mesopotamian records are written in cuneiform, the Egyptian in hieroglyphic—both employ hundreds of different signs, some standing for whole words and others for syllables. Their decipherment, one of the triumphs of modern archaeology, enables us to set the unfolding of biblical history in its broader Near Eastern context.

## PRIMEVAL HISTORY

How did civilization begin? Where did it begin? When did it begin? On these points there is today a fairly broad consensus. Civilization (literally, "the culture of cities") emerged when cities originated in the so-called "urban revolution" at some time in the fourth millennium B.C.E., beginning in Mesopotamia and spreading throughout the Near East. Certain other cultural developments were also involved: the construction of temples, palaces, and defensive walls; the accumulation of cattle, grain, and other forms of capital surplus; the invention of writing; the dramatic increase of craft specialization and the beginnings of industry, notably in textiles and metallurgy, and particularly the emergence of bronze as a principal medium for the manufacture of tools and weapons. Bronze replaced stone, or stone and copper, in this function and marks the end of the

(New) Stone Age or Chalcolithic (Metal and Stone) Age and the beginning of the Bronze Age.

These conclusions of modern scholarship were anticipated in a curious way by the biblical story of creation, or at least in its climax, the creation of man. The first man—whose name, Adam, is simply the word for "man" in Hebrew—is the ancestor of a succession of descendants who introduce the elements of civilization to the world: wealth in cattle and grain, city-building, metallurgy, and even music. Thus Adam may be intended to signal the creation of civilized man, or of civilization. And this is dated to the fourth millennium, specifically to 3761 B.C.E., by the internal chronology of the Bible, and located precisely in Mesopotamia. The history of civilized man according to the biblical conception begins in the legendary "Garden of Eden"—somewhere in the Valley of the Two Rivers, probably identifiable as a fertile area in southern Mesopotamia known in the cuneiform sources as *edin*.

Cuneiform sources also have various versions of the creation and of the origins of civilization. Like the biblical version, they belong to the realm of myth, that is to say they present an imaginary one-time occurrence in the remote past as the necessary and sufficient explanation for a continuing condition observed in current human experience. In one such scheme, history began with a succession of fantastically long-lived kings, each associated with a wise counselor who represents or introduces one of the basic arts and sciences of civilization. The first of these counselors was called Adapa, and is credited with the beginnings of astrology. In another myth, Adapa is offered the "bread of (eternal) life" and "water of (eternal) life" but refuses them, thus forfeiting once and for all mankind's chance to live forever.

Just so, the biblical Adam was permitted, even commanded, to eat of every tree in Eden, including presumably the tree of "eternal" life, but chose instead to eat from the one forbidden tree, thus bringing mortality to the human condition. But while such myths are not history, the combined evidence of cuneiform and biblical sources is nonetheless of historical value: it takes Israelite origins back to the beginnings of civilization, and sets the stage for the interconnections between "civilization and the Jews" that is to characterize the subsequent history of both.

In cuneiform sources the first eight (or ten) kings are followed by a great flood; in Genesis the first eight generations of man are succeeded by a universal flood, or Deluge. Such a flood is a familiar fixture in the mythologies of many peoples around the globe, but nowhere are the analogies to the Mesopotamian versions so many and so detailed as in Genesis. Moreover, the original inspiration of both these versions may be historical. (See Reading 1-1.)*

In Mesopotamia the flood very likely served as a metaphor, that is, as a symbolic representation of the "flooding" of the country by waves of new settlers early in the third millennium B.C.E. These newcomers were most likely uncivilized nomads or seminomads, perhaps originating in the Syrian Desert, depending hitherto on great flocks of sheep or herds of cattle that followed available pastureland from place to place, often in conflict with more settled farmers. But as they gradually learned about agriculture, they entered the more urbanized areas in which the farming population was concentrated. They came down the Euphrates and Tigris rivers from their homes in the desert, much like a flood, and even the name by which they were known sounded in the language then spoken in Mesopotamia (Sumerian) much like the word for flood. Their own languages (Amorite and Akkadian) were entirely different from Sumerian, but closely related to Hebrew, the language of the Bible.

In the Bible, the earliest history was told in the form of family history, with each generation linked to the next as father to son, and all responsible for each other. Here the same flood began as a purge of the earth from the pollution of its early violence, such as the murder of Abel by his brother Cain. It spared only Noah, the only one "blameless" in his generation, and his immediate family. When it ended, his descendants repopulated the known world. In keeping with this theory, entirely lacking in the cuneiform versions, these descendants were divided into three broad groups, descended respectively from the three sons of Noah (Shem, Ham, and Japheth). In a very general sort of way, they correspond to the speakers of the three great language families known to modern scholarship as Semitic, Hamitic, and Indo-European. The Israelites were destined to derive from the first of these groups, as were the Amorite and Akkadian speakers of Mesopotamia. Here, then, the flood, so far from symbolizing the disruptive and aggressive character of the Semitic newcomers, represented them as heirs of the original creation saved by divine intervention.

---

*Reading numbers refer to the *Source Reader* volume in *Heritage: Civilization and the Jews* published by Praeger Publishers in conjunction with this *Study Guide*.

In Mesopotamia, the arrival of the Semitic-speaking groups ushered in the so-called Early Dynastic Period (ca. 2900–2300 B.C.E.) during which the achievements of urban civilization were consolidated on a broad front. Kingship gradually became institutionalized as a hereditary office; trade and industry flourished; and arts and literature reached new heights. It was the institution of the city and of the city-state that made these and other achievements possible. The Mesopotamians duly admired that institution, enshrining their early history in a document ("The Sumerian King List") which is actually a detailed list of the cities (and their kings) that successively ruled Mesopotamia after the flood. The later Israelites, however, did not share the Mesopotamian veneration either of cities or of kings. According to the Bible, therefore, the call to "come, let us build a city, and a tower with its top in the sky, to make a name for ourselves, else shall we be scattered all over the earth" (Genesis 11:4)* merited divine displeasure. The tower was no doubt inspired by the fame of the Mesopotamian stepped temple-towers in Babylon and elsewhere (ziggurats), hence "tower of Babel." The penalty for the overweening ambition implied in its construction was twofold. Where once "all the earth had the same language" (Genesis 11:1), enjoying a kind of golden age of united speech such as is found also in Sumerian mythology, now the languages were confounded. The biblical tale thus attempts to account for the origin of the divergent language groups already implied in the family history of Noah.

But in addition, the very threat that the builders of city and tower had hoped to avert was visited on them by way of punishment, for "from there the Lord scattered them over the face of the whole earth" (Genesis 11:9). Translated into modern terms, Mesopotamia ceased to be the main focus of the story. More specifically, that focus moved from southern or lower Mesopotamia (Babylonia) to northern or upper Mesopotamia and its environs. This area today is located chiefly in northern Syria. It includes the upper course of the Euphrates River, its tributaries, and the lands lying west of it to the Mediterranean coast. Close to the Syrian Desert and far from the Sumerian city-states of the lower Euphrates valley, it was a natural area for settlement by the Semites. And indeed the descendants of

---

*All biblical translations are from *The Torah, The Prophets*, and *The Writings: A New Translation of the Holy Scriptures*, published by The Jewish Publication Society of America, Philadelphia: 1962, 1978, 1982.

Shem in the biblical narrative (Genesis 11:10–26) often echo in their personal names the geographical names of this region. Their common ancestor Eber is not only the forefather of all Hebrews (literally, "Eber-ites"), but also quite possibly a remote reflex of Ebrium. A ruler, or high official by that name, is conspicuous in the kingdom of Ebla, a prominent city-state which dominated all of the area in the twenty-fifth or twenty-fourth century B.C.E. according to the latest discoveries.

Thus ends the first period of Israel's protohistory, its "primeval history." It is not history at all, but rather a careful selection of mythological or legendary explanations—many of them shared with cuneiform sources—for some of the questions raised by the observation of the conditions of human life in general and of Israelite life in particular during later ages. It answers these questions by appeal to divine intervention at crucial times in the remote past. It funnels the human experience of this intervention in history from the universal to the particular, from the creation of (civilized) men to the election of the first patriarch, or legendary forefather of the Hebrews. Incidentally it shifts the geographical focus of the story subtly but inexorably from distant Mesopotamia to a point closer to the Holy Land.

## THE PATRIARCHAL PERIOD

In Mesopotamia, the balance of the third millennium was dominated by the empires of Akkad (ca. 2300–2100 B.C.E.) and Ur (ca. 2100–2000 B.C.E.). The Bible recalls the names of both these cities. Akkad was one of the "mainstays" of the heroic Nimrod (Genesis 10:10) who may perhaps be identified with the greatest king of the Akkadian (or Sargonic) dynasty, Naram-Sin. Ur of the Chaldeans (named thus much later in time) (Genesis 11:28 and 31; 15:7; cf. Nehemiah 9:7) was the birthplace or ancestral home of the first patriarch, Abraham. With him there begins the so-called patriarchal period, a period of some three hundred years (by the biblical chronology), spanning the lives of Abraham, his son Isaac, and his grandson Jacob. They are the subjects of traditional tales associated with the places of their sojourns (Genesis 12–36). Modern scholarship doubts that these three figures were demonstrably historical personages, or even that they were related to each other in the original versions of their stories. Hence the patriarchal period remains in the realm of protohistory, and the narratives about the patriarchs cannot claim to be genuine history. But the details of these narratives do contain many authentic clues to legal, geographical, and even historical data known from the independent testimony of cuneiform sources. On balance, this testimony best accords with the Old Babylonian Period (ca. 2000–1600 B.C.E.) as the original setting for the patriarchal narratives. While it is therefore impossible to write a history of the patriarchal period, one can highlight some of the features that it shares with the surrounding Near East in the Old Babylonian Period. This will be done here by way of illustrations drawn respectively from the realms of law, cult, and warfare.

In Babylonia itself, the Old Babylonian Period was characterized above all else by the elaboration of law. Judicious legal precedents were collected by a number of different kings, and promulgated in so-called codes of which the most extensive and famous was the "Laws of Hammurabi," the king who ruled at Babylon circa 1792–1750 B.C.E. Countless contracts, court cases, and letters furnish additional details of actual legal procedure. Both legal theory and practice are thus revealed in these sources. While the legal portions of the Bible furnish the closest biblical parallels, the patriarchal narratives provide additional analogues. Thus, for example, when Jacob fled to his kinsman Laban, he undertook to serve as herdsman for the latter's flock. In so doing, he "made good" the natural losses to the flock (Genesis 31:39) in the manner and in the very language of the Laws of Hammurabi and of an old Babylonian herding contract. (See Reading 1-2.) It may be noted in passing that the various legal parallels once alleged between the patriarchal narratives and the documents from ancient Nuzi (ca. fifteenth century B.C.E.) have more recently been questioned by most scholars.

Outside of Babylonia itself, the site that has yielded the most abundant and revealing evidence for this period is the great citadel of Mari on the Middle Euphrates River, at the border between the desert and the sown area. At this outpost of Mesopotamian civilization, the settled population encountered the seminomadic clans in search of pasture for their extensive herds. In their ongoing efforts to govern the relations between these two distinct and potentially antagonistic populations, the rulers of Mari used measures such as the census, ritual atonement, prophetic revelations, bans, and other techniques familiar from the Bible. Some measures are specifically associated with the patriarchs; when, for example, animals are killed in order to ratify a covenant between two warring tribes, we are reminded of the covenant which God concluded with Abraham (Genesis 15; cf. also Jeremiah 34:18f). (See Reading 1-3.)

The patriarchs covered considerable distances in their wanderings: from Ur in lower Mesopotamia to Harran, a caravan city (today in Turkey) whose very name means "crossroads," thence to the Land of Canaan (approximately modern Israel), and even into Egypt. Although extensive, these travels seem compatible with those recorded in the cuneiform inscriptions of the Old Babylonian Period which speak of traders' caravans, diplomatic embassies, or military campaigns, all using the network of well-traveled routes along the major rivers and between the major centers of settlement. The record of a particularly spectacular journey from Babylonia to the Syrian city of Emar may even be echoed in the one narrative that casts Abraham as a warrior—the story of the war of the four kings against the five including Sodom and Gomorrah (Hebrew: Amora) (Genesis 14).

The goal of the wanderings and of the patriarchal narratives themselves is never in doubt: it is Canaan, "the land that I will show you" (Genesis 12:1). If the primeval history climaxed when it was freed from its lower Mesopotamian origins, then the patriarchs repeatedly tried and ultimately succeeded in freeing themselves from their way-station in upper Mesopotamia and their sojourns in Egypt to establish a decisive claim on the land that was to be theirs by divine promise.

## JOSEPH IN EGYPT

About 1600 B.C.E., the Old Babylonian Period ended with the dramatic fall of the city of Babylon to Hittite invaders sweeping down the Euphrates River from their home in the highlands of Anatolia (modern Turkey). About the same time, the royal Egyptian capital of Memphis was captured by foreign invaders identified in the hieroglyphic sources as "rulers of foreign lands" (Hyksos). Some modern scholars regard these Hyksos as simply the westernmost branch of the same Semitic-speaking wave of Amorites as that which had moved eastward into Babylonia at the beginning of the millennium. The Egyptian sources are ambiguous, but they suggest that Asiatic invaders, whether or not of Semitic speech, gradually infiltrated Egypt in the same interval. Initially they were held at bay by a defensive wall erected where Egypt's eastern border meets the Sinai desert, named "Wall-of-the-Ruler, made to oppose the Asiatics and crush the Sand-Crossers." But gradually they were allowed to settle the eastern

Delta inside this frontier, and by 1600 they had displaced the legitimate kings of Egypt and reigned as pharaohs in their own right.

Given this background some would argue that the story of Joseph, which follows the patriarchal narratives in the Bible and forms the concluding position of the Book of Genesis (chapters 37–50), echoes these events. If it does so at all, however, it recasts them in its own style and to its own purpose.

According to the biblical account, then, the movement from Canaan to Egypt involved not a whole people but a family. Jacob, last of the patriarchs, had two wives and two concubines who among them bore him twelve sons and a daughter. His favorite wife was Rachel, and her two sons, born in his old age, were his favorite sons. One of them, Joseph, incurred the wrath of his brothers and was sold into slavery in Egypt. He thus paved the way for the rest of his family as from humble beginnings he rose, with divine help, to great heights. The adventures that attended Joseph's rise share many features with later tales in Egyptian and Aramaic (a Semitic language spoken throughout the Near East in the first millennium) and with other biblical tales of later date (e.g., Mordecai, Daniel; see p. 13). In the end, he became second in authority to the pharaoh himself, and thus was able to welcome his kinsmen into Egypt when famine drove them out of Canaan. He settled them in the land of Goshen, that is, presumably, the very area of the eastern Delta where the Hyksos had first gained a foothold in Egypt. The Book of Genesis— and with it the protohistory of Israel—ends with the aged patriarch blessing his sons, and with his death and the death of Joseph. (See Reading 1-4.)

It is difficult to reconcile this tale with the findings of historical scholarship. Its motive is clear: to form a bridge between the patriarchal narratives, told in terms of related individuals, and the history of Israel, told in terms of related tribes. At the same time the tale serves to move the geographical focus of this history once more: to explain why the Promised Land of Canaan was left behind and the history of the tribes of Israel begun in yet another foreign country—Egypt. These ends were accomplished by "renaming" Jacob: he becomes "Israel" (Genesis 32:29; cf. 35:10) and the sons of Jacob become the "children of Israel." The late, charming tale of Joseph artfully weaves all these strands together and forms a fitting third and concluding act to the protohistory of Israel—the first set largely in lower Mesopotamia, the second in Syria and Canaan, the third in Egypt.

## OPPRESSION AND EXODUS

The four-hundred-year span from circa 1600–1200 B.C.E. is known as the Late Bronze Age (the last phase of that stage of civilization when bronze served as a principal medium of manufacture). Throughout the Near East, this period witnessed the emergence of new ruling groups, often at the expense of Semitic-speaking predecessors. In Egypt, it largely coincided with the period of the "New Kingdom" or Empire. The pharaohs of this New Kingdom began the gradual expulsion of the Hyksos and the reestablishment of native rule in Egypt, and ended by crossing the frontiers and establishing Egyptian rule over the countries on their borders, including Canaan in the northeast.

A further distinguishing characteristic of this entire period was the pervasive presence throughout the Near East of persons designated in cuneiform and hieroglyphic sources as Hapiru or Habiru. These persons were of diverse ethnic affiliation, to judge by their names. But they shared a common social status as outcasts and aliens, uprooted from their ancestral homes by the disruptive arrival of newer population groups, a recurrent phenomenon in Near Eastern history. Thus dispossessed, the Habiru sought a new life for themselves either individually—by taking military or other service with the new ruling groups all over the Near East—or collectively—by banding together to take possession of the tracts of land which the ruling groups, with their bronze weapons and chariots, were unable to dominate, notably the hill country of Canaan. Indeed there are grounds to suppose that the "Hebrews" of the Bible are none other than these Habiru, or that portion of them which settled the Promised Land.

But the Bible uses this designation only sparingly with reference to Israelites—most often in a slightly derogatory sense, or when used by foreigners. When the curtain rises on the proper history of Israel in Exodus, the second book of the Bible, the designation used by the pharaoh is "the Israelite people" (literally "the people of the children of Israel;" Exodus 1:9). It is used by the unnamed new pharaoh "who knew not Joseph" (Exodus 1:8)—as well he might not, for by the Bible's own chronology, much of the four-hundred-year period of the Egyptian sojourn (Genesis 15:13; cf. Exodus 12:40) had elapsed. There ensued a period of oppression so burdensome that, in Israelite memory, Egypt was forever to be linked with the concept of slavery and forced servitude.

The pervasive and explicit reminders of the Egyptian oppression in later biblical passages are a powerful argument in favor of its historical truth, for it is inherently unlikely that a people should invent such an inglorious beginning for its own history. The biblical authors, it is true, did not mean to celebrate Israel, but rather God's might, acting on Israel's behalf. Yet the writers were quite capable of doing so within the broad outlines of actual events as shown by subsequent history. Nor is it reasonable to expect Egyptian records to document explicitly their treatment of the hated Asiatic intruders, whether these were the last of the Hyksos or the first of the Habiru. What these records do preserve is general descriptions of border-crossings by nomadic tribesmen from the east, their recruitment into labor gangs for construction projects, and the provisioning of these gangs with carefully allotted rations. These descriptions tally well with the general description in the Bible of the oppression (Exodus 1:13f; 5:6–18). (See Reading 1-5.)

The garrison-cities that the Israelites built for the Egyptians provide the most specific clue to the historical validity of the oppression. Pithom and Raamses (Exodus 1:11) can best be identified with sites in the eastern Delta called, in Egyptian, "house of [the deity] Aton" and "house of [the pharaoh] Ramses" respectively. The former provides a link with the so-called Amarna age of the fourteenth century B.C.E. when the pharaonic court moved to the city of Akhet-Aton (modern Amarna) and when the royal worship of the deified sun-disc (Aton) briefly threatened to overshadow the traditional Egyptian cults. The latter was named for Ramses II (ca. 1287–1221 B.C.E.) who, by virtue of the great length of his reign and the prodigious extent of his building operations, is a conceivable candidate for the unnamed pharaoh of the oppression.

The delicate balance of power crafted by international diplomacy in the Amarna age of the fourteenth century B.C.E. had depended on the mutual recognition of a few "superpowers" as "great kings"—notably Egypt (under the New Kingdom, specifically the Eighteenth Dynasty), Babylonia (under the Kassites), the Mitanni kingdom in Syria, and the Hittite empire in Turkey. Treaties governed the relations among these great powers and between them and the lesser kingdoms loyal to them (so-called vassal-states). Correspondence was exchanged chiefly in Akkadian, the international language of diplomacy at the time. Royal offspring were sent to foreign courts, the young princes in order to learn about other cultures and, incidentally, to serve as hostages for their fathers' good behavior; the young princesses in order to cement alliances by marriage.

All these arrangements began to come unhinged during the thirteenth century B.C.E. under the threat of new arrivals on the scene. Land-borne newcomers came from the Syrian desert—the latest wave of Semitic-speaking intruders called Arameans. From the sea came various Indo-European speaking groups, originating on the coasts and islands of Greece and settling the coasts of the Mediterranean Sea wherever they could find a foothold. The great powers began by attempting to enlist these "sea-peoples" in their own armies as diplomacy increasingly gave way to warfare, but they ended as victims of the new invaders, buying the invaders off or deflecting them elsewhere when they could, collapsing before them when they failed. By the end of the century the whole map of the Near East had changed again. The Hittite and Mitanni empires had disappeared, Kassite Babylonia was about to follow suit, and Egypt was greatly weakened.

It is under these conditions that the liberation of the Israelites from Egyptian oppression must be viewed. The event itself is not attested in any extra-biblical sources, but it fits well into the general picture of Egyptian weakness and preoccupation with the onslaughts of seaborne invaders at the end of the thirteenth century B.C.E. As usual, the biblical version introduces a personal element into the story. Moses, his brother Aaron, and his sister Miriam all figure prominently in the Book of Exodus. But many of the biographical details associated with them are of a legendary character and recur in numerous other folkloristic contexts. The birth of Moses, for example, is only one (albeit perhaps the oldest) of innumerable versions of the exposed child who is rescued by or returns to the royal court and ends up displacing or defeating the king. (**See Reading 1-6.**) Moses' speech defect provides a touch that is familiar from Sumerian literature. And the ten plagues (or seven according to Psalm 78) which Moses and Aaron invoke on the pharaoh are reminiscent of traditional Egyptian catalogues of natural disasters such as those that accompanied the breakdown of pharaonic power in earlier eras. (**See Reading 1-7.**)

In the biblical view, however, the basic agency of Israel's liberation from Egypt was not human but divine. It led to the exaltation not of a general or a king, but of the deity. And it entailed the emergence of the people as a collective entity based on the shared experience of a crisis overcome with divine help. This view fits convincingly into a contemporary Near Eastern pattern: a people or its king entrusting their fate to a deity; the trust dramatically vindicated by a decisive military victory; the victory in turn leading to the suppression of a rebellion, the repulsion of an invasion, the recovery of a cult statue, or the founding of a new dynasty.

In Israel's case the key event was the Exodus, the successful escape of the departing Israelites at the point of seeming entrapment between the pharaoh's pursuing chariotry and the Reed Sea. (This is the literal translation of the Hebrew name in Exodus 13:18, etc.; the traditional equation with the Red Sea is of doubtful validity.) And even if elements of the escape reflected standard military stratagems of the time on the one hand or miraculous embellishments on the other, the event itself became a fundamental part of Israel's own conception of its past. The Exodus was celebrated in some of its oldest poetry—briefly in the Song of Miriam and at greater length in the Song of Moses (both in Exodus 15). It was recalled at solemn convocations in biblical times and is narrated at the annual ritual of Passover to this day. It became the model for other deliverances from oppression and exile and for other triumphs of divine order over human or natural chaos. But it remained uniquely the warrant for God's exaltation above other divinities and for his enthronement as Israel's sovereign. In the words of the song: "Who is like You? O Lord, among the celestials . . . The Lord will reign for ever and ever!" (Exodus 15:11, 18).

## IN THE DESERT

In proclaiming God as their king the Israelites departed radically from Near Eastern usage in spirit but adhered closely to it in letter. In Egypt the pharaoh himself was regarded as a god, while nearly everywhere else a mortal king ruled by grace of the national or local god and was regarded as his steward on earth. With the growth of empires, sovereigns (suzerains) extended their sway over lesser client-kingdoms, and detailed the vassal's obligations in so-called suzerainty-treaties in which the sovereign assumed virtually divine status with respect to the vassal. And when an empire collapsed, such vassals were apt to declare their independence by shifting their allegiance from the foreign king to the native deity. (See **Reading 1-8.**)

Against this background we approach the momentous events at Mount Sinai involving, in essence, the sealing of a covenant between God and Israel. Israel now ratified its part of the bargain struck at the Reed Sea. In return for the divine deliverance there, they here assumed the role of vassals and recognized God as their sovereign without any earthly king to mediate between them. The relationship is defined and justified at the very beginning of the Ten Commandments (the "Decalogue"): "I the Lord am your God who brought you out of the land of Egypt, the house of bondage; you shall have no other gods beside Me" (Exodus 20:2f; cf. Deuteronomy 5:6f).

Was this Decalogue inscribed on two tablets, literally brought down from the top of Mount Sinai? Can this mountain be identified with any given peak on the desolate Sinai peninsula? Did the Israelites truly subscribe to its provisions with an "all that the Lord has spoken we will faithfully do" (Exodus 24:7)? These questions are basically unanswerable and are, in a sense, immaterial. What is crucial for the reconstruction of Israel's history is that her national consciousness was shaped by a succession of constitutive events: the deliverance from Egyptian bondage, the assumption of a covenantal obligation, and the conquest of the Promised Land. Without the Decalogue, or its equivalent, it is hard to conceive the formation of a nation out of the diverse tribes that had escaped Egypt or out of the mixed multitude (Exodus 12:38) or riffraff (Numbers 11:4) that had attached itself to them.

But the obligations assumed at Sinai involved more than the lofty imperatives and absolute prohibitions of the Ten Commandments. Ostensibly the entire body of detailed legislation called "the Book of the Covenant" (Exodus 24:7) was promulgated at this time. In fact, some of its provisions, notably the cultic ones, were clearly inspired by conditions that prevailed much later when the people were permanently settled and a central sanctuary was in operation. And other provisions, notably those of civil law, are strikingly paralleled in both letter and spirit by the collections of legal precedents issued long before by various Old Babylonian kings (see above). The laws of the goring ox, for example (Exodus 21:28–32, 35f), are already anticipated by the Laws of Hammurabi and, even more closely, by the earlier laws of the kingdom of Eshnunna. Other laws more relevant to the period of the desert wanderings were revealed to and through Moses during the subsequent traversal of the Wilderness of Sinai. (See Reading 1-9.)

Israel's desert wanderings, like the Exodus from Egypt, fit best into the migrations which characterized and helped to bring about the end of the Bronze Age (see above). These migrations included Arameans from the Syrian Desert east of the Promised Land, on the one hand, and Philistines settling the western coast of Canaan on the other. Israel felt a certain kinship with the Arameans, whose language was closely related to Hebrew. Indeed, the notion that "my father was a fugitive Aramean" became an article of faith before the sojourn in Egypt (Deuteronomy 26:5). But the Philistines were totally unrelated to Israel. They were first settled by the Egyptians as mercenaries in the Egyptians' Canaanite strongholds about 1190 B.C.E. Thereafter they competed with Israel for possession of the rest of the Promised Land. This area gradually acquired the name of Palestine (i.e., land of the Philistines). At the very outset of the wanderings, Israel was forced to avoid the "way of the land of the Philistines, although it was nearer" (Exodus 13:17). Instead, a circuitous route through the less heavily defended interior of the Sinai peninsula was chosen. A long halt was made at the oasis of Kadesh-barnea, a fortress guarding the border between the Sinai desert and the area of Philistine settlement. Representatives of the twelve tribes were despatched from there to spy out the land and reported that the land "does indeed flow with milk and honey," otherwise painting a glowing picture of its physical attractions in terms long used in Egyptian literature to describe Palestine. But the majority of the tribes hesitated to launch an invasion of the land from the south, again preferring a roundabout route through presumably friendlier territory. (**See Reading 1-10.**)

Thus perforce the wanderings had to detour to the east of the Promised Land, on the other side of the Dead Sea and the Jordan River. The Transjordanian territory was either traversed peacefully or conquered, depending on the success of the negotiations with the kings who ruled its various parts. The most extensive negotiations involved Balak, king of Moab, a people related to Israel by long tradition (cf. Genesis 19:37) with whom they were most often on a hostile footing. Balak engaged the services of Balaam, a visionary, in a vain attempt to curse the Israelites and thus presumably to impede their further progress (Numbers 22–24). The report of this event is often suspected of having been embellished, but it has gained a certain literary validity through recent discoveries in Transjordan: the figure of

Balaam ben Beor recurs on a seventh-century B.C.E. inscription from that area as a master of visions and curses. (See Reading 1-11.)

At the end of these wanderings two and a half tribes accepted as their inheritance those portions of Transjordanian land already conquered. Then they all stood poised on the eastern bank of the Jordan River, ready to assume the inheritance of the land that they believed had been divinely promised to them. Moses, the aged leader, was vouchsafed a distant view before he died. His mantle of leadership passed to Joshua.

## WHEN THE JUDGES RULED

Before the end of the thirteenth century B.C.E. Israel had gained a foothold in the Promised Land. Its name occurs for the first time outside the Bible on a stela (stone slab) of the Pharaoh Merneptah (ca. 1220–1211 B.C.E.). It is mentioned there in the context of settled cities and peoples on Egypt's Asiatic frontier. (See Reading 1-12.) Beyond this single testimony, however, archaeology has not yet been able to furnish unambiguous evidence for the date, the nature or even the validity of Israel's conquest of the Promised Land. The Iron Age now dawned to bear witness to the gradual replacement of bronze by iron, but Israel did not share in this advance; for the time being the new medium remained a Philistine monopoly (I Samuel 13:19–21). And attempts to correlate the destruction of specific sites with the beginning of the Iron Age and the coming of the Israelites have often enough been unsuccessful. This is most notably true of Jericho, the first fortress likely to have been encountered by any army crossing the Jordan River nearest the point where it flows into the Dead Sea. Excavations at Jericho strongly suggest that the site was entirely unoccupied at the time.

What then are we to make of the Book of Joshua, which carries on the thread of the narrative where the Book of Numbers, and its repetition in Deuteronomy, left off? It recounts in detail the dramatic destruction of Jericho, followed by the systematic reduction of the other walled cities of Canaan, and the absorption of their lands by the Israelites. Each of the tribes not already awarded land on the other side of the Jordan (nine and a half in all) received land on this side by the casting of lots.

This conception of the conquest is in striking contrast to another and much briefer version but one with equal biblical authority

(Judges 1). According to this version the Israelites did not at once dispossess the inhabitants of the great fortified cities, but contented themselves with the hill country and unfortified settlements. Given their inferiority in armor and chariotry, they had to rely on superior strategy or other devices to gain the upper hand over the indigenous population. Nor was this population rooted out; rather it was gradually absorbed into the emerging Israelite majority. The archaeological record can better be reconciled with the realistic version of the conquest in Judges 1 than with the idealized one in Joshua.

During the first two centuries of the Iron Age (ca. 1200–1000 B.C.E.), Egypt, as graphically and even humorously documented by the tale of Wen-Amon, gradually lost its traditional influence and interest in Asiatic affairs. At the same time Babylonia and Assyria became preoccupied with wars against each other. Thus neither hieroglyphic nor cuneiform sources throw much light on affairs in Palestine or Syria at this time. True, the area had meantime invented a script of its own. Indeed, it was much simpler than either of the other scripts. Via Phoenician and Greek it was destined to become the basis of our own modern alphabet. But few inscriptions in this new "West Semitic" script antedate the first millennium. Hence the early stages of the Israelite settlement in the Promised Land must be reconstructed largely from the biblical account, in particular the Book of Judges.

According to that source Israel was at this time organized into twelve tribes. These tribes occupied separate parts of the land on both sides of the Jordan and followed separate policies in each part. Only occasionally did a group of tribes make common cause against a common threat, whether this threat came from the native population or from other newcomers. In such cases the tribes in question rallied around a leader who by virtue of his bravery, skill or other talents was able to achieve a military victory. These "charismatic" leaders were called "judges," and followed their triumphs in battle with a brief period of civilian rule. Twelve such judges are known, distributed (more or less) over the twelve tribes. Few if any of them can be connected securely with events recorded in extra-biblical sources. (**See Reading 1-13.**) But some of their stories have gripped the popular as well as the artistic imagination: Deborah, a mother in Israel who celebrated her victory in song; Gideon who refused the offer of kingship; Jephthah whose fateful vow had to be paid by his daughter; Samson who courted Delilah and perished with the Philistines.

None of the judges was succeeded by a son (though Gideon's son made the attempt), and none commanded the allegiance of all the tribes. Their common loyalty was, as before during the period of the wanderings and conquests, to the unseen God of Israel. And their common visible link was apparently the ark or box which was believed to contain the sacred tablets of the law received at Mount Sinai. According to one theory, a shrine containing this ark was established at a succession of sanctuaries all located in the central highlands where it could be conveniently reached by all the tribes who dwelled round about. This institution is sometimes referred to as an "amphictyony" or "league of those dwelling around" a central sanctuary, analogous to later Greek examples. A closer analogy may, however, be furnished by earlier Mesopotamian experiments in uniting previously independent city-states that divided the upkeep of a central sanctuary on the basis of the twelve months of the year. This may explain the persistence of the number twelve in the tribal system of Israel. By thus uniting the separate tribes for common worship, the basis was also laid for concerted action in the realms of military action and political organization. Even as the sons of Jacob had become the Children of Israel, so now the tribes of Israel were ready to emerge as the nation of Israel.

## THE EMERGENCE OF KINGSHIP

Kingship was one of the fundamental constituents of ancient Near Eastern civilization. In Mesopotamia it was thought to have come down from heaven at the beginning of history and again after the Flood. The Egyptians believed that their first king was the sun god Re: he handed the kingship on to other gods, the last of whom was incarnate in all the pharaohs of Egypt from the beginning of the historical period. Elsewhere the conception of royalty followed one or the other of these two models. Rule by kings was well-nigh universal. Rule by the people (the Greek idea of democracy) was unknown in the Near East. Rule by God (theocracy) was unique to Israel.

But even in Israel, theocracy was more of an ideal than a reality. As we have seen, the tribes of Israel resorted repeatedly to temporary military leaders during their struggles to settle the Promised Land. And even these could not unite them sufficiently or rule them efficiently. Pressures mounted to conform to the prevailing constitutional pattern. They converged in the person of Samuel, a figure who in some sense represented the last of the judges and the first of the prophets. Faced with the twin threats of Philistines on the west and Ammonites on the east, the tribes demanded, "Appoint a king for us, to govern us like all other nations" (I Samuel 8:5). Samuel countered with a classic defense of theocracy and a warning of the evil consequences of monarchy (I Samuel 8:11–17; cf. 10:25). But the people insisted, "We must have a king over us, that we may be like all the other nations" (I Samuel 8:19f). (**See Reading 1-14.**)

Samuel responded by anointing Saul as first king of Israel. Saul's physical stature and military prowess matched the charismatic qualities of the earlier judges. And he surpassed them in his ability to unite all the tribes and led them to victory over both Philistines and Ammonites. Although Saul remained to the end a simple man of the people, he established some of the trappings of a royal court on his ancestral lands within the territory of his tribe. For example, he established the dynastic principle: Jonathan was his heir-presumptive. When Jonathan and his two brothers died in battle against the Philistines, and Saul committed suicide rather than face capture (ca. 1000 B.C.E.), another son succeeded to the throne.

Thus the monarchic principle was introduced to Israel. Despite initial misgivings and Saul's tragic end, the principle survived, ready to be strengthened. To begin with, the prospects appeared bleak. The southern tribe of Judah anointed David the son-in-law of Saul as its own king. David had distinguished himself as a warrior but had fallen out of favor at the court. The northern tribes at first followed Saul's surviving son but, after seven years, made David their king as well.

David thereupon proceeded to consolidate the monarchy beyond anything his predecessors had achieved. By a clever stratagem he captured the apparently impregnable citadel of Jerusalem and, rather than assigning the city to his own tribe of Judah or any other tribe, he made it his own royal city and thereby the capital of what was at last truly a united monarchy. He thoroughly defeated the Philistines, recovering the ark they had captured (see p. 22), and installed it ceremoniously in his new capital. Thus Jerusalem at a stroke became the successor of the old tradition of a central sanctuary housing the cultic symbol of the tribal confederation.

In other matters of state the new king was equally astute. He created an army loyal to himself, completed the subjugation of the native population, secured the kingdom's boundaries by treaties and

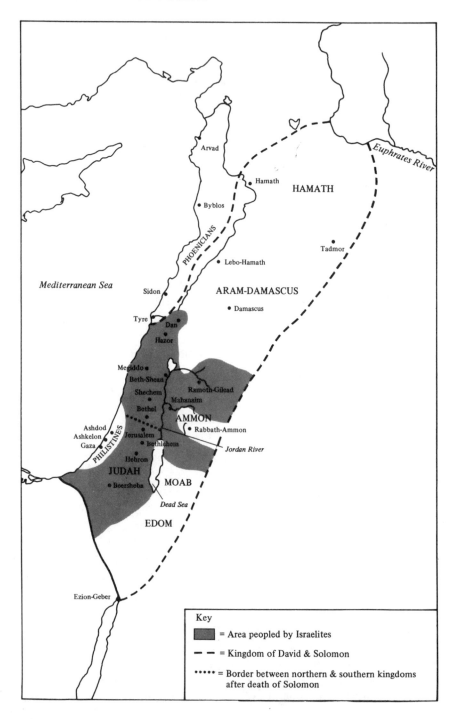

**Map 2    The United Israelite Monarchy Under David and Solomon**

alliances, and extended them by conquest. His biggest triumph was over his Aramean contemporary Hadadezer (II Samuel 8 and 10). This enabled him to reach the Euphrates River and incorporate most of Syria into his growing kingdom.

In addition to his military prowess, David was famed as "the sweet singer of Israel" (II Samuel 23:1). He was the supposed author or subject of numerous poems preserved in the Book of Psalms and elsewhere, some of them celebrating highlights of his life both before and after his accession. (See Reading 1-15.) He was mindful of the ethical behavior demanded by the God of Israel even if he did not always adhere to it. Beginning with David, prophets became a regular fixture at the courts of Israel. They dared to call even kings to account for immoral conduct and laid the foundation for subsequent literary prophecy with its high ethical content.

One area in which David met with almost continuous reverses was that of personal and family relations. His marriage to Saul's daughter Michal turned out badly; his marriage to Bathsheba involved the surreptitious murder of her husband; the first child of their union died as an infant. His firstborn son raped his half-sister, daughter of David by yet another wife, only to be murdered in turn by her brother; the latter then raised the banner of revolt against his father and paid with his life for the attempt. Even with these contenders out of the way, the remaining sons (and their respective mothers) struggled with each other for David's favor. It required prophetic intercession before David decided in favor of Bathsheba's son Solomon. Yet for all his human shortcomings, David passed into later tradition as the ideal king, the model for all successors even after the fall of the kingdom and the end of the dynasty he had founded.

## THE SOLOMONIC EMPIRE

The period of circa 1100–650 B.C.E. is referred to in Egyptian history as the Third Intermediate Period. It was the third (and longest) of those interludes when the centralized power of the pharaohs broke down and the pharaohs' authority had to be shared with other dynasties, with rival claimants to the throne, or with powerful provincial governors. Under such circumstances Egypt could not effectively wield influence abroad. The same label is sometimes applied to post-Kassite Babylonia in the roughly contemporaneous interval (ca. 1150–700 B.C.E.) between the end of Kassite rule and the beginning of Assyrian domination there. During most of this long span of time Babylonia was totally unable to play a role in the international affairs of the Near East. With Syria and Anatolia previously neutralized, the way was open for Israel to assume the status of a major power in its own right. It rose to the occasion most conspicuously during the reign of Solomon (ca. 965–925 B.C.E.).

Solomon, whose very name means "his peace," "had peace on all his borders round about" (I Kings 5:4). These borders preserved and even extended those already reached by David. This was achieved without resort to warfare. Instead, Solomon relied on the threat posed by a newly organized standing army, complete with chariotry, and the promise of dynastic marriage. The latter notably involved Egypt, breaking long precedent. Not only was a daughter of the pharaoh allowed to marry the Israelite king, but she brought him territory, probably the last Egyptian holdings in Asia, as dowry. Thus Solomon's kingdom embraced all the lands between the Euphrates River and the Sinai peninsula, a realm of truly imperial extent.

As a man of peace, Solomon was entitled, in the biblical view, to surpass his father in another respect—as temple builder. Solomon selected Jerusalem for this purpose, and erected there the first permanent sanctuary to Israel's God. The work began in his fourth year of rule (ca. 960 B.C.E.). Its completion seven years later was followed by elaborate seven-day dedication ceremonies (I Kings 8:65f.; cf. II Chronicles 7:8f). Almost twice as much time was required for the palace that Solomon built for himself and his "seven hundred royal wives" (I Kings 11:3), albeit with less fanfare (I Kings 7:1). It must have been correspondingly larger and more elaborate. (See Reading 1-16.)

For both these unprecedented building operations Solomon made good use of his foreign contacts. In particular, the allied King Hiram of Tyre supplied both raw materials and skilled labor. But unskilled labor had to come from the Israelites who were forced to endure conscription into labor battalions as well as military units, confirming all the drawbacks of kingship that Israel had been warned of when it first demanded a king (see p. 23). To facilitate these and other transformations, Solomon reorganized the whole governmental structure of the kingdom. He abolished most of the old tribal boundaries and replaced them, at least in the north, with twelve new provinces. Each of these was responsible for filling the royal coffers during one month (I Kings 4:7). Analogous systems existed then in contemporary Egypt and had been used in Mesopotamia over a thousand years earlier. Thus he cleverly retained the old principle of tribal organization but broke up old tribal loyalties while assuring a steady income for the royal household. (**See Reading 1-17.**)

Solomon's diplomatic and administrative gifts were matched by his intellectual endowments. His wisdom was legendary and the Queen of Sheba (Saba) was said to have come all the way from distant Arabia to test it. Supposedly he composed 3,000 proverbs and more songs than even David (I Kings 4:32). Within the Hebrew Bible, much of the Book of Proverbs and all of Ecclesiastes and the Song of Songs were attributed to him, and postbiblical Jewish literature added to this list, though with considerably less justification. All in all the Solomonic empire achieved first rank in political and cultural terms a scant two generations after the introduction of kingship in Israel.

But for all its grandeur, it was not destined to outlive him. Tribal loyalties remained strong, and the burdens of taxes and inscription weighed more heavily on the ten northern tribes (Israel) than on the two southern ones (Judah). The former appealed to Solomon's successor to ease their burdens, and he duly consulted with "the elders" and "the young men," each in turn (I Kings 12; cf. II Chronicles 10). Of these two consultative groups, the former counseled restraint. But the latter advised confrontation and, following ancient literary precedent, their counsel prevailed. The northern tribes therefore proclaimed their traditional rallying-call: "To your tents, O Israel!" (I Kings 12:16; cf. II Samuel 20:1). They anointed a king of their own and put an end to the United Monarchy. For the next two centuries (ca. 920–720 B.C.E.), there was to be a divided monarchy—Judah in the south and Israel in the north. (**See Reading 1-18.**)

## THE KINGDOM OF ISRAEL

Israel, whether united or divided, was not alone in taking advantage of the weakness of the traditional centers of power during the Early Iron Age. Far to the east of the Euphrates River, straddling the Tigris River, lay the kingdom of Assyria. Already in the fourteenth century its rulers had begun to challenge the great powers. In half a millennium of nearly constant warfare they had developed its military capacities to unprecedented heights. However, they were thwarted by mountainous terrain from expanding northward into Anatolia (Turkey) or eastward into Iran, and a certain respect for the older culture of Babylonia usually made them reluctant to penetrate southward. But westward the way lay open, and westward the course of their empire took its way. Inexorably the Assyrians thus came into contact and competition with the northern kingdom of Israel, which was striving to maintain or restore the Solomonic empire in Syria.

At first there was no hint of the troubles to come. The new Israelite kingdom was preoccupied with internal problems, and none of its rulers was able to establish an enduring dynasty. Effective leadership seemed to lie in prophets like Elijah and Elisha, who repeatedly sought to warn the northern kings against involvement with their immediate neighbors, notably in Phoenicia (Lebanon) and Syria. The seductions of the pagan cults encountered through such involvements, they were afraid, would wean Israel away from the worship of its own true God.

But the accession of Shalmaneser III of Assyria (858–824 B.C.E.) changed the nature of the threat. Given his unambiguous designs on the lands of all the kings of the area, the kings had no alternative but to join in a grand alliance against him. Israel was a prominent member of the alliance that confronted the great conqueror, no less than five times between 853 and 841 B.C.E. In effect, the allies fought Shalmaneser III to a standstill, and for a time they enjoyed a respite from the Assyrians, who contented themselves with accepting their tribute. Shalmaneser had himself thus pictured together with the prostrate king of Israel on a black obelisk, the first monument presumably depicting an identifiable biblical personage. He is there named "Jehu son of Omri," though in fact Jehu (841–814 B.C.E.) had put an end to the house of Omri. Under his successors the northern kingdom was thus more appropriately referred to as Samaria, after the capital city which Omri had built. (See Readings 1-19 and 1-20.) The long reign of Jeroboam II (793–753; sole ruler since 781 B.C.E.) even saw a restoration of Israel's borders almost to their Solomonic extent. But a new breed of prophets arose, whose words have been preserved in biblical books bearing their own names. Beginning with Amos, they warned of the fragile character of political independence—in effect of the temporary nature of the respite. They coupled these warnings with denunciation of the rich new cosmopolitan life indulged in by the newly emerging royal-urban society. They condemned the foreign cults, conspicuous consumption, expropriation of small landholders, and exploitation of the landless poor. They urged a return to the simple life Israel had known in the premonarchic days on penalty of sharing the fate of other kingdoms whose reach had exceeded their grasp. (**See Reading 1-21.**)

Their words truly proved prophetic. Whether because they were ignored or, on the contrary, as a novel theory would have it, because they were only too well heeded, Israel began an economic and military decline. At the same time Assyrian power experienced a new resurgence beginning with Tiglath-pileser III (744–727 B.C.E.) which was to keep it permanently involved in the affairs of Israel and Judah until all three states had vanished. The new king himself invaded the northern kingdom and annexed half of its territory, including all that lay east of the Jordan. He sent much of the population into exile in Assyria or to distant provinces of its growing empire, thus exposing Israel to a policy of state to be encountered many times again. In 722 B.C.E. Samaria, the capital of Israel, fell to the Assyrian armies, and the entire northern kingdom was incorporated into the Assyrian provincial system. (**See Reading 1-22.**)

## THE KINGDOM OF JUDAH

The southern kingdom, meantime, had led a somewhat quieter, more sheltered existence. The Davidic dynasty was firmly established in Judah, and son succeeded father in nearly unbroken succession. Egypt was generally too weak and Assyria still too distant to cause alarm. Initially the main threat came from the kindred kingdom of Israel. When Israel allied itself with the Arameans of Syria, Judah even turned to Tiglath-pileser of Assyria for help. But the fall of Israel had a profound effect on the southern kingdom, perhaps heightened by an influx of refugees from the north. The words of the prophets no longer fell on deaf ears. In Judah the prophets were ultimately to help shape royal policy.

With Israel incorporated into Assyria, Judah now bordered on the insatiable empire. The first blows were directed against the Philistine cities on the coast which barred the way to Egypt, the greater prize. But Judah could not remain a bystander for long. In 701 B.C.E. Sennacherib of Assyria invaded Judah, destroying all its walled cities. Only Jerusalem itself was spared. It seemed to King Hezekiah (716–687 B.C.E.) that he owed his salvation to divine intervention. Isaiah the prophet, who had counseled him to hold fast, was vindicated, and the king inaugurated a series of religious reforms that expressed his gratitude. Even the illness that racked the last fifteen years of his life did not shake his faith. He addressed God by means of a letter-prayer, familiar in Assyrian and Babylonian usage, and appointed his son Manasseh as co-regent. (See Reading 1-23.)

Manasseh was able to maintain a precarious independence from Assyria by, in effect, swearing vassalage to her king. Though religious reforms lapsed during his long reign (696–642 B.C.E.; sole reign since 686), they were resumed with even greater zeal by Josiah (639–609 B.C.E.), who was considered second only to David as a model king. A "book of the law" (or "scroll of the teaching," I Kings 22:8) was discovered in the Temple in Josiah's eighteenth year (622 B.C.E.) and promulgated by him. It is generally thought to be the core of the biblical Book of Deuteronomy. Under its provisions the local cults, permitted until then, were abolished and the sacrificial cult centralized once and for all in the temple of Jerusalem. Once more God became Israel's sovereign overlord, and Deuteronomy the vassal-treaty that confirmed the relationship. Some of its provisions clearly paralleled the treaties between the Assyrian kings and their vassals. This is notably true of the curses foreseen for violations of the treaty. In a political sense, then, Josiah was implicitly declaring his independence from Assyrian vassalage. (See Reading 1-24.)

Indeed, the Assyrian Empire was in decline. Josiah took advantage of the situation to extend his rule and his reforms to the territory of the former northern kingdom. But greater powers were waiting in the wings. Marching north in a last, unsuccessful effort to save his Assyrian ally, Neco, the new pharaoh of a newly recovered Egypt, was met by Josiah on the ancient battlefield of Megiddo, whether for battle or in peace is not certain. In either event, the pious king was slain for his pains (609 B.C.E.). Four years later Neco in turn was defeated by a resurgent Babylonia at the Battle of Carchemish. The Babylonian armies were led by Nebuchadnezzar and, in him, the Near East found a new empire-builder. Two of his major campaigns were directed against Jerusalem. The first, in 597 B.C.E., was duly chronicled by the Babylonians in words supplementing the biblical account but surprisingly similar to it. The second, in 586 B.C.E., ended in the complete subjugation of the city, the exile of the rest of its principal citizenry, the destruction of the First (Solomonic) Temple, and the end of the First Commonwealth. (See Reading 1-25.)

# THE PROPHETIC ROLE

Thus ended Israel's brief experiment with kingship. In fact, the institution of kingship, so typical of the Near Eastern states, lasted little more than four centuries under Israelite and Judaean auspices. Brief revivals of kingship were attempted subsequently—and the hope of an ultimate restoration of the Davidic dynasty was never totally abandoned—but another institution, more peculiarly Israelite in origin and character, proved more enduring. This was prophecy.

Apart from Moses, the first prophet according to the biblical conception was Samuel who himself had, however reluctantly, anointed the first king. But Samuel and his immediate successors were prophets in an older mold: "seers" whose behavior was thought to mark them as possessed by the divine spirit and whose actions as much as their words were designed to convey the divine message. They were often surrounded by bands of disciples and exercised a fascination over wide segments of the population by claiming, or being perceived as having, the power to work miracles.

In due time such early prophets found a hearing also at the royal court, where some ingratiated themselves by endorsing royal policy. But others followed Samuel's example and dared to hold even kings to the ethical standards demanded by Israel's God. Thus the prophet Nathan reproved King David for his devious designs on Bathsheba, and Elijah similarly confronted King Ahab of Israel for high-handedly appropriating Naboth's vineyard. But these and many other named and unnamed early prophets are still known to us only through the tales associated with them or the brief denunciations recorded in their names.

Beginning early in the eighth century B.C.E., a new kind of prophecy emerged, first in the northern kingdom and then in the south. This was literary prophecy, a conception of the inspired man of God, whose public statements were accepted as divine messages worthy to be recorded for all posterity. This new form of prophecy was less concerned with foretelling the future than with forthtelling the word of God. It did not so much predict as "confront man with the alternatives of decision." According to Amos, the consequences of choosing the wrong alternative could be the very end of the flourishing northern kingdom. Before the end of the century history vindicated this prophecy, and the southern kingdom therefore paid greater heed to Isaiah, the first of the "major" prophets. Isaiah's messages, often frankly political, cast him as a clarion call of conscience at the courts of four successive kings.

Jeremiah encountered royal resistance to prophetic counsel. In the tumultuous days preceding the fall of the southern kingdom, he found his writings burned, his property confiscated, his life in danger, and himself imprisoned. His "Jeremiads" (lamentations) were unwelcome warnings of doom in a period desperately in need of hope.

With that hope dashed by destruction and exile, a new role emerged for prophecy. Words of reproach were replaced by expressions of consolation. The third of the major prophets, Ezekiel, upheld the spirits of the exiles with visions of a rebuilt temple and a restored cult. A second Isaiah (or a nameless prophet whose words were added to those of the first Isaiah) interpreted exile itself as a testimony to the universal power of God, who employed foreign nations to carry out the divine design for Israel. If one nation had exiled the people, another would restore Israel. And late prophets like Haggai and Zechariah would encourage the work of restoration.

From first to last Israelite prophecy provided a unique vehicle for imparting a highly ethical component to Israelite life. Prophets were not always in competition with kings or priests or lawgivers; often, indeed, they were equally concerned with statecraft, cult, and law. But they demanded that all these spheres be infused with a high moral content. They thus elevated the institution of prophecy far above the simple role of frenzied seers with which it had begun.

---

*Editor's Questions*
**AFTER VIEWING AND READING**

- How did the Mesopotamian and Egyptian cultures contribute to the history of the ancient Israelites?
- Do the biblical accounts and archaeological evidence merge to give a coherent account of the Israelites' conquest of Canaan?
- Why were the judges unable to defend the Israelites against the Philistines?
- Did David and Solomon's kingdom contain the seeds of its eventual decline?

- Compare Assyria and Babylonia's rise to power and describe how their military exploits affected the Israelite kingdoms.
- Identify three Israelite prophets. Did they preach identical messages? Were there differences in their styles and behavior?

SUGGESTED READINGS

Roland de Vaux, *The Early History of Israel,* trans. by David Smith (Westminster Press, 1978)

Tomoo Ishida, ed., *Studies in the Period of David and Solomon and Other Essays* (Yamakawa-Shuppansha, 1982)

Morris Silver, *Prophets and Markets: The Political Economy of Ancient Israel* (Kluwer-Nijhoff Publishing, 1983)

E.A. Speiser, ed., *At the Dawn of Civilization* ( = The World History of the Jewish People, ed. Benjamin Mazar, vol. 1) (Rutgers University Press, 1964)

Robert R. Wilson, *Prophecy and Society in Ancient Israel* (Fortress Press, 1980)

# 2

## The Power of the Word

William W. Hallo

*Editor's Suggestions*
BEFORE VIEWING THE SHOW

Examine Map 3, which shows the extent of the Hasmonean state in the second century B.C.E., and Map 4, which notes the major Jewish population centers in the Mediterranean world from the first through the fifth centuries C.E.

*Overview of the TV Program*

The kingdom of Judah was destroyed by Nebuchadnezzar, and many Israelites and their nobility were exiled to Babylon. There they reestablished their lives and learned how to worship their God in a strange land. They were now called Jews, people who had come from the kingdom of Judah. The Babylonian Empire fell with the conquests of Cyrus, who allowed the Jews to return to their homeland. Some took advantage of his offer, and after a number of difficult years they were able to rebuild the Temple in Jerusalem.

Like the Babylonian Empire, the Persian Empire was also defeated in war. This time the conqueror was Alexander the Great. His victory meant not only the supremacy of Hellenic power but also the spread of Hellenistic civilization throughout the empire. The Jews, as other peoples, learned from Hellenistic culture. But they disagreed among themselves what the desirable limits of Hellenistic influence on the Judaean population should be. A civil war erupted broadening into a revolt against the Jews' Hellenistic overlords. The victories, led by Judah the Maccabee, led to the purification of the Temple, an act which was commemorated by the holiday of Hannukkah.

The Maccabees founded the Hasmonean state, and the new Jewish state grew and became more powerful. With the rise of the Roman Empire, Judaea came under its control in 63 B.C.E. Within the Jewish religion a number of sects developed, each practicing according to its own beliefs.

Roman rule became harsher and the Jews were oppressed economically and politically. Men appeared and declared themselves the messiah—the long-awaited redeemer of the Jewish people; these individuals claimed they would save the Jews from Roman domination. A great revolt erupted in 66 C.E. against Rome, but in four years Jerusalem was captured and the second Temple destroyed. Some Jews continued fighting, as did those at Masada, while others followed Yoḥanan ben Zakkai, leader of the Pharisee sect, who sought a policy of accommodation with Rome. He emphasized the continuation of the Jewish faith through the study of Jewish law and the practice of good deeds, and he believed that Judaism could survive without a temple. Still, Jews smarted from their loss and another rebellion, led by Simon Bar Kokhba in the next century, suffered devastating defeat in 135 C.E.

*Watch for . . . and Think about*

Note the ruins of the Babylonian Empire. Why was it hard for the Jews to mix with Babylonian society?

Observe the glories of Greece and Hellenistic civilization. What did the Jews find attractive in this culture and what repelled them?

You will glimpse a model of the second Temple erected in Jerusalem. Do you see Hellenistic influence in its architecture?

After the defeat in 70 C.E. by the Romans the Arch of Titus was erected in Rome. What did it symbolize?

WHILE READING THE *STUDY GUIDE* AND *SOURCE READER*

Look for the following:

- Jeremiah comforting the Babylonian Jewish exiles.
- Cyrus' policy toward the Jews.
- Where Jews lived outside of their homeland. Identify Diaspora.
- The attempt of the Jews returning to rebuild the Temple. What problems did they face? Identify Yehud, Judaea, and the Samaritans.
- Ptolemies, the Seleucids, and Judah Maccabee. Why did the Maccabees revolt against the Seleucid rulers? Were they successful?

- The stages of Roman rule in Judaea. Identify Herod, the pro-curators, and Messiah.
- The forms Judaism took during the last two centuries B.C.E. and the first century C.E. Identify synagogues, sects, Pharisees, Sadducees, and Essenes.
- The issues that concerned the Jews living in the Diaspora during Roman rule.

## THE BABYLONIAN EXILE

Civilization originated in the Near East with the beginning of the Bronze Age and spread rapidly both westward and eastward. By the end of that age it reached from the Atlantic Ocean to the Pacific. But throughout the Bronze Age and the Iron Age that followed, civilization's geographical center remained the Near East in general and Mesopotamia or Babylonia in particular. That made Babylonia peculiarly open to the winds of change that blew all around it. And in the sixth century B.C.E., change was definitely in the air. The entire civilized world was in an intellectual ferment. To the west, the pre-Socratic philosophers of Ionia (western Turkey) were stirring the Greek-speaking world. To the east Zoroaster in Iran, Buddha in India, Confucius, and possibly Lao-Tse, in China, were laying the foundations of whole new systems of thought and belief. Time and place thus conspired to make sixth-century Babylonia the natural epicenter of a world in transition. And it was precisely here that Judaean exiles now found themselves.

The new environment was not uncongenial. Universally feared and detested by its subject peoples, and beset by powerful new enemies from the mountains on its northern and eastern borders (especially the Medes and Persians), the mighty Assyrian Empire had collapsed completely (609 B.C.E.), and a succession of Chaldean kings had restored the ancient glories of Babylon one last time (625–539 B.C.E.). These kings continued the Assyrian policy of mass deportations of conquered populations, and well might the Psalmist lament: "By the rivers of Babylon, there we sat, sat and wept, as we thought of Zion" (i.e., Jerusalem; Psalm 137:1). (See Reading 2-1.) But Jehoiachin, the exiled king of Judah, was provisioned from the royal coffers and eventually released from prison (II Kings 25:27). (See

Reading 2-2.) And life in Babylonia offered its own compensations. No doubt many exiles heeded the injunctions of the prophet Jeremiah to "build houses and live in them, plant gardens and eat their fruit, take wives and beget sons and daughters . . . and . . . seek the welfare of the city to which I have exiled you and pray to the Lord in its behalf" (Jeremiah 29:5–7). Jeremiah himself, exempted from exile by the Babylonians, accompanied another group of refugees to Egypt instead—where they all vanished (Jeremiah 43:7). But Babylonia proved more hospitable. On the soil whence Israel derived its ancestry other prophets arose to comfort the exiles, notably Ezekiel and a "second Isaiah." They reconciled the loss of political independence with a new vision of religious universalism. The God who had liberated Israel from Egyptian bondage and covenanted with it to be his peculiar people—the God who had freed Israel from Assyrian sovereignty and made it his own vassal—that God had not abandoned his people to Babylonian captivity. He was the Lord of all peoples, and used them as his instruments. In due time, he would find a new instrument to effect Israel's release from captivity. This new conception of a universal deity ruling over all peoples—and demanding faithful obedience from all individuals—was to be as far-reaching in its ultimate effect as any of the intellectual upheavals beyond the borders of the Near East. The Exodus from Egypt had inspired Israel to acknowledge its God as its sole sovereign and thus inaugurated monotheism, but in a limited form which still allowed for the possibility of other deities ruling over other peoples. The Babylonian exile, and more particularly the deliverance from exile, established the belief in an all-inclusive monotheism which was to be adopted far beyond the limits of Israel.

## THE JUDAEAN RESTORATION

Deliverance came sooner than anticipated. Jeremiah had forecast an exile of seventy years (Jeremiah 25:11f.; 29:10; cf. II Chronicles 36:21). But the end of the Chaldean Empire was hastened by its last king, Nabonidus, whose strange policies were remembered in the Book of Daniel (though there attributed to Nebuchadnezzar) and in even later Jewish writings, and the policies were equally puzzling and even unpopular among his Babylonian contemporaries. (See Reading 2-3.) Meantime the Medes and Persians had united under a powerful new leader, Cyrus the descendant of Achemenes, and were forging a new Persian (or Achemenid) empire under his auspices.

Jews and Babylonians alike welcomed Cyrus as a relief from the apparent madness of Nabonidus, and even employed curiously similar language to express themselves. (**See Reading 2-4.**) In 538 B.C.E., less than fifty years after the second exile, Babylon opened its gates to the new master of the world.

Cyrus did not disappoint the hopes pinned on him. He respected Babylonian traditions and turned Babylonia into one of the richest and most favored provinces of the growing new empire. And he secured the loyalty of his innumerable subject-peoples, not by terror and deportation like his predecessors, but by returning them to their ancestral lands, allowing them to restore their native cults and extending a measure of autonomy to them. These enlightened policies, proclaimed in a lengthy inscription, applied to numerous exiled populations and the cult-statues of their deities. (**See Reading 2-5.**) Nor were they simply "campaign promises," to be forgotten once Cyrus was safely entrenched. Records of otherwise insignificant communities, such as a group of Arameans from the town of Neirab in Syria, show that resettlement was effected.

Thus there is no reason to doubt the essential validity of the verse with which the Hebrew Bible concludes (II Chronicles 36:23; cf. also in Ezra 1:1–4): "Thus said King Cyrus of Persia: The Lord God of Heaven has given me all the kingdoms of the earth, and has charged me with building Him a house in Jerusalem, which is in Judah. Anyone of you of all His people, the Lord His God be with him and let him go up." According to the detailed biblical statistics nearly 50,000 exiles took advantage of this offer immediately. And others took advantage of the permission to remain behind in Babylonia, where they had managed to find a hospitable new home, and to assist the immigrants (literally "ascenders") with material and moral support. Thus was born that distinctive pattern which was to characterize Jewish history ever since: a well-entrenched Diaspora community content to remain in exile while praying for the eventual restoration of Zion as a homeland and supporting those willing to go up and make the attempt.

## THE EMERGING DIASPORA

The conquests by Cyrus and his successors created an empire larger than any the world had yet seen. "A hundred and twenty-seven provinces from India to Nubia" (Esther 1:1) were subject to one sovereign. They were ruled by governors (satraps) with considerable autonomy and were linked to each other by a highly developed road system. Although royal rescripts (formal announcements) may have been sent "to every province in its own script and to every people in its own language" (Esther 3:12, 8:9), the fact is that one script and language began to be current throughout the empire under royal auspices, and that was Aramaic. Jews also began to use this language and its script. Thus they could communicate with each other back in their own land or scattered throughout the provinces. Of the various Diaspora communities, three are particularly worthy of notice.

The first was Egypt. Far up the Nile from the places settled by the Judaeans of Jeremiah's time (see p. 38), a settlement of Jews lived on the southern border of Egypt. They had probably arrived there in the seventh century B.C.E., when Egypt regained its independence from Ethiopian and Assyrian rule. Certainly they were indifferent to Josiah's reforms of 622 B.C.E.—for they constructed a temple in defiance of Deuteronomy's centralization of the cult at Jerusalem. The temple was located on an island in the middle of the Nile, opposite the city of Syene (modern Aswan; today site of the Aswan Dam). When the Persians conquered Egypt, they engaged these Jews as mercenary soldiers, first to guard the frontier between Egypt and Nubia and soon enough, no doubt, to help control the local population as well. The latter responded by pillaging the temple, and the Jews appealed to their brethren in Judaea and Samaria for help. Their ultimate fate is unknown; perhaps they returned there as the exilic prophets had prayed (Isaiah 49:12 as read in the Dead Sea Scrolls; cf. Ezekiel 30:6, Jeremiah 44:28). (See Reading 2-6.)

A better fate was in store for the exiles who chose to remain in Babylonia. Here the Jews were quickly and fully integrated into the thriving commercial life of the country. A great banking house such as "Murashu and Sons" at Nippur, though not itself Jewish, dealt on many occasions with persons with distinctly Jewish names. The transactions are recorded in numerous documents of the fifth century B.C.E., still written in cuneiform but now often bearing endorsements in Aramaic. (See Reading 2-7.) Most of the Jews farmed modest-sized parcels of land. But some enjoyed higher status, and the descendants of the exiled king Jehoiachin continued to serve as rulers of the exiles (exilarchs) according to later tradition. Certainly the community met no such untimely end as the successive settlements in Egypt.

The situation in Iran proper was again different. Here, at the center of the Persian Empire, Jews might aspire to high office, but they were also particularly vulnerable to court intrigue. Both situations are reflected in the story of Mordecai as preserved in the biblical Book of Esther. The story is set in the reign of Xerxes (485–465 B.C.E.) at the capital city of Susa (Shushan). Essentially it is a creative variation on the theme of the success story of the wise vizier already encountered previously in the case of Joseph (see p. 13). In the absence of significant contemporary documentation from Susa, it must serve as the principal source for life in this Diaspora. And in fact it preserves authentic touches as in the use of lots or dice (*purim*) to determine high affairs of state. (**See Reading 2-8.**) It may therefore be regarded as another prescription for life in the Diaspora. Like Joseph in Egypt and Daniel in Babylonia, Mordecai in Persia exemplified the possibility of adhering to the ancestral faith even while rising to high estate in an alien environment. More than that, it illustrated the new mission that Judaism had assumed as a theological consequence of the prophetic interpretation of recent history: to spread the teachings of God to all humanity, to become a light to the gentiles (cf. Isaiah 49:6).

## THE SECOND TEMPLE

The former kingdom of Judah (in Hebrew: Yehudah) had meantime become Judaea (in Aramaic: Yehud), a small province within the great Fifth Satrapy of the Persian Empire called "Beyond the River" (i.e., west of the Euphrates; cf. Ezra 6:6, etc.).

The exiles who had returned there from Babylonia (and perhaps Egypt) joined the Judaeans (mostly poor) who had stayed behind to build a new life for themselves. Initial prospects seemed bleak. The people were impoverished, the temple destroyed, Jerusalem desolate, Judaea shrunk in size from the kingdom of Judah, and the restoration of kingship a hope deferred to an ever more distant future when, it was believed, a descendant of the house of David would again be God's anointed (Hebrew: *mashiach*; hence Messiah, the hoped-for king of the ultimate restoration). "Messianism" gradually replaced the lost causes of political independence and Davidic kingship.

All the more effort, by contrast, went into religious restoration. Imperial permission and even financial support were secured to rebuild the temple on its ancient sacred site. The Jewish governor of Judaea, the high priest, and prophets like Haggai and Zechariah all encouraged the work and persevered over the objections of jealous neighbors and suspicious officials. In the sixth year of King Darius

(515 B.C.E.) the new temple was completed and dedicated, and the sacrificial cult reinstated. (**See Reading 2-9.**)

A wholly new configuration emerged from these developments. The distant Persian monarchy demanded political loyalty but tolerated religious autonomy. Thus sporadic attempts to restore the Davidic dynasty were doomed to failure, and effective local power passed into the hands of the priesthood. Prophecy, which had for so long been a concomitant to kingship, now ceased as a vehicle of communication with the divine, and a class of learned scribes rose in its place to hand down and interpret the accumulated legal and prophetic teachings of earlier generations. A true theocracy was born in which God was the veritable sovereign and the priesthood his earthly lieutenants even though there was no overt challenge to the secular authority of the Persian administration.

The emerging leadership reflected these new realities. Ezra combined the role of priest and scribe, while Nehemiah, raised at the Persian court, came to Jerusalem as a governor loyal equally to the foreign emperor and to his Jewish origins. Ezra observed the New Year's festival by reading the "Scroll of the Teaching of Moses" (or "Book of the Law of Moses") to the entire people assembled in Jerusalem, in what appears to have been the first institutionalized use of the recently completed Pentateuch. The Pentateuch prescribed both secular and ritual behavior, and its official adoption marked, in a sense, the emergence of Judaism as a formal religious doctrine out of the diverse traditions that had shaped Israel's heritage. Meanwhile, Nehemiah completed the work of rebuilding the city by reconstructing its ruined walls, an achievement documented by recent excavations.

Among those who had watched the temple rebuilding with mixed feelings were the Samaritans. Heirs to the territory of the defunct northern kingdom of Israel, they occupied its ancient capital of Samaria and the surrounding countryside. In the eyes of the Judaeans, they were pagan descendants of exiles from conquered Babylonian cities brought in by the Assyrians more than a century earlier. But in their own eyes, they were Israelites—albeit with a difference. Their Bible (confined to the first five books, or Pentateuch) exhibited many differences in chronological, geographical, and other details all designed to show that the central sanctuary was destined, not for Jerusalem, but for Mount Gerizim near Samaria. There they maintained (and maintain to this day) a sacrificial cult in competition with that of Jerusalem. A schism developed and never healed. Under the leadership of Nehemiah and Ezra in the fifth century, special precautions were taken at Jerusalem to prevent (and even to undo) intermarriage between adherents of the two faiths. (See Reading 2-10.) Little is known of either community in the fourth century, except that the breach widened. As the Persian Empire began to decline before the growing power of the Greeks (who alone had withstood the tide of Persian expansion), the Judaeans wisely threw their support to the new invaders. The Samaritans opposed them, and many of them perished for their pains in the caves around Samaria where they had fled for safety. The papyrus documents which they took with them for safekeeping provide a precious glimpse into their last years. (See Reading 2-11.)

## THE PROMISE OF GREECE

In certain curious ways the history of Greece paralleled that of Israel. Both peoples shared and reshaped some of the oldest Mesopotamian myths; both believed they had originated far from their present homelands and acquired them by conquest; both looked back to fabled lawgivers at the beginning of their own collective experience; both had shared in the intellectual ferment of the sixth century B.C.E. Greeks were scattered in colonies all around the Mediterranean Sea, far from Athens and the other cities that had sent them forth; Jews were as widely dispersed from Jerusalem in the Diaspora (the very word is Greek) of the Persian Empire. Numerous Greeks and Jews had served that empire as mercenaries, artisans, and officials. They admired the strength of the Empire but knew its weaknesses. Now they were ready to make common cause in assuming its inheritance—to mingle the best of Greek and Near Eastern civilization in that peculiar mix known as Hellenistic culture.

These may be, then, among the reasons why, in 332 B.C.E., the Jews were as eager to welcome the Greeks as they had been two centuries earlier to welcome the Persians. The newcomers were led by the youthful Alexander of Macedon, so charismatic a combination of looks, learning, and luck that he swept all before him. Many of those he conquered were prepared to accord him divine honors, and even the Jews were willing (to this day) to name their children after him. Alexander completely defeated the Persian Empire and succeeded to all its domains. His realm, however briefly, even exceeded it in extent, incorporating as it did the Greek world on its western border and parts of India on its eastern frontier. Throughout this enormous realm cities were founded on the model of those in Greece, and Greek culture, including the Greek language, was widely adopted.

These developments survived Alexander's early death (323 B.C.E.), and the subsequent division of his realm among the generals of his armies. Judaea at first fell to the share of Ptolemy, who established a Greek dynasty in Egypt. Partly by choice and partly by force, Judaeans flocked by the tens and hundreds of thousands to settle in Egypt, particularly in Alexandria. In this, one of the greatest cultural centers of the Hellenistic world, they soon formed a sizable and distinct portion of the population. They were free to maintain their separate traditions, but learned to absorb many Greek ones as well. They produced a Greek translation of the Bible (the *Septuagint*) and of many other Jewish writings. Some of these have been preserved in the Christian Bible and elsewhere through these efforts. In Philo of Alexandria (25 B.C.E. to 50 C.E.) they produced an original thinker of the first order who strove to reconcile Jewish and Greek thought in his extensive writings (see p. 54).

Ptolemaic rule in Judaea lasted until 200 B.C.E., illuminated in part by records of an Egyptian official. (**See Reading 2-12.**) Then the land fell under the control of the Seleucid kingdom, which had inherited much of Alexander's Asian conquests, including Babylonia and Syria. Jerusalem was thus reunited with the eastern Diaspora. But relations with the new Greek (or "Syrian") overlords deteriorated rapidly. The Seleucid rulers were determined to impose Greek patterns of culture and conduct. But only the Hellenizers among the Jews were prepared to abandon their own traditions. In terms not unlike their Babylonian contemporaries, they depicted the Seleucids as merely the latest in a succession of rulers who too were bound to pass from the scene. (**See Reading 2-13.**) Such predictions replaced earlier prophecy, which was believed to have ceased in the time of Ezra, and assumed the form of apocalyptic or dramatic revelations of the future. In the Hebrew Bible, they are attributed to Daniel.

The opposition to the Seleucid Greeks, however, also assumed more concrete forms. Under Judah Maccabee, the standard of revolt was raised. After some years of intensive fighting, the first objective was secured in 164 B.C.E.: the temple was recaptured from the Syrian troops that had occupied it, cleansed and rededicated. The festival of Hannukkah ("(re)dedication") celebrates this occasion to this day. (**See Reading 2-14.**) But for all their mutual antagonism, Jews and Greeks continued to interact creatively during the Seleucid period. Among many other legacies of the age, the Jews adopted the Seleucid Era (which began in 312 B.C.E.) as a system of dating. They held on to it even after it was replaced by the Christian or common era (C.E.) in the European West and the Muslim Era in the Near East; not until approximately the eighth century C.E. did they replace it with the Jewish Era of Creation.

The apocalyptic visions of Daniel are the latest writings incorporated in the Hebrew Bible. The vagueness or incorrectness of Daniel's predictions of events after 164 B.C.E. serves, in critical opinion, to date them to that year. With these events, then, biblical history comes, in a sense, to an end. What follows is epilogue, culled from sources other and later than the Hebrew Bible. These include the *Apocrypha*, or Jewish writings incorporated in the Christian Bible, and the histories of Josephus. Josephus wrote in Greek, attempting to interpret to the Greek-speaking world the entire history of Israel. He thus did for this history what other Hellenistic writers had done for the native traditions of Egypt, Babylonia, and Phoenicia. But only Josephus' writings are preserved in full, and they are particularly detailed for the events now unfolding.

## THE HASMONEANS

### by Shaye J. D. Cohen*

The rededication of the temple in 164 B.C.E. was followed by twenty years of fighting and negotiating between the Seleucids and the Maccabees (or the Hasmoneans, as the leaders of the revolt were called by the Jews). Not until 142 B.C.E. was independence achieved and the last Seleucid soldier removed from Jerusalem. The Maccabean cause was aided immeasurably by the weakness of the Seleucid government. Harassed by the Romans in the west and by the Parthians in the east, beset by internecine strife and political instability, the Seleucid empire was incapable of stopping the Maccabees, whose

---

*Dr. Cohen has written the remainder of chapter 2.

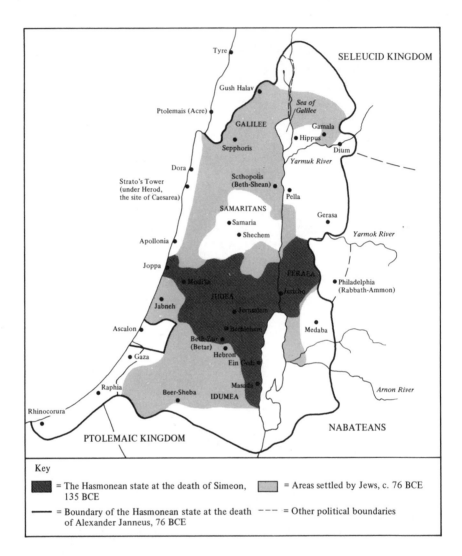

**Map 3    The Hasmonean State**

war for religious freedom won them not only religious freedom but also an independent state of impressive dimensions. Having conquered Samaria, Galilee, Idumaea, much of the Transjordan, and many cities along the coast, the Maccabean conquerors of the latter part of the second century B.C.E. created a state which rivaled that of King David and King Solomon. The Maccabees justified these conquests by the argument that the Jews were merely reclaiming their ancestral land, which had been promised to them by God. (**See Reading 2-15.**) Many of the new subjects of the Maccabean state were persuaded or compelled to adopt the Jewish religion, because God's land had to be populated by God's people. The Maccabean empire reached its zenith during the reign of Alexander Jannaeus (103–76 B.C.E.).

Success, however, was fleeting. In 63 B.C.E. Pompey marched into Jerusalem at the head of his Roman legions. The Jews had invited Pompey to arbitrate the rival claims of the two sons of Alexander Jannaeus to succeed their father, but even without an invitation Pompey would have found an excuse to impose Roman domination on the Jews. The Romans had been expanding eastward ever since the third century B.C.E., and there was no way that the Jews could have stopped them. With the Roman conquest came the reduction of the territory under Jewish control and the loss of political independence.

In the span of two generations the Maccabees rose from outlaws to kings, from ordinary priests to high priests, from rustics to aristocrats. Their fall was just as precipitous: in one generation they lost it all. They never attained the unanimous support of the Jews, many of whom supported Judah's struggle for religious freedom but opposed his usurpation of political leadership. The Maccabees were social upstarts, country priests who had ousted the aristocrats of the city of Jerusalem. Although they had neither the pedigree nor the social standing to become high priests and kings, the Maccabees ultimately assumed both offices. The opposition became violent during the reigns of John Hyrcanus (134–104 B.C.E.) and Alexander Jannaeus, who had converted the Maccabean state—founded on the basis of zeal for Jewish law—into a typical petty principality of the Hellenistic east. But one achievement will always be to their credit: they saved the monotheistic faith. Judah and his followers were imbued with Hellenistic culture, but they, unlike the Hellenizers, recognized the limits of Hellenization. They were prepared to adopt and adapt

Hellenistic culture to the needs of Judaism, provided that these influences would enrich Judaism and not destroy it. By preventing Judaism from becoming another local variation of the polytheism of the Semitic east, they saved Judaism and, ultimately, Christianity and Islam, the two monotheistic faiths which would emerge from Judaism.

## THE THREAT OF ROME

The initial contacts between the Romans and the Jews were friendly. The Romans had supported Judah the Maccabee and his followers in their struggle against the Seleucids. Pompey's entrance into Jerusalem was in response to an invitation from the Jews themselves. But 63–31 B.C.E. was a period of great instability in Rome which witnessed the collapse of the Republic and the birth of monarchic rule. The Romans needed a ruler who could keep the peace in Judaea while maintaining loyalty to Rome. Since they were the focal point of the nationalist aspirations of the Jews, the Maccabees could no longer be trusted. The Romans therefore chose a new dynasty of Jewish rulers who would owe their august status to the Romans alone. They chose Herod, known to posterity as Herod the Great. After a shaky start, Herod became the sole ruler of Judaea and other portions of Palestine during his lengthy career (37–4 B.C.E.).

Herod was a man of contradictions. He was a Jew of Idumaean extraction; his detractors called him a "half-Jew." He saw himself both as king of the Jews and as the cosmopolitan ruler of all the peoples of Palestine. He rebuilt the temple in Jerusalem (the temple mount which still forms the center of Jerusalem is the work of Herod), aided the Jews in the Diaspora when they needed help and usually observed Jewish law when dealing with his fellow Jews. But in his private life he did not observe the Jewish traditions, and even in public did many things that offended Jewish sensitivities. The magnificent temple was capped with a Roman eagle, and the city of Jerusalem was equipped with a stadium. Unsure of the loyalties of his Jewish subjects, he sought the support of the numerous pagans who lived in Palestine by building temples and cities for them (the most famous of which is Caesarea). The pagans of other areas also benefited from his largess. He bestowed gifts upon many cities of the east and even helped to support the Olympic games. Herod's greatest failure was his relationship with those closest to him. He suspected everyone, especially his own children, of plotting his downfall. He built fortresses throughout the country (the most famous of which is Masada) and killed several of his wives, many of his children, and numerous members of the aristocracy. Herod's brutality, high taxes (needed to pay for all his building projects), irreligiosity, and obsequiousness to the Romans did not endear him to the Jews. Upon his death in 4 B.C.E. the first murmurings of anti-Roman rebellion were heard.

The spirit of revolution died down for a while but returned in the forties C.E. with increasing force. In 66 C.E. a full-scale war broke out between the Romans and the Jews of Palestine. The causes of the war were many and varied. Not long after Herod's death the Romans decided to abolish his kingdom and to rule Judaea directly. They appointed administrators, known as *procurators* or *prefects*, who were poorly equipped for their task. Obtuse, stubborn, brutal, insensitive, and corrupt, they represented Roman imperial administration at its worst. Even the emperors did not always realize that the Jews were different from all other peoples. The mad emperor Caligula (37–41 C.E.) decided to erect a statue of himself in the temple, and would have implemented his plan had he not been opposed by the governor of Syria and had he not been assassinated at an opportune moment. Roman maladministration, then, was partly to blame for the events of 66 C.E. On the Jewish side there was high unemployment and much social unrest. Many revolutionary groups directed their energies primarily against the wealthy and the aristocracy. Many Jews, believing that God would soon destroy the Roman Empire and replace it with the rule of his anointed king (the Messiah), were prepared to risk all since the end was imminent. The result was war and catastrophe. In 67 and 68 C.E. the Roman general Vespasian reconquered the entire countryside and in 70 C.E. his son Titus reconquered Jerusalem and destroyed the temple.

The Jews lost the war because they had started it without sufficient advance preparation. A series of riots in 66 C.E. became a war for which no one was prepared. There was no central leadership; the numerous revolutionary groups fought each other with even greater ferocity than they fought the Romans. Many Jews opposed the war altogether—and these were not just the wealthy and the aristocracy. Peasants, too, feared that they would lose all they had in a war with Rome, and sober people of all social classes realized that armed conflict with Rome was futile if not impious. They believed that God would destroy the Roman Empire at the appropriate moment and that there was nothing that the Jews could do to hasten the appointed time. In the Jewish historical tradition, from rabbinic antiquity until the rise of Jewish nationalism in the nineteenth century, the heroes of the war are not the revolutionaries who failed, but the quietists who succeeded, in ensuring Jewish survival. The fanatics of Masada, who continued to fight the Romans even after the temple was destroyed, accomplished nothing. They committed suicide, but suicide was not an avenue to the future. (**See Reading 2-16.**)

## RELIGIOUS FERMENT

The period between the rise of the Maccabees (160's B.C.E.) and the destruction of the temple (70 C.E.) witnessed many important religious developments. Some of these have been touched upon already: the flowering of apocalyptic literature, the growth of speculations about the end time, and the struggle concerning the proper limits of the adaptation of Hellenistic culture. Another important development is the emergence of sectarianism. When Jews gathered to pray and study together they formed *synagogues* (literally, "assemblies"). When they gathered in small organizations and asserted that only the members of the group correctly understood God's will and God's law, they formed *sects* (literally, "schools of thought"). The best-known sects are Pharisees, Sadducees, Essenes and Christians (or Jewish-Christians). (**See Reading 2-17.**)

The most extreme of all the sectarians were the Essenes. Admission to the community was granted to prospective members only after a three-year probation and a ceremony in which the initiate swore to obey all the rules of the sect and not to reveal any of its secrets to outsiders. The Essenes led lives of purity and prayer, avoiding all intercourse with women, surrendering all their private property, and following a strict monastic existence. They regarded the temple in Jerusalem as unclean and its priesthood corrupt, and looked forward to the future time when a new temple would be erected by God and the proper sacrificial cult restored. Probably the largest Essene community was at Qumran, near the Dead Sea, where Bedouin shepherds and modern-day archaeologists have made many spectacular discoveries. Not all Essenes lived at Qumran or followed such rigorous separation from their fellow Jews, but the Essene ideal was to minimize contacts between the "sons of light" (as they called themselves) and the "sons of darkness."

Many of these Essene ideas have close parallels in early Christianity. The founder of Christianity, Jesus, was a holy man, preacher, and teacher—a social type commonly found in Palestine in the first century. When he was not performing healings, he taught piety and ethics. His followers saw him as a prophet and/or messiah, but the Romans and the high priests saw him as a troublemaker, and the Romans crucified him. (See Reading 2-18.) This did not dampen the spirits of Jesus' followers because they believed that he was resurrected. They formed a sect to await his return which, they thought, would occur imminently. Virtually all of these followers were Jews, and the conduct of most of them was well within the bounds of ancient Judaism. To what extent the historical Jesus spoke or acted against the observances of the Jewish religion is not very clear, but it is likely that the majority of his early followers continued the traditional observances and differed from their fellow Jews in the same manner that all Jewish sects differed from each other and from the masses. This situation did not last long. With the influx of gentiles into the sect, the growth of the idea that faith in Jesus as Messiah was a substitute for the Jewish customs, and the emergence of a trinitarian conception of God, Christianity became a separate religion.

The animosity which characterized the relations between the different factions of ancient Judaism can be seen clearly in the Essene attacks on the temple and the priesthood, and in the Christian attacks on the Pharisees (notably Matthew 23). The Pharisees, who, some scholars suggest, should be considered a "party" rather than a sect, emphasized the observance of the ancestral traditions, notably the laws of purity, priestly tithing, and the Sabbath. Like the Christians and the Essenes they believed in the resurrection of the dead and the immortality of the soul. They were very influential even if the number of those who actually belonged to the group was rather small. The Sadducees, their arch-rivals, did not accept the Pharisaic traditions, did not believe in the resurrection of the dead, and did not enjoy widespread support.

Although numerous aspects of Jewish sectarianism in antiquity are obscure, three points seem reasonably clear. First: the sects, like the synagogue, represent the democratization of Judaism. The practices of Judaism were not to be restricted to the priesthood in the temple but were to be observed by all Israel. Second, all the sects (except, perhaps, the Sadducees) stood in an uneasy relationship with the temple and the temple cult. The Essenes opposed it; the Pharisees tried to transfer the laws of purity from the temple precincts to the table of the lay Israelite; and the Christians prayed in the temple even as they told stories of its purification by Jesus and of its imminent destruction. Third, the vast majority of Jews belonged to no sect at all. They were plain people whose folk religion probably had little in common with the learned traditions and ethereal speculations of the sectarian fringe.

## THE EXPANDING DIASPORA

A Greek author of the first century B.C.E. remarked that "it is not easy to find any place in the civilized world that has not yet received this nation [the Jews] and in which it has not made its power felt." The origins of the Jewish *Diaspora* (literally, "dispersion" or "scattering") have been treated briefly above, but some Jews left their homeland in order to better their economic status. Judaea was a hilly and rocky country, and its excess population had to look for opportunities elsewhere. Other Jews were mercenaries in the armies of the Persian and, later, of the Hellenistic Empires. Many Jews were captured during the numerous wars which took place on Palestinian soil during the fourth and third centuries B.C.E. and were taken to distant countries to be sold as slaves. The nucleus of the Jewish community of Alexandria apparently was formed by the prisoners of war sent home by Ptolemy the First. The Jewish community of Rome, which became prominent only after Pompey conquered Judaea in 63 B.C.E., seems to have had similar origins. Last, in times of persecution and distress, many Jews must have left Judaea for haven in other countries.

As a result of all these factors the Jewish Diaspora grew and by the second century B.C.E. attained significant dimensions. (**See Reading 2-19.**) Its major centers were Babylonia (whose community was established by the exile of 587 B.C.E.), Alexandria in Egypt, Rome, and Antioch in Syria. In addition to these major centers, there were numerous smaller communities throughout the towns and villages of Syria, Asia Minor (modern Turkey), and North Africa. Once these communities were founded, they grew both by natural increase (since the Jews, unlike the Greeks and Romans, did not practice infanticide) and by the conversion of gentiles to Judaism. Diaspora Jews, notably in Rome, eagerly sought to propagate their faith among their

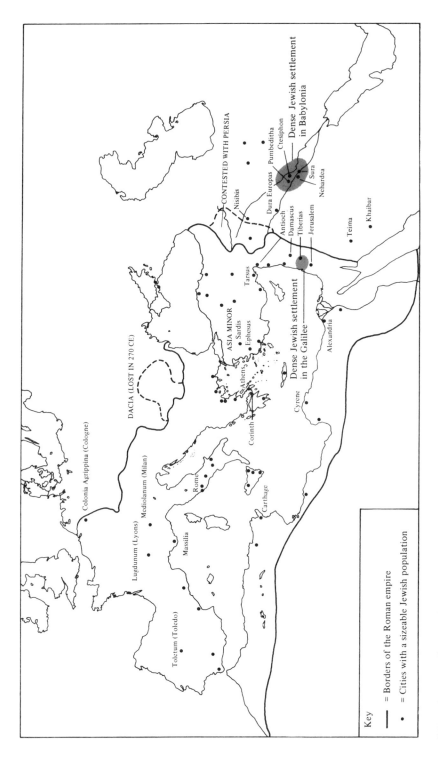

Key

— = Borders of the Roman empire

• = Cities with a sizeable Jewish population

**Map 4  Jewish Population Centers, First to Fifth Centuries C.E.**

Pumbeditha
Ctesiphon
Dense Jewish settlement in Babylonia
Sura
Nehardea
Dura Europos
Nisibis
CONTESTED WITH PERSIA
Khaibar
Damascus
Antioch
Tiberias
Teima
Jerusalem
Tarsus
Dense Jewish settlement in the Galilee
ASIA MINOR
Sardis
Ephesus
Alexandria
Athens
DACIA (LOST IN 270 CE)
Cyrene
Corinth
Colonia Agrippina (Cologne)
Rome
Mediolanum (Milan)
Carthage
Lugdunum (Lyons)
Massilia
Toletum (Toledo)

gentile neighbors. The reasons for this missionary impulse, inherited from Judaism by Christianity, are not known, but the success of the mission is evident. The Jews were expelled from Rome several times for "infecting" the Romans with their customs. Many gentiles, who did not wish to undergo the dangerous, painful, and (to them) embarrassing ritual of circumcision, opted to "fear the Lord" from afar and to become "God-Fearers" or "sympathizers" with Judaism.

Jewish life in the Diaspora had its share of problems. The cultural clash between Judaism and Hellenism was even more intense here than it was in the homeland. Some Jews were invigorated by the conflict and wrote in Greek, which testifies to their ability to live in two worlds simultaneously. The best-known Greek-Jewish author is Philo, a philosopher and biblical exegete of the first century C.E., who tried to find the fundamental ideas of Greek philosophy in the five books of Moses. In the Middle Ages generations of Jewish, Islamic, and Christian philosophers were still grappling with the questions first raised by Philo. Other Jews, however, were unable simultaneously to abide by the words of both Plato and Moses. They became apostates, like the extreme Hellenizers in Judaea during the time of the Maccabees, and rejected Judaism. Philo's own nephew abandoned all loyalty to the Jews and Judaism for the sake of a career in the Roman civil service.

The other major issue confronting the Jews of the Diaspora was civil rights. Recent archaeological discoveries show that the Jews of Sardis (in Asia Minor) in the second and third centuries C.E. owned a synagogue which was the city's largest building (it was the size of a football field), and which loomed over the city square. Members of the synagogue were city magistrates. This, then, was a prosperous and secure community. Other communities, especially in the first century B.C.E. and the first century C.E., were not nearly as secure. In the cities of Syria, western Asia Minor (the coast of modern Turkey), Palestine, and, especially, in Alexandria, the relationship between the Jewish communities and their Gentile hosts was very tense. The tension occasionally erupted into violence. As usual, the details are obscure, but the fundamental issues are reasonably clear. The Jews demanded both equality and tolerance: they wanted to be the same as their neighbors but they also wanted to be different. They wanted the rights of citizenship, but they also wanted special exemptions because of the peculiarities of their faith. "If the Jews wish to be Alexandrians, why don't they worship the gods of the Alexandrians?" was the reply, and the battle was joined. In Alexandria an anti-Jewish political party was formed which disseminated anti-Semitic propaganda. The issue was resolved by the emperor Claudius against the Jews. Individual Jews could obtain citizenship in Alexandria, but the Jewish community as a whole had to be content with tolerance, not equality.

A larger and more important issue than citizenship in the cities was citizenship in the Empire. In 212 C.E. the emperor Caracalla decreed that all the inhabitants of the Roman Empire, including the Jews, were to receive the rights of citizenship. Centuries later, when they were persecuted by the Church, medieval Jews often turned to the state for protection, contending that, as citizens, they should be able to enjoy the rights guaranteed by Roman law. In the long run the edict of Caracalla had much greater impact than did the decision of Claudius.

---

*Editor's Questions*
AFTER VIEWING AND READING

- Did the Babylonian exile end with Cyrus' call for the return of the Jews to their homeland? Why did some remain?
- What type of religious worship was established by the Jews on the island of Elephantine?
- How did Ezra and Nehemiah help consolidate the renewed Jewish settlement in the Holy Land? Who were the Samaritans and why did they cause problems for the Jews?
- How did Daniel respond to the conflict between the Hellenizers and the Jews who wished to follow their own traditions closely?
- Why was the festival of Hannukkah instituted?
- Did the preaching of Jesus correspond with the ideals of the Jewish sects that flourished in the first century C.E.?
- What were the options faced by the Jews after the Temple was destroyed in the year 70 C.E.?

SUGGESTED READINGS

Roland de Vaux, *Ancient Israel: Its Life and Institutions,* trans. by John McHugh (McGraw-Hill, 1961)

John H. Hayes and J. Maxwell Miller, *Israelite and Judaean History* (Westminster Press, 1977)

W. Stewart McCullough, *The History and Literature of the Palestinian Jews from Cyrus to Herod: 550 B.C. to 4 B.C.* (University of Toronto Press, 1975)

David M. Rhoads, *Israel in Revolution 6–74 C.E.* (Fortress Press, 1976)

Morton Smith, *Palestinian Parties and Politics that Shaped the Old Testament* (Columbia University Press, 1971)

Victor Tcherikover, *Hellenistic Civilization and the Jews* (Jewish Publication Society, 1959; also paperback reprint)

# 3

## The Shaping of Traditions
## (First to Ninth Centuries)

_David B. Ruderman_

_Editor's Suggestions_
BEFORE VIEWING THE SHOW

Examine Maps 4 and 5, of the Jewish population centers, in the _Study Guide_ and refer to them as needed.

_Overview of the TV Program_

Jewish communities in the first century C.E. were to be found in Judaea, throughout the Roman Empire, and in Babylonia. The Pharisees, an important group within Judaism, believed that the customs of the Jewish people would help them survive the destruction of the Temple. Over time some of these traditions were organized in the _Mishnah_, a work which became the foundation for the continued development of the Jewish religion. In Judaea a preacher named Jesus traveled the countryside, and some Jews believed him to be the long-awaited messiah. At first these individuals, later called Christians, formed a sect within Judaism. However, when Paul spread the message of Christianity throughout the Roman Empire, many gentiles (non-Jews) flocked to the new religion. Paul didn't require them to follow Jewish laws and traditions, and slowly the Jews and Christians drifted apart.

After years of Roman persecution of the Christians, emperors arose who were favorable to the new religious group, and by the fourth century Christianity became the official religion of the Empire. When the Empire fell in 476 C.E., the Church became the major stabilizing force within that society and kept many of the Roman traditions alive.

In Babylonia and in Palestine Jews continued to study their traditions, and commentaries were written on the _Mishnah_ which were compiled in the _Talmud_. This rich amalgam of laws and folklore was destined to be interpreted again and again.

In the seventh century in the Arabian peninsula, the third great monotheistic religion emerged as Muhammad of Mecca preached and set the groundwork for the rise of Islam. At the time of Muhammad's death, most of the peninsula was under his control, and within a hundred years his followers had conquered territories stretching from Persia in the east to Spain in the west. Ninety percent of the Jews lived under Islam and carried their own customs wherever they settled in the new Islamic empire.

In Spain the Jews established their communities under Muslim rule, while further north in Christian Europe Jews were invited to help the economy by encouraging trade. Rulers, such as Louis the Pious, favored this policy, although churchmen like Agobard of Lyons were aghast at the growing influence of the new Jewish communities.

*Watch for . . . and Think about*

Look closely at the synagogues where the Jews worshipped in the Holy Land and in the Diaspora. How would you compare them? What do they reveal about Jewish life inside and outside of Israel?

Observe the mosques of Islam and contrast them with the buildings seen at the end of the show that are associated with Charlemagne. Can you imagine the texture of life in these two dissimilar societies?

WHILE READING THE *STUDY GUIDE* AND *SOURCE READER*

Look for the following:

- The political and religious responses to the destruction of the Temple in Jerusalem. Identify *mizvot, nasi.*
- The "parting of the ways" between Christianity and Judaism. It was a gradual process. Identify gentiles, and the *adversos Judaeos* tradition and its goal.
- *Halakhah* and *Midrash.* What kinds of materials do the *Mishnah, Baraita* and *Talmud* contain?
- How the new religion of Islam developed and how its attitudes toward Judaism were formulated. Identify *Koran, dhimmis.*

- Why Jews moved from Muslim countries to Christian Europe. What was the Church's response to this new migration?

---

## IN THE AFTERMATH OF THE TEMPLE'S DESTRUCTION

To all appearances, the humiliating defeat of the Jews and the destruction of Jerusalem and the Temple at the hands of the Romans in 70 C.E. seemed to mark the bitter end of Jewish life in Palestine. By 73 the last rebel fortress at Masada, overlooking the southwest shore of the Dead Sea, could no longer withstand the overpowering might of the Roman legions. Eleazar ben Yair, the leader of the Masada band, openly acknowledged to his soldiers the futility of further resistance and the inevitable conclusion to be drawn from the funereal scenario of Jerusalem's ashes. Flavius Josephus (first century C.E.), in the seventh book of his history, *The Jewish War*, attributes the following words to Eleazar: *

> And where now is that great city, the mother-city of the whole Jewish race, intrenched [sic] behind all those lines of ramparts, screened by all those forts and massive towers, that could scarce contain her munitions of war, and held all those myriads of defenders? What has become of her that was believed to have God for her founder? Uprooted from her base she has been swept away, and the sole memorial of her remaining is that of the slain still quartered in her ruins! Hapless old men sit beside the ashes of the shrine and a few women, reserved by the enemy for basest outrage.
>
> Which of us, taking these things to heart, could bear to behold the sun, even could he live secure from peril? Who such a foe to his country, so unmanly, so fond of life, as not to regret that he is still alive today? Nay, I would that we had all been dead ere ever we saw that holy city razed by an enemy's hands, that sacred sanctuary so profanely uprooted! . . . let us have pity on our-

---

*Flavius Josephus, *The Jewish War*, trans. H. St. J. Thackeray, Cambridge, Mass. and London: Harvard University Press, 1961, Loeb Classical Library, vol. 3, pp. 611–613.

selves, our children and our wives, while it is still in our power to find pity from ourselves. For we were born for death, we and those whom we have begotten; and this even the fortunate cannot escape.

**(See Reading 3-1.)**

For Eleazar, the ultimate Jewish response to Roman abasement and servitude was martyrdom. To live without the Temple, without political sovereignty, without human dignity, was for him no life at all, either for the individual or the entire nation.

So single-minded and rigid a reaction to Jerusalem's disaster stands in marked contrast to that of Eleazar's countryman Rabban (rabbi) Yoḥanan ben Zakkai. Having saved his own life and those of his followers by submitting to Roman control—even when Jerusalem was laid waste—Yoḥanan elected a strategy for collective survival rather than collective suicide. Yoḥanan reportedly had once proclaimed: "Happy are you, O Israel! When you obey the will of God, then no nation or race can rule over you!" (*Mekhilta de R. Ishmael*, Baḥodesh 1). To him Roman political domination could not destroy the human spirit of politically vanquished Jews as long as they remained steadfast to their covenant with God. Not even the seeming finality of Jerusalem's utter devastation would lead Jews to relinquish their will for life:*

> Once as Rabban Yoḥanan ben Zakkai was coming out of Jerusalem, Rabbi Joshua followed him and beheld the Temple in ruins.
> "Woe unto us," Rabbi Joshua cried, "that this place, the place where the iniquities of Israel were atoned for, is laid waste."
> "My son," Rabban Yoḥanan said to him, "be not grieved. We have another atonement as effective as this. And what is it? It is acts of loving kindness, as it is said, 'for I desire mercy, not sacrifice'." (Hosea 6:6)

**(See Reading 3-2.)**

To Yoḥanan ben Zakkai and the subsequent generations of rabbis who followed him, the events of 70 C.E., despite their tragic consequences, also constituted a new opportunity, a new challenge for the

---

*J. Goldin, trans., *The Fathers According to Rabbi Nathan* (New Haven: Yale University Press 1955), p. 34.

rebirth and revitalization of Jewish life. In the aftermath of the Temple's destruction, the program of the Zealot faction was discredited; they had led the nation down a path of death and destruction that had ended at Masada. But ben Zakkai and his disciples salvaged a new seat of Jewish learning in the town of Yavneh, and with it a new lease on life to restructure the foundations of Judaism.

Yoḥanan's blueprint for communal survival was firmly rooted in the ideological assumptions of the Pharisees, a program which had evolved long before the Temple's destruction. Having emerged as a political party within the Palestinian community during the reign of the Hasmonean dynasty (before 66 B.C.E.), the Pharisees introduced a new religious ideology and social organization to the Jewish community years before the defeat of 70 C.E. Their most dramatic innovation was the gradual transfer of religious authority from the priests associated with the Temple service to the rabbinic sages.

To legitimate their claims to be the exclusive spokesmen for Jewish tradition, the Pharisaic rabbis reread the sacred texts of Judaism in order to underscore their central and exclusive prerogatives to mold Jewish norms and values. Their most transparent formulation of their new stake to leadership in the Jewish community is found in the rabbinic text *Mishnah Avot*, (Ethics of the Fathers) (1:1): "Moses received the Torah on Sinai, and handed it down to Joshua; Joshua to the elders; the elders to the prophets; and the prophets handed it down to the men of the Great Assembly." They considered the latter to be related to the Pharisees, which assured them an uninterrupted chain of sacred tradition from Moses to their immediate ancestors. Not surprisingly, they linked their own authority to the prophets and altogether excluded the priests with their competing claims to authority.

The rabbis assumed to speak for a sacred tradition which they felt was complete itself without need of modification or extension: "You shall not add on to what I command you or take anything away from it, but keep the commandments of the Lord your God that I enjoin upon you" (Deuteronomy 4:2). Yet their most ingenious innovation was to implant in the *Torah* a mechanism for its own rejuvenation and reformulation. They conceived of God's bestowal of the law on Sinai as a two-dimensional operation—a written text, and in addition its interpretation, elaboration, and refinement, transmitted orally. The concept of a twofold law infused new life into the divine legislation, allowing it to adjust and modify itself to the exigencies of

Jewish life in subsequent centuries. While the written text was fixed and immovable, the oral law was pliable and modifiable, ready to harmonize the apparent contradictions between the generalized prescriptions of the written text and the specific requirements of individuals and communities. The written law marked a single moment in history; the oral law was unbound by time. It constituted the continuous revelation of God's will—past, present, and future. The Pharisees insisted that only the rabbis, the acknowledged experts on God's revelation, were empowered to interpret and expound the law. By enshrining the concept of the twofold law in Judaism, the rabbis ensured their own unrivaled place as the sole expositors of the divine will. Rabbinic authority became synonymous with divine authority.

The Pharisees not only enhanced the generative powers of the law; they also effected a major transformation in the way the law was practiced. They instituted an enlarged system of *mizvot* (divine commandments) which became the prerogative of all Jews rather than reserving them to a single priestly class. The commandments of Judaism were all of equal importance; they were the domain of every segment of the community, rich or poor. They ensured the democratic participation of the entire society in God's world, breaking the priestly monopoly of divine service.

The system of *mizvot* underscored the importance of each individual and his religious responsibilities. The worth of each person depended not on birth or power but on what he accomplished in the area of divine service. The system of *mizvot* provided a program of personal salvation for everyone. The rabbis argued that the good—those who observed the divine commandments—would be rewarded in the next world, while those who ignored the commandments would be punished.

The Pharisees, in short, had provided Yohanan ben Zakkai with a master plan for the survival of Judaism even before the Temple had been razed. Their strategy included a new concept of divine law with a written and oral component; a system of fluid transmission, exposition, and elaboration of God's revelation; a new leadership class of rabbis supplanting that of the priests; and the democratization of Jewish life through a system of ritual and moral demands, ensuring the personal salvation of every member of the Jewish community.

With the destruction of the Temple in 70 C.E. the Pharisaic program for Jewish life flourished. So total was the Pharisaic success that after 70 Pharisaism was equated with Judaism; Pharisaic ideology and institutions were enshrined in Jewish culture. This task became the crowning achievement of Yoḥanan ben Zakkai and his successors.

Yoḥanan ben Zakkai presided over the community of Yavneh for the first decade after the Temple's destruction, and under his leadership the work of physical and spiritual reconstruction began. Despite the loss of life and property engendered by the war, much of the Jewish community outside Jerusalem had remained essentially unmolested. Moreover, Roman policy demonstrated increasing confidence in the new rabbinic leadership and growing tolerance of the community's activities. Under such favorable conditions the authority of the rabbinate in Yavneh steadily increased. Yoḥanan's successor, Rabban Gamaliel II, gained official recognition from the Roman authorities as head of the Jewish people and, reportedly, visited Rome with a delegation of his close rabbinic associates.

During the last decades of the first century C.E., the sages of Yavneh thus were free to carry out their major program of reconstruction and consolidation. With the destruction of the Temple, synagogues—already in existence prior to 70—now assumed critical importance as the center of Jewish learning, prayer, and social activity. Prayer, study, and ethical deeds now became worthy substitutes for Temple sacrifices. Moreover, the synagogue assumed the cherished prerogatives of the Temple: within its confines, the ram's horn was sounded on the New Year, the rituals of the major Jewish festivals were performed, and the priestly benediction was recited. Thus the rabbis sought to minimize the discontinuities with the past by the conspicuous presence of traditional symbols and ceremonies.

Yavneh became the center of a new rabbinic leadership, and there the rabbinic legislative and judicial body, the Sanhedrin, was reconstituted and presided over by Gamaliel II who took the title *nasi*. The Sanhedrin assumed supreme legislative and judicial control over the Jews living in Judaea and eventually throughout the Diaspora. It claimed the right to set the Jewish calendar, thus regulating the individual and collective observance of Jewish life within and outside Judaea. It completed the process whereby it was determined which books were to be included in the Hebrew Bible and which to be left out. The work of shaping, summarizing, and consolidating the teachings of the earlier Pharisaic rabbis continued with augmented intensity. The legal controversies between the dominant pre-70 schools of the rabbis Hillel and Shammai were almost always resolved in favor of Hillel. The rabbis also standardized the daily and Sabbath prayers and the Passover seder ritual, and infused a new historical meaning into the major holidays of the Jewish year, a meaning which reflected their own awareness of the Jewish past and present. Within two decades of the debacle of 70 C.E., the Yavneh leadership had succeeded in restructuring a mutually beneficial political relationship with Rome, a powerful social organization and religious program for Palestinian and Diaspora Jewry, and a new and bold vision of a universal Jewish faith, transcending the limitations of Temple, land, and sectarian divisiveness. (See Reading 3-3.)

## THE GROWING ESTRANGEMENT BETWEEN CHRISTIANS AND THE JEWS

The dramatic consolidation of rabbinic authority at Yavneh left a decisive imprint on the development of Christianity as well. Prior to the destruction of the Temple, the Christians were basically a Jewish messianic sect like other Jewish messianic sects, claiming to represent the true Israel in opposition to the official priesthood, the Temple, and the law. With the crucifixion of Jesus and with the growing disappointment over the fact that the overwhelming majority of Jews and their leadership remained apathetic or antagonistic to Christian teaching, the Christians began to distance themselves from the rest of the Jewish community. Yet the established leadership of the community hardly noticed them, since they constituted no serious threat to the communal welfare. Most of the Judeo-Christian synagogues in Jerusalem still demanded total attachment to Jewish law even while believing in the messiahship of Jesus. After 70, however, these groups with their antipathy to Jewish law became more visible. When the Judeo-Christians of Jerusalem fled to the town of Pella rather than participate in the war against Rome, their break with the rest of the Jewish community, which was under Roman siege, became flagrantly apparent.

The growing alienation of the Judeo-Christians from Judaism was attributable to a large extent to antagonisms that had been festering within Christian circles since the death of Jesus (ca. 30 C.E.). The crucifixion itself had created a formidable crisis for Christian faith. Seen in the context of Jewish messianic teaching, Jesus' death constituted an undeniable paradox. If Jesus was in fact the Messiah, how was it possible for him to expire on a cross? If he was the Messiah, why was he incapable of saving himself as well as others, of eradicating evil, and of overthrowing Roman rule? To most of the Jews the matter was closed, but to his disciples Jesus' shocking death immediately required a novel explanation in terms of faith.

The explanation that arose in the aftermath of the crucifixion was that Jesus inevitably had to suffer and be rejected by the official religious leadership of Israel, who had caused him to be executed, so that he might be resurrected on the third day to sit at God's right hand. By combing Hebrew scriptures and by reading into Jewish history a pattern of an apostate Israel—which had always rejected its prophets and even killed them—the disciples were able to make some religious sense out of the crucifixion. As proof, key passages, like Isaiah 52–53, Psalms 22 and 100, and many others, could be interpreted as adumbrations of Jesus' own encounter with the unbelieving Jewish people. (See Reading 3-5A.)

The theme that the Jews had always killed their prophets and that it was therefore natural for them to murder Jesus finds its best expression in the parable of the vineyard (Mark 12:1–12; Matthew 21:33–46; Luke 20:9–19). In this revealing narrative, the vineyard owner (God) leaves his vineyard (Israel) in the hands of tenants (the Jews). He occasionally sends his servants (the prophets) to obtain his share of the fruit. The unfaithful tenants, however, kill the servants until the owner decides to send his own son to represent his interests. But "they took him and killed him and cast him out of the vineyard." What follows is the biblical verse, Psalm 118:22, referring to Jesus: "The stone that the builders rejected has become the cornerstone."

The vineyard text provided an ideological framework par excellence to legitimize Christian revelation in Jewish terms. The Jewish rejection of Jesus and his execution, supposedly at the hands of the Jews, represented the inevitable culmination of Jewish crimes against God and humanity. The paradox of the crucifixion was no paradox at all. It was necessary for Jesus to atone for the sins of mankind; it also was necessary for him to die at the hands of the Jews. Rather than a statement of historic reality, the deicide charge arose out of the critical need to polemicize with the Jewish religious tradition in order to authenticate Christian belief in the years following Jesus' death.

The teachings of the apostle Paul constituted an additional factor in the growing alienation of Christianity from Judaism. Paul's message underscored the growing divergence between the religions of the old and the new covenant, between material Israel and spiritual Christianity, between the present reign of the *Torah*, and the ultimate vindication of the Church. Furthermore, Paul's direction of Christianity toward the conversion of gentiles living throughout the Roman Empire went beyond the limits of Jewish blood and community and ultimately led to an unavoidable enmity between the new Christian groups and the Jewish communal leadership. Paul's juxtaposition of "the believing Gentile" with "the unbelieving Jew," in which the former was worthy of a salvation from which the latter was excluded, was too distasteful a pill to swallow for Paul's former coreligionists. Even with the most tolerant and benign Jewish-Christian interaction, such pronouncements could not have gone unanswered by the official Jewish leadership.

On the contrary, in the wake of the disaster of 70, the rabbinic leadership of Yoḥanan ben Zakkai and Gamaliel II was in no mood for such a provocative challenge to the validity of their interpretation of Judaism. In an age in which reconstruction and centralization of rabbinic authority were uppermost in their minds, the dissenting voices of Paul's followers, protesting the viability of Jewish law and the rabbinic understanding of salvation, were patently intolerable. In a community still trying to come to terms with the Temple's destruction as a blow to Jewish faith, the Pauline challenge had to be met with decisive action. From the rabbinic perspective what was required was conformity of practice and belief, which was now being violated by the Christian insurrection. The rabbis felt obliged to respond forcefully to the circles of Christian dissent in order to preserve intact their own vision of Jewish survival and to legitimate themselves as the exclusive spokesmen of the divine will.

Thus the final clash, the inevitable parting of the ways, arose at a critical moment in the transformation of both rabbinic Judaism and Pauline Christianity. At the point where the rabbis had all but gained universal acceptance in the Jewish community of their path to individual salvation through their notion of a twofold law, the followers of Paul offered the hope of salvation through a redeeming Christ to a swelling constituency of gentiles living outside the confines of Jewish society. The rabbis could no longer allow so conflicting a view of salvation as Paul's to coexist with their own sanctified conception within the Jewish community. In the last years of the first century C.E., Gamaliel II is said to have ordered his associate, Samuel the Small, to compose a malediction against sectarians, especially Judeo-Christians, to be recited daily by every Jew. The *birkat ha-minim* (benediction of God who condemns the sectarians) is currently the twelfth blessing of the eighteen traditional weekday benedictions recited in the synagogue. Having undergone many changes in subsequent centuries, in its present form the benediction contains no reference to heretics and Judeo-Christians. But the original Palestinian prayer was most explicit: *

> May there be no hope for apostates. Mayest thou uproot the kingdom of arrogance speedily in our days. And may the Judeo-Christians and other heretics perish instantly. . . Praised art thou, O Lord, who subdueth the arrogant.

The "benediction," as it was called euphemistically, constituted a malediction, which meant that a Christian could no longer participate in a Jewish congregation without, in effect, cursing himself. The break between Jews and Christians became final and official.

The expulsion of the Judeo-Christians from the Jewish community created a further crisis for Christian identity. It also ushered in a more intense period of rivalry and hostility between the two faiths, both of which claimed to be the true faith of Israel as they zealously pursued potential converts.

A clear reflection of the new level of antagonism is found in the fourth canonical Gospel according to John, composed roughly at the beginning of the second century C.E. More than any other work of the Christian canon, this Gospel later served to encourage and buttress anti-Judaic sentiments. Written after the other three "synoptic" Gospels (so called because of their many agreements in subject, order, and language), Matthew, Mark, and Luke, it effectively expressed some of the central theological convictions of early Christianity. At the same time, the motif of opposition between the Jews and Jesus was made more explicit than it had been in any of the other Gospels. In the synoptic Gospels, the term Jew usually appears as a neutral term. In John, "Jews" are singled out as the principal oppressors of Jesus: "This was why the Jews crucified Jesus" (John 5:16); "Away with him, away with him, crucify him" (John 5:18, as spoken by the Jews). In the earlier Gospels, the chief priests or elders are responsible

---

*Leon J. Liebreich, trans., *Weekday and Sabbath Liturgy*, typescript, Hebrew Union College—Jewish Institute of Religion, 1965, p. 85.

for the crucifixion; in John, the Jews are singled out as the killers of Christ.

The most violent expression of hostility toward the Jews is found in the eighth chapter of John, in which Jesus is said to have said the following during a lengthy dispute with the Jews:

> You are of your father the devil, and your will is to do your father's desires. He was a murderer from the beginning and has nothing to do with the truth, because there is no truth in him . . . If I tell you the truth, why do you not believe me? He who is of God hears the words of God; the reason you do not hear them is that you are not of God.

(John 8:44–47)

**(See Reading 3-5B.)**

The vilification of the Jews in the Gospel of John, the labeling of the entire Jewish nation as Christ-killers, and their explicit designation as children of the devil gave ultimate theological expression to the roots of anti-Jewish attitudes in the continuing Church tradition. In subsequent generations the Church fathers unhesitatingly employed similar themes in their efforts to demonstrate the veracity of the Christian faith by underscoring the perversities and blindness of Judaism.

From about the second to the sixth centuries, *adversos Judaeos* ("testimonies against the Jews") tracts emerged as an essential part of the literature of the early Church fathers. These collections of Christian testimonies, with passages culled from the Old Testament to demonstrate Christian beliefs, focused on two major themes: the rejection of the Jews and the choice of the gentiles, and the inferior status of Jewish law and practice.

Hippolytus of Rome, writing in the third century, perceived the Jews as criminals and surpassed even John in his revulsion toward them:*

> Why was the Temple made desolate? Was it on account of the ancient fabrications of The Calf? Or was it on account of the idolatry of the people? Was it for the blood of the prophets? Was it for

---

*Hippolytus, "Against the Jews," 7, trans. Rosemary Ruether, *Faith and Fratricide.* New York: Seabury Press, 1974, p. 128.

the adultery and fornication of Israel? By no means, for in all
these transgressions they always found pardon open to them. But
it was because they killed the son of their Benefactor, for he is
coeternal with the Father.

*(Contra Judaeos, 7)*

As in the vineyard parable, Jewish history was seen by this priest
as a continuous trail of Jewish crimes, culminating in the murder of
the Son of God.

John Chrysostom, writing at the end of the fourth century, could
easily correlate his intense dislike for Jews of Jesus' day with his feelings regarding those contemporary Jews living in close proximity to
his Christian community in Antioch:*

I know that many have high regard for the Jews and they think
that their present way of life is holy. That is why I am so anxious to
uproot their deadly opinion . . . . A place where a prostitute
offers her wares is a house of prostitution. But the synagogue is not
only a house of prostitution and a theater, it is also a hideout for
thieves and a den of wild animals. . . . But the Jews have not the
faintest idea of such [spiritual] things, living for their stomachs,
all agape about the present, no better off than pigs and goats,
ruled only by licentiousness and excessive gluttony. One thing
only they know—how to stuff themselves and get drunk. . . .

**(See Reading 3-6.)**

What all these church writers had in common was a program-
matic way of reading the biblical text. They read all statements of
divine wrath as referring to Jews and all statements of divine compas-
sion as referring to Christians. They viewed the Old Testament as a
text for anti-Judaism on the one hand and Christian self-glorification
on the other. The fourth-century Syrian father Aphrahat, comment-
ing on Hosea 2, wrote, for example:†

*John Chrysostom, "Homilies Against the Jews," I, 3, 4, trans. Robert L.
Wilken, in Wayne A. Meeks and Robert L. Wilken, *Jews and Christians in Antioch
in the First Four Centuries of the Common Era.* Missoula, Mont.: Scholars Press,
1978, pp. 89, 90, 93.

†Aphrahat, "Demonstrations against the Jews," trans. Jacob Neusner, *Aprahat
and Judaism*, Leiden: E. J. Brill, 1971, p. 63.

> Israel has played the whore, and Judah has committed adultery.
> And the people which is of the peoples (the Church) is the whole
> and faithful people, which has gone down and adhered to the
> Lord.

This one-sided interpretation was easily extended to discussions of the material-oriented Jewish statutes in contradistinction to the spiritualized Christian one. Amos' telling condemnation "I hate, I despise your feasts, and I take no delight in your solemn assemblies" (Amos 5:21) and similar prophetic utterances referred, in Christian eyes, to the futile observance of the ritual law by "carnal" Jews in opposition to the spiritual and uplifting mode of Christian practice. Divine service could only be realized in the Church through the agency of its new priesthood and its own rites, which had replaced and superseded those of Aaron.

The *adversos Judaeos* tradition thus became a vital concern of Christian exegetes, serving an intrinsic need to affirm their own faith by disaffirming that of the Jews. At least at their inception, anti-Judaic sentiments were directed less at arguing with or converting Jews than with asserting a specific Christian identity by deprecating the Jewish one. For the rabbis, on the other hand, the denial of Christianity was no longer an issue of great interest after having removed the Judeo-Christians from the synagogue at the time of Gamaliel II. At most, the occasional signs of anti-Christianity in rabbinic writings were expressions of an extrinsic need to defend Judaism against Christian vilification.

Despite the pervasiveness of anti-Judaic themes in Christian sermons, biblical commentaries, and theological tracts, the Jews were rarely butchered or assaulted by Christians throughout the first ten centuries of the common era. More often than not, the Christian attack against Judaism remained a war of words. The Christian clergy, with few exceptions (e.g., John Chrysostom), usually attacked Jews more as abstract theological monsters than as real members of contemporary society. Yet Christian theological attitudes toward the Jews and Judaism ultimately had an impact on social and political policy as well.

The turning point was the conversion of the emperor Constantine to Christianity at the beginning of the fourth century. Christianity gradually was transformed from a persecuted faith into the official religion of the Roman Empire. The rivalry between Judaism and Christianity was no longer one of two minority faiths, the latter more often persecuted than the former. With the ascendancy of Christianity as the official religion of the Roman Empire, pagan religions became illegal and the treatment of Judaism became less favorable. Previously, Jews had enjoyed a special protected status under imperial Rome; they had been exempted from all forms of pagan worship and were allowed relative economic freedom. By the beginning of the fifth century, however, their political and economic status worsened, first under the new statutes of Theodosius II, and later under the revisions of Justinian in the sixth century. Shorter recensions of the code of Justinian were later incorporated into canon law and eventually served as the basis for the emerging legal status of Jews in medieval Christendom. (See Reading 3-8.)

The specific prohibitions relating to Jews in both fifth- and sixth-century codes included the following: the Jews were prohibited from owning Christian slaves, from proselytizing Christians, from impeding other Jews from converting to Christianity, and from marrying with Christians. Jews were excluded from all civil and military offices and were allowed neither to act as lawyers and judges nor to hold any authoritative position over Christians. They also were forbidden to build new synagogues or repair old ones. The public performance of their rites was restricted, and they were singled out for special taxation.

In the fifth century as well, occasional outbursts of persecution and destruction of Jewish life and property were not uncommon in Palestine and Asia Minor. The new legal restrictions and the new signs of physical assault undoubtedly were related to the abusive rhetoric of the Church fathers. Theology had deleteriously affected the political and economic status of Jews in the Roman Empire but still only to a limited degree. The new prohibitions against the Jews never intruded upon their day-to-day lives. They continued to function as a legal group with imperial sanction. In some instances ecclesiastical officials even cautioned restraint in dealing with the Jews and protested against excessive violence directed at their community. Thus the net effect of church theology and social policy toward the Jew was primarily social estrangement and a perception of them as depraved, but there was no plan to exterminate them. (See Reading 3-7.)

Most representative of the emerging position of Jews in Christian society in late antiquity and subsequently throughout the early Middle Ages was the view of St. Augustine (354–430). Augustine's attitude—rather than that of Chrysostom and others like him, whose verbal assaults could easily have been translated by extremists into physical abuse—eventually became the dominant theological view of the Church toward the Jews living in its domain. Rather than charging that the Jews should be killed, Augustine described a place among the living for them, albeit a life of misery and depravity. Since the Jews killed Christ, they deserved death, but like Cain, who murdered his brother Abel, they were not to die but rather were doomed to wander the earth as witnesses of the ultimate truth of Christianity. Jews were to exist with a pariah status, always present to testify to the final triumph of the Church. When Christ returns, the Jews would finally acknowledge their error, convert to Christianity, or be condemned to final damnation: *

> . . . not by bodily death shall the ungodly race of carnal Jews perish. For whoever destroys them in this way shall suffer sevenfold vengeance, that is, shall bring upon himself the sevenfold penalty under which the Jews lie for the crucifixion of Christ. So to the end of the seven days of time, the continued preservation of the Jews will be a proof to believing Christians of the subjection merited by those who, in the pride of their kingdom, put the Lord to death.

The Jewish-Christian debate, with all the mutual condemnations and antagonisms it engendered over the centuries, need not obscure, however, the pervasive influence of rabbinic civilization on Christianity (and eventually on Islam as well). The Hebrew Bible, understood by the rabbis as an eternally valid scripture, became the foundation and source of subsequent spiritual and intellectual creativity in both religions. Christianity faithfully transmitted to the Western world the Bible's singular passion for monotheism, its elevation of the worth of the individual in God's eyes and its preoccupation with ethical obligation as a fundamental dimension of fulfilling God's will. Despite the prolonged antipathy which developed between the two sibling faiths, Jews and Christians continued to share a system of mutual values and beliefs. Ironically, heated expressions of mutual recrimination and contempt often served to conceal this common ground of familiarity and shared universe of discourse.

---

*St. Augustine, "The Writings Against the Manichaeans," in *A Select Library of Nicene and Post-Nicene Fathers of the Christian Church*, 1887, IV, p. 187, Wm. B. Eerdmans Publishing Co., Buffalo, N.Y.

# THE EMERGENCE OF RABBINIC LAW AND CULTURE

Despite its enduring significance, the Christian schism, from the rabbis' perspective, represented a minor, albeit painful, distraction from their major religious and political agenda. While Christianity flowered in the first five centuries of the common era, rabbinic civilization entered its most fertile and creative period, first in Palestine and later in Babylonia. The final result would be both a monumental literary output and a sweeping legacy for medieval Jewry.

In the period immediately following Gamaliel II's leadership in Yavneh, however, the future of Jewish life in Palestine and throughout the Roman Empire did not seem so promising. The rabbinic strategy of accommodating Jewish national aspirations and peaceful coexistence with Roman authority soon appeared to come unraveled. Despite the efforts of the rabbis of Yavneh to discredit the program of the Zealot faction which had engulfed that group in the debacle of 70 C.E., revolutionary and messianic agitation in Judaea and throughout the Diaspora never evaporated. Between 114–117 C.E. the Jewish communities in Cyrene, Alexandria, Cyprus, and Mesopotamia unsuccessfully rebelled against Roman rule in the wake of the Roman emperor Trajan's attempt to extend his empire to the Persian Gulf.

Trajan's successor, Hadrian, soon gave up the areas his predecessor had conquered to secure peace with the Parthian Persians and introduced a period of stability and reconciliation within his empire. His reign, however, was marked as well by a third major revolt of the Jews against Roman occupation, this time centering in Palestine itself. Apparently having given the Jews false hopes of rebuilding their Temple, Hadrian called off the project and may have decided instead to rebuild Jerusalem as a pagan city, dedicated to Hellenistic culture. The Jews, led by Simon Bar Kokhba, a formidable warrior with messianic illusions, were no match for the powerful Roman forces or the Roman political leadership. Despite a spirited resistance, the rebels were soundly defeated at Betar in the summer of 135. Hadrian, in response, issued a series of crippling decrees prohibiting Jews from living in Jerusalem, now renamed Aelia Capitolina, executed the illustrious rabbinic scholar Akiva bar Yosef (Bar Kokhba had already died in battle) and some of his rabbinic associates, and prohibited the teaching and practice of Judaism throughout Palestine.

The seemingly ominous consequences of the Bar Kokhba revolt were short-lived. Hadrian died three years later and his successor,

Antoninus Pius, immediately relaxed the tensions between the Roman government and its Jewish subjects by rescinding the decrees regarding the practice of Jewish ritual and study. The rabbis who assumed the leadership of the Jewish community in Palestine reciprocated in kind, launching a new conciliatory policy toward the Romans, reminiscent of that of Yoḥanan ben Zakkai in the aftermath of the Temple's destruction. They shifted their own seat of intellectual and political activity to Usha and to other towns in the Galilee where the majority of the Jews in Palestine then resided. The rabbinic legislative and judicial body, the Sanhedrin, was reconstituted by Simeon, the son of Gamaliel II, who served as *nasi*. Simeon shared his power with a distinguished circle of rabbinic authorities, among them the learned rabbi Meir, who had faithfully mastered and transmitted the legal teaching of his martyred teacher, Akiva bar Yosef. Under Simeon the sages of Usha systematically collected and refined the legal conclusions of past generations, preparing a foundation for the editing of a comprehensive legal code in the next generation.

Throughout the second century C.E. and well into the third, the Jews of Palestine continued to enjoy favorable treatment from Rome, particularly under the Severan emperors (193–235 C.E.). Judah, Simeon ben Gamaliel's son and successor as *nasi*, enjoyed even more political power and material prosperity than his father. Endowed with the authority to collect taxes, to appoint rabbis, and to represent the Diaspora Jewish community as well as his own in Palestine, Judah ha-Nasi assumed the status of a miniature emperor. He ruled until his death in 217 C.E. as the exclusive head of the Jewish community in Palestine and the Diaspora and the chief representative of the Jews to the Roman government.

The crowning achievement of Judah ha-Nasi was the redaction of the *Mishnah*, completed around 200 C.E. A law code, textbook, and condensation of the vast body of orally transmitted rulings of centuries of Pharisaic and rabbinic leadership, the *Mishnah* represented the culmination of rabbinic legal interpretation of the sages of Palestine. It also constituted a new basis for future interpretation and commentary on the part of succeeding generations of rabbis. (**See Readings 3-4A and 3-4B.**)

Although based on earlier rabbinic interpretations of the Bible, the *Mishnah* itself is hardly a biblical commentary. Instead its editor sought to organize the rabbinic interpretations of essentially legal rulings (*halakhah*) in the Bible according to their subject matter rather than following their original historical order in the biblical text itself. Accordingly, the *Mishnah* constituted a novel reordering of traditions of Jewish law, breaking with the organizational principles that marked both earlier and later rabbinic compilations of legal rulings of the Pentateuch called *Midreshei Halakhah*. It also constituted a bold condensation and refinement of earlier rabbinic decisions. Certain earlier Pharisaic and rabbinic rulings were omitted by Judah in the *Mishnah*. In this way, Judah attempted to define categorically the precise meaning of Jewish normative tradition, but he was only partially successful. While subsequent generations of rabbinic scholars gave ultimate priority to Judah's edited *Mishnah*, those external traditions (*beraitot*) not incorporated in the *Mishnah* nevertheless reflected other legal opinions contemporaneous with those of Judah. These were collected carefully by later sages and eventually edited in a work known as the *Tosefta*. Although of lesser authority than the *Mishnah*, the *Tosefta* was regularly consulted by later rabbis and thus gave expression to the democratic traditions underlying rabbinic interpretation and codification.

The *Mishnah* is divided into six *sedarim* (orders), each subdivided into *massekhtot* (tractates), which are again subdivided into chapters and paragraphs (*mishnayot*). The subject matter of the *Mishnah*'s *sedarim* vividly reflect the wide-ranging interests of rabbinic law, encompassing every aspect of human life and daily activity. The modern demarcation between mundane and holy had no significance in a law code whose authority was derived from no less a source than the divine revelation at Sinai.

The six orders include *Zeraim* (seeds), which treats agricultural matters, except for its first tractate on liturgy; *Moed* (holidays), which treats the holy days of the Jewish calendar; *Nashim* (women), regarding marital and family law; *Nezikim* (damages), analyzing property and criminal law; *Kodashim* (holy things), on laws of Temple sacrifice; and *Teharot*, explaining laws regarding ritual uncleanness.

The editor of the *Mishnah* in Judaism, like the editors of the New Testament in Christianity, saw his holy code as a natural embodiment of the divine word, God's revelation, as expounded and filtered through succeeding generations of religious teachers. Both the New Testament and the *Mishnah*, while originating in the Hebrew Bible, came to supplement and supplant their earlier legal formulations. Both Judaism and Christianity are unintelligible without the intermediary function of the *Mishnah* and the New Testament respectively. Rather than seeing either book as a conscious rupture from the past, from their scriptural font, both rabbis and Christian teachers understood these authoritative supplements as mere reflections of the original divine intention, mere transparent explications of what the original biblical text had always intended. Of course, the parallel place of the *Mishnah* and the New Testament in the histories of Judaism and Christianity also underscores the widening chasm separating the two faiths that existed by the beginning of the third century. Christianity had virtually broken with the law of the Pharisees in the name of a higher spiritual and institutional authority, the Church. Judaism had come to enshrine Pharisaic values and norms as the cornerstone of religious life and intellectual activity.

Despite its monumental significance for Jewish life in the first centuries of the Christian era, the *Mishnah* reflected one of the dimensions of rabbinic spirituality and self-expression. It never assumed the position of frozen, unchallenged canon. Alongside the rapid evolution of legal (*halakhic*) exegesis and codification there developed the dramatic proliferation of rabbinic homily, theological speculation, and ethical teachings. The latter were embodied in rabbinic interpretations of biblical narrative, called *Midreshei Aggadah*. As in the case of *Midreshei Halakhah*, these rabbinic commentaries follow the order of the biblical verses. Thus one of the most important of these commentaries, *Midrash Rabbah* (the Great Midrash), is organized according to the five Books of the Pentateuch and the five scrolls of the *hagiographa*: Song of Songs, Ruth, Lamentations, Ecclesiastes, and Esther. Many of the *Midreshei Aggadah* derive ultimately from sermons originally preached by rabbis in the synagogue or in their academies. Although edited and revised as late as the fifth through the twelfth centuries, they originate to a large extent in the Palestinian Jewish community during and immediately after the compilation of the *Mishnah*. (**See Reading 3-4C.**)

The homiletic *Midrashim* gave full expression to the rabbis' attempt to communicate the values of Judaism. They discoursed on God and his relation to man, on the reasons for his commandments, on the meaning of divine providence in relation to human freedom, on the juxtaposition of good and evil in the world, on the purpose of human suffering and on the secrets of divine creation and messianic culmination. Like life itself, the rabbinic ruminations embedded in the *Aggadah* are undisciplined, rambling, and even contradictory.

They testify to the openness and diversity of rabbinic thought and self-expression. Like the *Tosefta*, they tend to undermine the conservative, fixed image of Jewish normative life as embodied in the *Mishnah*. The *Midreshei Aggadah* reveal glimpses of a dynamic Jewish cultural experience never insulated from external influence; a rabbinic landscape that included encounters with Greek and Roman philosophy and law, with ancient mystical traditions, as well as with popular expressions of religion, magic, and superstition. They reflect too the emerging need of Jewish exegetes, especially in Palestine, to parry and refute Christian interpretations of the Hebrew Bible. The *Aggadah* thus supplied the rabbis of Palestine and later in other communities with an idiom for the expression of their deepest convictions about Judaism's relevance and enduring legacy in the changing social and intellectual universe of the Roman Empire of late antiquity.

In the more restricted realm of the *halakhah*, Judah ha-Nasi's code never functioned as the editor had perhaps intended, as the definitive conclusion of the revelatory process which had evolved from Sinai. On the contrary, the later generations of rabbis in the academies of Tiberias, Caesaria, and Sepphoris utilized the *Mishnah* as a new stimulus for further discussion, elaboration, and untapped exegetical creativity. Indeed, after the death of Judah ha-Nasi, the relatively tranquil conditions of Jewish Palestine were abruptly transformed. By the third century, the Roman Empire had experienced considerable political decline, economic impoverishment and contraction, leading to a steady deterioration of the physical life of Jews living within its borders. In the fourth and fifth centuries the gradual political victory of Christianity within the Roman Empire, as we have seen, also spelled the eventual decline of Jewish political and social status. In the fifth century, despite the discriminatory legislation of the Theodosian code and occasional provocations by religious Christians, Jews succeeded in maintaining their institutions of rabbinic learning and transmission although somewhat diminished in scope and vitality.

By the fifth century the rabbis of Palestine edited their discussions and elaborations of the *Mishnah* in a work called the Jerusalem or Palestinian *Talmud*. Although less complete and polished than its Babylonian counterpart, reflecting the growing hardships of Jewish communal life in Palestine in the third and fourth centuries, it still constituted a work of considerable achievement. The Jerusalem *Talmud*, which is only a quarter the size of the Babylonian *Talmud*, is nevertheless a multivolume work, consisting of the *Mishnah*, followed by an elaborate amplification of the *Mishnah* called the *Gemara*. In the case of both works, written in Palestine and Babylonia, the *Mishnah* and *Gemara* together are called collectively the *Talmud*. The Palestinian work never achieved the status of the larger *Talmud* written in Babylonia. Nevertheless, it became an authentic source of independent legal, social, and religious attitudes in its own right, reflecting an indigenous Palestinian tradition of Jewish *halakhic* development and constituting a revealing mirror of Jewish civilization in Palestine for over two hundred years following the death of Judah ha-Nasi.

By the time the Jerusalem *Talmud* had been completed, however, the rabbis of Palestine were well aware that their community, with all its cultural aura evoked by memories of its splendorous past, no longer remained the center of Jewish life. For the first time in Jewish history, the Palestinian leadership saw their authority and their spiritual dominance eclipsed by a new and creative circle of rabbis living outside Israel in the area of Babylonia then under Persian rule.

Since the period of the destruction of the first Temple in 586 B.C.E., Jews had inhabited the Babylonian region. But only with the establishment of the Arsacid dynasty of the Parthian Persians in the second half of the second century B.C.E. do the first signs of Jewish cultural and institutional life in that area become visible. Still much later, at the end of Parthian rule in Persia, does evidence exist for the official recognition of the Jewish community by the local government. In the second century C.E. or perhaps earlier, the Parthian king recognized the *resh galuta* (head of the exile: exilarch), a Jewish official who claimed Davidic descent stemming back to the Babylonian captivity of 586, as the legal head of Babylonian Jewry. The exilarch became the chief political representative before the Persian court, the collector of taxes, and the supervisor of the Jewish judicial system.

During the Hadrianic period, a number of Palestinian rabbis settled temporarily in Persia; a few even remained. From the second century as well, Babylonian Jewish students studied in Palestinian academies, and official contacts between the Palestinian *nasi* and the local Babylonian community were not infrequent. Judah ha-Nasi's editing of the *Mishnah* provided a further stimulus for the development and transmission of rabbinic law and ideology in Persia, as it had done for the Palestinian community. With the availability of a reliable, easily transportable summation of the rabbinic body of works of the Land of Israel, the emerging rabbinic class of Babylonia slowly became less dependent on the academies of Palestine for the exposition of Jewish law. The *Mishnah* became the central text for rabbinic study in Persia, encouraging the elucidation of the Palestinian canon in the light of the newly evolved circumstances of Jewish living in the Diaspora.

By the third century Babylonian Jewry reached a further state of maturity and independence from Palestinian rabbinic institutions with the founding of the academy of Sura by Rav, a student of Judah ha-Nasi. Samuel, Rav's contemporary, headed at the same time the academy at Nehardea. When Nehardea was destroyed by mid-century, the academy of Pumbedita assumed the dominant status of its predecessor.

The Sassanian Persians conquered the Parthians in 226 C.E. and ruled until the rise of Islam in the middle of the seventh century. With the exception of occasional disruptions, which affected Jewish life in the third and much later in the fifth century, the Sassanians continued the tolerant policies of the Parthians; the Jews were recognized as an official minority and the titular status of the exilarch was confirmed. Most importantly, the rabbis of Babylonia were able to shape, in an unparalleled manner, a Jewish community guided by values transmitted by them and directed by laws and institutions of their own design. The history of Babylonian Jewry is consequently the history of the transformation of the largest and most influential Jewish community in the Diaspora into a religious community molded in the image of the rabbis. It is a history of the rise to prominence of rabbinic institutions of learning and legal formulation; the adaptation of Palestinian Jewish law to the needs of Babylonian Jewry; and finally the composition and redaction of a Babylonian *Talmud* that would become the central corpus of all rabbinic teaching for future generations. At Sura and Pumbedita and in other Babylonian centers, the heirs of Yavneh's Pharisees with their comprehensive strategy for Jewish communal survival ultimately achieved their most enduring accomplishment.

The sages of Sassanian Persia lived and worked in a stimulating cultural and political environment where they were obliged to define the nature of Judaism and the limits of their own political power. From within the cultural milieu of Persia, the rabbis responded to the challenge of the Persian Zoroastrian religion, which recognized two deities, one good and the other evil. They also absorbed mystical and magical notions of the universe, experimented with local medicinal practice, and flirted with astrology and various mystery cults. Under a centralized governmental authority, the rabbis were forced to define the limits of their own power over the Jewish community. Only in Jewish ritual and ceremonial law was their authority unchallenged. In civil law the law of the government became synonymous with *Torah* law (*dina de-malkhuta dina*, the rabbinic ruling literally meaning "the law of the state is the law"). In both the cultural and political spheres the rabbis demonstrated their acumen for accommodation and adjustment without violating the uniqueness and vitality of their spiritual and intellectual principles. (**See Reading 3-4D.**)

The principles were embodied compellingly and imaginatively in the pages of the Babylonian *Talmud*. Despite the external signs of editing, the *Talmud* still preserves an air of freshness and spontaneity in its deliberations. It is a work which discusses Jewish law but it is more than a law book. It begins with the *Mishnah* and *Baraita*; it is also stories and ethics and homilies; and it is especially debate, both between contemporaries and between rabbis of different eras and places, who nevertheless share a unity of purpose which transcends a particular time and place. The *Talmud* pursues hypothetical possibilities with the same rigor as realistic eventualities. It views argumentation and intellectual acuity as part and parcel of the holy process of determining Jewish norms. It mixes freely abstract logical reasoning with biographical and episodic digressions. Rabbinic discussion wanders innocently from perspicacious elucidation to irritating minutiae to the chitchat of everyday encounter. But to the discerning student, the *Talmud* reflects an overarching unity, a self-consistent and harmonious record of God's revelation to his chosen people.

Above all, the *Talmud* represents an invitation to uninterrupted learning, an "oral law" never closed or canonized but open to continuous elaboration, refutation, and counterrefutation. The rabbis left both a work of law and an educational program. Scholarship and intellectual achievement together with ritual observance and ethical behavior led ultimately, in their eyes, to spiritual fulfillment and sanctity. "Our merciful father," the rabbinic liturgy proclaims, "inspire us to understand and to discern, to perceive, to learn, and teach, to observe, to do and fulfill lovingly all the instructions of the *Torah*."

The rabbinic age in Jewish history, like the patristic age in Christian history to which it corresponds, thus played a decisive role in the shaping of a new religious culture. Like the Church fathers, the rabbis produced a body of theological speculation, a legal code, a homiletical and ethical literature, a liturgy, and a scriptural exegesis, which established the classical foundations of their historic faith. Both religions offered similar but diverging responses to a world plagued with societal instability and human anxiety. Both established, in the course of some five hundred years, the social organization and theological orientation which would serve as the underpinning of the two religious communities for years to come.

## JUDAISM AND THE RISE OF ISLAM

The first half of the seventh century marks a cataclysmic transformation in the histories of the peoples of the Middle East and eventually of those living throughout the entire Mediterranean basin and beyond. In the year 622 C.E., a religious visionary named Muhammad fled his native city of Mecca in the Arabian peninsula for the northern town of Yatrib, later to be called Medina. This migration, the *hijra*, signified an important step in Muhammad's steady rise to power, his proclamation of the new religion of Islam, and his eventual conquest of lands and peoples in the name of his newly revealed faith. In the ten years that followed until his death in 632, he captured Medina and Mecca and drew together a militant army of the faithful ready to do battle for Allah (Muhammad's God) and his self-proclaimed prophet. Upon Muhammad's death his successors sought in a series of bloody battles to unify the entire Arabian peninsula under the banner of Islam. Conquests led ultimately to the mass conversion of thousands of captives living in Arabia. The leaders of the new Muslim state next turned eastward to Persia, northward to Syria, and westward to Egypt and North Africa. By the beginning of the eighth century Islam could claim a vast empire that stretched from the western extremities of India to the Pyrenees mountains of northern Spain.

By 661 C.E. the Umayyad dynasty succeeded in consolidating under its rule these expansive territories, holding an enormous and variegated population. It established its capital in Damascus, Syria, and held onto its impressive holdings for nearly a century. By 750 C.E., however, it was riddled with insurrection and instability; it was then overthrown by a new dynasty of the rival Abbasids, who founded their own capital in Baghdad in the general vicinity of ancient Babylonia.

Even in more isolated settings the Jews were never impervious to their surroundings. Nevertheless, the Islamic conquest created an overwhelming change in the social, political, economic, and cultural landscape of which they were a part. Its consequences for Jewish life were far-reaching. As early as the initial years of Muhammad's sojourn in Mecca and Medina, he undoubtedly established intimate contacts with Jews. A substantial Jewish settlement in the Arabian peninsula already had existed in pre-Islamic times, both in the south, in Yemen, and in Mecca and Medina and in the Hijaz region of the northwest. In Mecca he first met Jewish merchants with whom he conversed, absorbing a considerable body of Jewish lore. In Medina (Yatrib) he discovered a community dominated by the conspicuous presence of three Jewish tribes. At first he was rebuffed by these Jews since they could find nothing in his new monotheistic faith that appealed more than their own. Understandably he was taken aback by their indifference and hostility and he took revenge on them by the sword. (**See Reading 3-10.**)

But at the same time he was deeply indebted to the Jews, as the written record of his revelation of the *Koran* amply testifies. In the forty-eight suras of the *Koran* written in Mecca, Jewish influence is especially pervasive. Not only did Muhammad appropriate Abraham and Moses (as well as Jesus) as prophets of the new faith who preceded the seal of Muhammad's prophecy; he also freely utilized Jewish concepts and literary motifs throughout Muslim scripture. No doubt he also had access to Christian materials from which he drew consciously and unhesitatingly. Whether he was more strongly influenced by Judaism or Christianity is difficult to determine, given the imprecise nature of the materials the written text preserves, as well as the imprecise character of the modes of transmission by which the teachings of the two great faiths reached him. What is clear, however, is that rabbinic Judaism left a fundamental imprint on Muhammad's religion just as it had on Christianity.

Islam was most indebted to Judaism in its theory of divine revelation. Both religions begin with the assumption of the divine disclosure of a book; in Judaism it is called the *Torah*, or *al kitab*, and the *Koran* in Islam. Islam also appropriated from Judaism the idea of a twofold law—a written text and an oral one—called in Islam the *Hadith*. It, as at the rabbinic academies, developed its own rules of interpretation, its own legal schools, and its own institutions for the codification of religious law. As in Judaism, the study of law became a supreme form of divine worship. Like Judaism, Islam glorified the religious leader whose authority derived from his knowledge of divine law. Both Judaism and Islam subsequently emerged as religions of statute in which the believer fulfills himself through the observance of divine commandments as understood by the legal scholars of his religion. In this latter sense, Judaism reveals an even greater affinity to Islam than to Christianity, which emphasized faith over action. (See Reading 3-11.)

Other than the evidence of the *Koran*, little is known about the initial contacts between Jews and Muslims during the first one hundred years of Islamic rule. What is discernible, however, is the legal situation of the Jewish minority which was already determined by the middle of the seventh century. Jewish political status under Islam was established under the same principles bearing on other non-Muslims. The Jews were part of a protected minority called *dhimmis*, which included Christians, Zoroastrians, and a few other faiths. In return for payment of a poll tax (*jizya*) and for accepting other discriminatory practices, the *dhimmis* received assurances of religious tolerance and security for their lives and property. Most importantly, their religious communities were allowed to live under their own jurisdiction without excessive governmental interference. The *dhimmis* faced restrictions in government service, in erecting new houses of worship, in public religious practices, and in other areas confirming their social inferiority. But most of these constraints had already been present in Roman, Byzantine, and Persian law. Moreover, with the exception of the often debilitating poll tax, most restrictions were often ignored. The Jews were not always restricted occupationally; some were even prominent as government officials and as physicians. Other than a number of isolated outbursts of hostility against the Jews—most notably the persecutions by the deranged Caliph al-Ḥakim in Egypt at the beginning of the eleventh century, and the atrocities of the Berber tribes, the Almohades and Almoravides, in the eleventh and twelfth centuries in Spain—the Jewish community remained unmolested by Muslim society through most of the Middle Ages. Unlike their coreligionists in Christian lands during the Middle Ages, Jews were not singled out as a special group, nor were they charged with deicide. Islam never displayed any intrinsic theological need to validate its own faith at the expense of Judaism. In this sense the religious and social climate was usually healthier for Jews living in the medieval Muslim world than in that of the Christians.

By the second half of the eighth century and the beginning of the ninth, documentation of Jewish life under medieval Islam becomes more plentiful and the composite portrait the sources yield becomes more precise and detailed. The most dramatic historical discovery of source material about the Jewish community is that of the *genizah*, a huge warehouse for storing obsolete Hebrew books and other documents, written in colloquial Arabic but with Hebrew characters, found in Fustat (Old Cairo), Egypt, at the end of the nineteenth century. This hermetically sealed chamber contained thousands of documents describing the political, economic, social, and religious life of Jews living not only in Egypt but throughout the entire Islamic world primarily from about the beginning of the ninth through the twelfth centuries.

The Cairo *genizah* provides overwhelming evidence of a commercial revolution within the Jewish community of the Muslim world. Jews, having left farming, entered urban communities to engage in international trade along with hundreds of other professions associated with the new explosion of goods and services of the ninth and tenth centuries. The *genizah* documents describe both occupational diversity as well as social mobility. As one historian describes them, the Jews became "a Mediterranean people," distinctly middle class, whose social liaisons and cultural horizons were enhanced by their new economic success.

The magnitude of Jewish economic activity indicated by the *genizah* provides additional perspective for understanding a single source of information about Jewish merchants in previous centuries. At the end of the ninth century, a Muslim geographer described the existence of a group of long-distance traders who lived in the eighth century, called the Radanites, apparently from a region near Baghdad. (See Reading 3-12.) These merchants, trading in slaves and luxury goods, traveled from the Middle East to the Slavic regions of the north, across Europe to Spain, finally returning home via North Africa. They also traveled to the Far East, to India, and to China. In a period with relatively few links between East and West, this notable group functioned as intermediary between the two continents and foreshadowed the vigorous mercantile activities of Jewish businessmen of the period of the *genizah*.

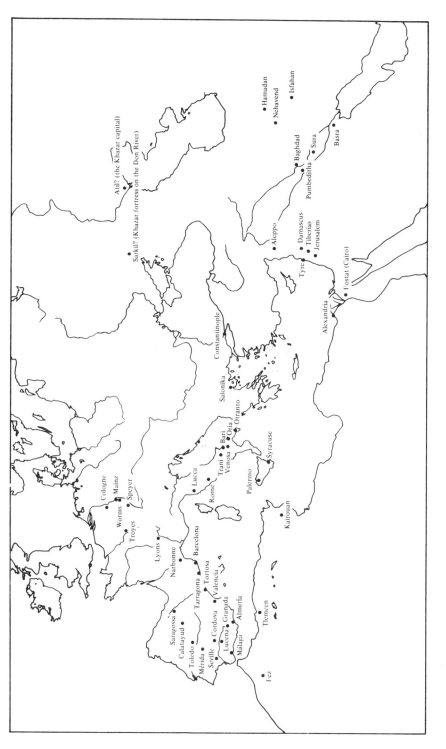

Map 5  Jewish Population Centers, Seventh to Eleventh Centuries

Atil? (the Khazar capital)
Sarkil? (Khazar fortress on the Don River)

Hamadan
Nehavend
Isfahan

Baghdad
Pumbeditha
Sura
Basra

Aleppo
Damascus
Tiberias
Jerusalem
Tyre
Fostat (Cairo)
Alexandria

Constantinople

Salonika

Otranto
Oria
Bari
Trani
Venosa
Syracuse
Rome
Palermo
Lucca

Cologne
Mainz
Speyer
Worms
Troyes
Lyons
Narbonne
Barcelona
Tarragona
Tortosa
Valencia
Saragossa
Calatayud
Toledo
Mérida
Seville
Cordova
Lucena
Granada
Málaga
Almería
Tlemcen
Fez
Kairouan

85

The *genizah* provides more than a glimpse into economic activity. It is a treasure house of social history providing a unique vision of members of a community who were essentially middle class, representing a broader cross section than any other equivalent medieval population. It describes a web of social and political activities across the Muslim empire between Jews and Jewish communities and Muslims, between men and women, families and friends. These records portray a dynamic human civilization with intense social mobility and interaction, the knowledge of which explodes the myths of Jewish isolation and insularity in the medieval world. They highlight as well the sophisticated organization of Jewish communal life in a satellite community such as Egypt as well as in the political nucleus in Baghdad. Indeed, viewed together with the previous literary and archival documents, the *genizah* archives enable us to reconstruct in a relatively detailed manner the functioning of the Jewish community as a vital and dynamic subcommunity within the Islamic world.

The sources do not allow us an uninterrupted glance at the functioning of the Jewish community from Talmudic times to the rise of the Abbasid capital in the eighth century. Nevertheless, it seems safe to suggest a certain degree of continuity despite the disruptions wrought by the Muslim conquest. From the beginning of the Abbasid period, the exilarch (*resh galuta*) is still mentioned as the titular head of Baghdadian Jewry. The academies of Sura and Pumbedita, both in the environs of Baghdad, were revived and functioned as centers of rabbinic learning and codification as they had in previous centuries. The head of the academy was called a *gaon* (plural, *geonim*), whose authority both in Baghdad and throughout the Abbasid reign outstripped that of the exilarch. (See **Reading 3-13.**)

A precious Hebrew chronicle of the early tenth century written by one Nathan the Babylonian provides a revealing portrait of the academies of Baghdad and the power of the *geonim*. At the height of Abbasid power the academies were highly centralized institutions. Their heads were usually selected from a limited number of families. They presided over a highly structured academy of seventy members whose admission was severely restricted. In contrast to the situation in Talmudic times, one's position and power in the academy was more often dependent on family status than rabbinic expertise. The *geonim* wielded considerable power in determining Jewish life through their writing of rabbinical *responsa*, legal answers to queries addressed to them from all corners of the Diaspora. The *geonim* also enhanced their authority by channeling it through local authorities in Egypt, North Africa, and elsewhere in a kind of diocesan organization network.

Perhaps the most powerful force in the political world of Baghdad Jewry, even more powerful than the *geonim* themselves, were select families of court bankers, especially two which rose to prominence by the early tenth century, the Aaron and Netira families. By virtue of their considerable economic standing at the caliphate court, they were able to exercise substantial influence in the political affairs of the Jewish community. Aware of that power, Nathan explicitly refers to their crucial weight in determining the outcome of the disputes between the two *geonim* and the exilarch, which had crippled Baghdadian Jewish affairs in the early years of the century.

The *genizah* gives also a rich portrait of the functioning of local Jewish communities outside Baghdad. In most large towns, two synagogues existed, one with loyalty to a Palestinian rabbinate, which was undergoing its own revival in the ninth and tenth centuries, and one loyal to Baghdad. The two congregations, however, functioned as one, electing a board of elders who appointed various community officials. The community organization functioned effectively in collecting taxes, in offering a wide array of social services unavailable through the Muslim government, and in running its own educational and judicial systems. The continuous thread of Jewish self-government, especially at the local level, remained unbroken from antiquity through the Middle Ages, despite the external changes in the political regimes to which the Jews were subject.

Political and economic interaction between Jews and Muslims was translated into cultural dialogue as well. Baghdad of the ninth and tenth centuries was both the fiscal and cultural center of the Western world. Of particular importance was the revival of Greek philosophical and scientific learning at the courts of the Abbasid caliphs. The Aristotelian works, together with other classics of Greek philosophy, were translated into Arabic, discussed, expounded upon, and made to address the present reality through penetrating commentaries and contemporary philosophical treatises. Most remarkable was the impact of the Greek learning on Islamic theology. The truths of divine revelation had to be reconciled with those of Plato and Aristotle, the latter assuming an almost canonical status in the minds of the new Arabic philosophers. The result was the school of philosophers associated with the *Kalam* (especially the school of the Mutazilites) who assumed that there could be only one universal truth, not two, and who strove to harmonize their own faith with rational thought as conceived by Greek philosophy. Their theologizing led to the systematization of Islamic religion, to the cloaking of beliefs—ultimately impenetrable by rational demonstration—in rational proofs, often arbitrarily and artificially conceived.

The best example of the penetration of Islamic thought into the Jewish community is found in the writings of the illustrious *gaon* of Sura, Saadia Gaon (882–942). Born in Egypt, Saadia traveled briefly to Aleppo and perhaps Palestine before arriving in Baghdad in 921. There he rose meteorically to power, assuming the *gaonic* office of Sura and engaging in a bitter struggle with the exilarch, David ben Zakkai. Saadia's effort to reassert the tottering authority of the Sura academy, which involved the entire leadership of the Jewish community, including the Aaron and Netira families, eventually ended in his defeat and coincided with the general political decline of both Muslim and Jewish Baghdad. (See **Reading 3-13.**)

Saadia's stormy communal and literary careers offer a rare opportunity to observe the vigorous political and intellectual universe of a community through the prism of an individual. Saadia saw himself as the foremost representative of rabbinic Judaism in his era and expended all his energy in defending it against its detractors. As a young man of twenty-three he wrote his first polemical work against the Karaites, a sectarian group that had challenged the authority of the rabbis to interpret the *Torah*. Founded by one Anan ben David around 760, the Karaites emerged as a powerful movement during Saadia's lifetime, producing a rich literature in Arabic and Hebrew in such areas as law, biblical interpretation, Hebrew philology, and philosophy. Ironically, Saadia's anti-Karaite work stimulated a virtual outpouring of theological response on the part of Karaite thinkers and served to fortify the determination of their leaders to challenge the rabbinic domination. (See **Reading 3-15.**)

In another debate Saadia defended the exclusive right of Baghdadian rather than Palestinian rabbis to determine the calendar and life cycle of the Jewish community. He composed a prayer book, translated the Bible into Arabic, and wrote extensive biblical commentaries in which he fulminated against Islam, the Karaites, and rationalist skeptics within the Jewish community. His major work was his philosophic treatise, *The Book of Beliefs and Opinions*, written in Arabic as a reinterpretation of the principles of Judaism in the context of the discussions of the Kalam Mutazilite school of Muslim philosophy. (**See Reading 3-14.**) In the light of the apparent incongruities between faith and reason, Saadia undertook a systematic description of the Jewish religion, attempting to demonstrate the authenticity and rationality of the divine revelation as understood by the rabbis. For Saadia, Judaism's validity rested on its demonstrability. Subjective certitude was no longer enough; a Jewish religious thinker was required to substantiate what was already revealed. In so doing, Saadia advocated that philosophy (the acquisition of truth by rational means) was itself the highest religious goal of Judaism, a position that was reaffirmed by later Jewish philosophers throughout the Middle Ages. Saadia's multifaceted activities and concerns thus patently illustrate the dramatic metamorphosis of Jewish social and cultural life in the dynamic setting of tenth-century Islam.

## THE BEGINNING OF JEWISH SETTLEMENT IN NORTHERN EUROPE

Another consequence of the Muslim conquest and its subsequent transformation of Jewish society was the gradual immigration of Jews into northern Europe. Radanites and other Jewish merchants who undertook long-distance trading ventures from the Middle East through Byzantium and especially Italy, northward and westward, may have constituted the nucleus of small Jewish settlements in western Europe, noticeably visible by the ninth century. A paucity of sources before this period makes it difficult to account for the emergence of Jews in these new regions in the north. What seems clear, however, is that small Jewish communities first appear in Europe strung out along trade routes. A large-scale migration of Jews from Muslim countries to Catholic Europe never actually took place, but a gradual, modest trickle of Jewish merchants who eventually opted for permanent settlement in these new, underdeveloped areas seems plausible in explaining the Jewish entrance into northern and western Europe.

By the ninth century, however, firm evidence exists to account for Jewish colonization in western Europe. Beginning with the Carolingian period, Charlemagne and his son, Louis the Pious, made a special effort to attract Jewish traders to their northern French and German possessions. Three extant charters from this era, written to individual Jews, offer them the promise of imperial protection for their lives, limbs, and property and allow them to live "according to their own law." The charters are colored by the feudal concepts of a contractual relationship between lords and their vassals, as, for example, the one written to an Abraham of Saragossa, who "has entrusted himself into our hands and after an oath we have received and hold him under our protection." The charters, in describing the Jew as a kind of royal vassal, were significant in establishing an important precedent for the legal definition of Jewish status in Christian Europe. Whatever their situation beforehand, in return for the fiscal and administrative benefits they would provide feudal lords of later kings, the Jews could now claim the benefit of physical protection and a stipulated position within feudal society. Out of such mutual economic self-interest, Jews were able to fashion a stable relationship with ruling Christian authorities, one unrelated to theological concepts affecting previous Jewish-Christian liaisons.

Of course, the emerging medieval Church was not oblivious to the growing presence of Jews in the midst of Christian Europe. As early as the sixth century, Pope Gregory the Great had already reiterated the Church's position on the Jews which would become the dominant theological position of Roman Catholicism at least until the period of the Crusades. On the one hand, Gregory disapproved of synagogue burnings and forced baptisms of Jews; on the other hand, he remained a faithful heir of the *adversos Judaeos* tradition, advocating the social segregation and expounding on the inferiority of Jews. With few exceptions, this posture, already articulated by Augustine a century earlier, was reasserted by later Church spokesmen.

In the ninth century, Agobard, the archbishop of Lyons, voiced alarm at the emerging feudal "anarchy" of the Carolingian order. He objected to the preferential treatment afforded Jews at court, the promotion of their trade at public fairs, their ownership of Christian slaves, and their growing influence over Christians. From his canonical and theological perspective, the new charters were undermining his conception of the ideal position of the Jews as socially inferior and separate from the Christian body politic. His contemporary, the churchman Amulu, raised similar objections and even went beyond Agobard in attempting to introduce Christian sermons into the Jewish synagogue. But neither Agobard nor Amulu nor any other church officials succeeded in upsetting the relatively tolerant circumstances affecting Jewish life in early medieval Europe. (**See Reading 3-16.**)

Thus by the early Middle Ages the Jewish community, extended throughout the Christian and Muslim worlds, emerged as a semiautonomous corporation with considerable rights and responsibilities to administer its own law and to live according to the norms of its ancestral heritage. Moreover, Judaism itself, in its encounter with Christianity and Islam, had surfaced mature, resilient, and creatively responsive to the constantly changing social and cultural circumstances of the past ten centuries. It had weathered the recriminations and challenges to its survival emanating from both Christian and Muslim societies; it had discovered the strategies to live—indeed, to flourish—within each civilization. The new stimuli of the two great religions had injected new vitality, new cultural resources and priorities, into Jewish culture. Armed with the Talmudic legacy of Babylonia and Palestine, the *responsa* and philosophical defenses of *gaonic* leadership and the economic and political know-how to endure, Jews had implanted themselves securely in the soil of Europe, North Africa and the Middle East. No doubt their Temple still lay in ruins; the Jewish people remained scattered throughout the world, and their Messiah still "tarried." Nevertheless, Yoḥanan ben Zakkai's modest blueprint to counter Jewish social and cultural extinction had achieved far more than its architect could ever have imagined.

---

*Editor's Questions*
AFTER VIEWING AND READING

- A noted historian has written that there were two roads leading out of Jerusalem in the year 70 C.E., one led to Masada and the other to Yavneh. What does he mean? Do you agree?
- How did Paul's preaching further separate the Jews from Christians? How did the rabbis respond? What did Christianity's position toward the Jews become by the end of the sixth century?
- How did Jewish customs and traditions develop from the compilation of the *Mishnah* to the final editing of the *Talmud*? What other writings are extant today from the rabbis?
- What role did Judaism play in the rise of Islam? How did the Muslims, as reflected in the pact of Umar, treat the Jews?

How did the *resh galuta* and the *geonim* help govern the Jews who lived under the Abbasid caliphate?

• What were the charters that Charlemagne and Louis the Pious offered the Jews? Why did this policy upset Agobard of Lyons?

---

## SUGGESTED READINGS

S. D. Goitein, *Jews and Arabs: Their Contacts Through the Ages* (Schocken, 1964)

S. D. Goitein, *A Mediterranean Society: The Jewish Community of the Arab World as Portrayed in the Documents of the Cairo Geniza* (4 vols.) (University of California Press, 1967–84)

Judah Goldin, *The Living Talmud: The Wisdom of the Fathers* (Mentor, 1957)

Jacob Neusner, *First Century Judaism in Crisis: Yoḥanan b. Zakkai and the Renaissance of Torah* (Abingdon Press, 1975)

Jacob Neusner, *There We Sat Down: Talmudic Judaism in the Making* (Abingdon Press, 1972)

Rosemary Ruether, *Faith and Fratricide: The Theological Roots of Anti-Semitism* (Seabury Press, 1974)

Milton Steinberg, *As a Driven Leaf* (Behrman House, 1939)

# 4

## The Crucible of Europe
## (Ninth to Fifteenth Centuries)

### David B. Ruderman

*Editor's Suggestions*
**BEFORE VIEWING THE SHOW**

Examine Map 6 in the *Study Guide* for the details of Jewish settlement in Europe in the late Middle Ages.

*Overview of the TV Program*

"The Crucible of Europe" describes Jewish life in Muslim Spain and the Jews' great cultural achievements. Maimonides, who spent most of his adult life in Cairo, was heir to these traditions. In northern Christian Europe, the Jews were mainly merchants and developed their own unique religious customs. Although their Christian neighbors considered them alien and accused them of killing Jesus, the Jews were invited to help build new cities and develop urban economic life.

When the Christians conquered Spain, the Jews' "golden age" came to an end, but the Jews continued their cultural life and helped the new rulers translate Arabic works into their own language. Meanwhile, in the rest of Europe Jews were separated from Christians, subjected to violent attacks, and eventually expelled.

Anti-Jewish sentiment spread to Spain where Jewish communities were devastated in 1391 and many Jews converted to Christianity. The government established an Inquisition to investigate the religious sincerity of the Jewish converts to Christianity and then at the end of the fifteenth century expelled the professing Jews.

*Watch for . . . and Think about*

Look for the palace of the Alhambra and the synagogues Santa María la Blanca and El Tránsito. Did Muslim architecture influence the design of Jewish synagogues?

Note the statuary representation of Judaism as a blinded beautiful woman, the walls that surrounded the Jewish quarters, and the drawings of Jews wearing special badges and pointed hats. Were Jews considered aliens and was Judaism respected in Christian European society?

See the illuminated manuscripts and graphics depicting Jewish scholars engaged in study and in performing other religious rituals. What was the nature of Jewish religious and intellectual life in Europe during this period?

WHILE READING THE *STUDY GUIDE* AND *SOURCE READER*

Look for the following:

- The Jewish culture created in Andalusia (Muslim Spain). How did it emerge? Who helped sustain it? What were the activities pursued by those who participated in this culture? Identify Sephardim, Jewish philosophy, and Jewish law.
- The Crusades and how they affected the European Jewish communities. Identify Ashkenazim.
    The legal status of the Jews and their economic activities in the twelfth and thirteenth centuries. Identify blood libel and disputation.
- The subjects the Jews studied in France, Germany, and England. What types of books did Jewish authors write? Identify mysticism.
- What happened to Spanish Jewry in 1391. Identify *conversos* and Inquisition. Who were Ferdinand and Isabella, and how did their policies affect the Jews?

---

## THE FLOWERING OF JEWISH CIVILIZATION IN MUSLIM SPAIN

In describing his native Spain in the tenth century C.E., Said al-Andalusi, a Muslim writer, noticed especially the achievements of one particular Jew named Ḥasdai ibn Shaprut (905–75). A prominent physician, employed by the caliphs of Cordova, Ḥasdai "was the first to open for Andalusian Jewry the gates of their [own] science of jurisprudence, chronology, and other subjects." Consequently, the Jews of Spain no longer had to depend on the Jews of Baghdad in order to adjust their religious calendar and "in order to learn the law of their faith." (See Reading 4-1.)

Al-Andalusi's astute remarks about Ḥasdai ibn Shaprut signal a major cultural and political transformation for Jews living in Andalusia (the Muslim name for Spain) and particularly at the Umayyad Court at Cordova in the middle of the tenth century. In this period, as al-Andalusi testifies, the Spanish Jewish community began to assert its independence from the dominance of Baghdadian Jewry. By declaring Spanish Jewry's prerogative to determine its own mathematical calculation of the Jewish calendar, Ḥasdai virtually assumed the right of the Spanish Jewish community to establish its own autonomous political, economic, and religious status. Al-Andalusi's comments, confirmed independently by Jewish sources, point to a development within Andalusian Jewry directly related to the gradual erosion of political power and cultural vitality of Baghdadian Jewry's institution, the gaonate, by the second half of the tenth century. This cultural and political change within the Jewish world corresponded as well to a similar shifting of power from east to west within the entire Muslim Empire.

Al-Andalusi correctly emphasizes the pivotal role of Ḥasdai ibn Shaprut in effecting the transformation. Although Jews had lived in Spain for centuries and had even played a supporting role in facilitating the Muslim conquest of the Iberian peninsula at the beginning of the eighth century, no Jew had risen to so prominent a position in Spanish society as Ḥasdai. Ḥasdai's success as diplomat and courtier to the caliphs Abd al-Raḥman III (912–61) and al-Ḥakam (961–79) stemmed primarily from his considerable skills as a physician. Gaining the confidence of the caliph through his medicine, he was eventually appointed director of customs and given some responsibility for delicate diplomatic negotiations with the kingdoms of Byzantium, the Holy Roman Empire, and Navarre.

Ḥasdai's political power allowed him to function as the leading figure within the Spanish Jewish community. Claiming the title nasi, the honor originally bestowed on the heads of the Palestinian Sanhedrin Ḥasdai acted as the chief patron of the Spanish Jewish community and its principal spokesman before other Jewish communities. In his latter role, Ḥasdai corresponded with the Jews of Byzantine Italy, southern France, and Sicily. He also tried to establish a liaison with the king of Khazaria, an empire between the Black and Caspian seas, whose royal household apparently had converted to Judaism by Ḥasdai's time.

Ḥasdai's role as a patron of arts and letters helped to establish the unique literary ambiance that marked the efflorescence of Jewish culture in medieval Spain. Imitating the customs of his fellow Muslim courtiers at Cordova, Ḥasdai promoted the composition and recitation of secular poetry by distinguished Hebrew poets. He especially commissioned his personal secretary, Menahem ibn Saruk, and the latter's rival, Dunash ibn Labrat, to write for him. Dunash consequently introduced, for the first time, the use of Arabic meter into Hebrew poetry. (See Reading 4-6.)

Ḥasdai's patronage served to establish a new Jewish attitude to poetry. For centuries, beginning in Palestine, Hebrew poets had written poems exclusively for the purpose of prayer. Inspired by the Arabic example, Menahem, Dunash, and their successors wrote poems in Hebrew to flatter or entertain their patrons—without regard to liturgical use. The professional Hebrew poet asserted his own national and cultural distinctiveness by writing poems according to the model of Hebrew rather than Arabic scriptures. But by composing poems on love, on wine, on women, and on the glorification of nature, he celebrated a life-style and the values of an elite society that was indistinguishable from its Islamic counterparts. The professional poet, writing for a literate Hebrew public, espoused the ideal of appreciating literature for its own sake, independent of any religious purposes. He also functioned as a political propagandist, using biting satire or obsequious flattery to curry the favor of his cultural patron. (See Reading 4-5.)

Most of all, Ḥasdai's cultural interests helped shape the emerging self-image of a Jewish courtier class that would dominate Spanish Jewry for generations to come. For this group of Jewish literati, knowledge of the *Torah* alone did not make the complete Jewish gentleman. Their courtly bearing and their dignified social status were the result of systematic training in literature, science, and philosophy. They attempted to harmonize Jewish learning and "Greek wisdom" as Saadia had done in Baghdad, but in their curriculum of Jewish and "Greek" studies they also strove to realize a social as well as an intellectual ideal. Scholarly attainment in both traditional and secular fields of learning led ultimately, in their mind, to a nobility of character, to the forging of a complete human being who embodied the best of Jewish and Muslim culture. More than any other source, the numerous poems of the Spanish Hebrew poets came to extol and to propagate the virtues of this new Jewish elite.

Nobility and social advantage, however, did not weaken their relationship to their community and its cultural resources. Spanish Jewry produced Talmudists who also wrote Hebrew poetry and Arabic philosophy and remarkably well-rounded philosophers who also mastered the *Talmud*. This integration of learning coincided as well with a noticeable social integration. The ideal Jewish courtier placed his political power and social rank at the service of the Jewish community. Nobility thus required community activity. Cultural elitism could not mean social estrangement. In this regard Hasdai's activity on behalf of the Jewish community became the model for aspiring Jewish courtiers. The fate of the Jewish people, so they thought, rested on the shoulders of their privileged class, whose sense of *noblesse oblige* required their untiring efforts on behalf of the entire community. Of course, few courtiers were capable of realizing so lofty an ideal; later generations would complain bitterly about the blatant disregard of the courtier class for the communal welfare. Nevertheless, the ideals of Hasdai's cultural program were solidly ingrained in the attitude of aspiring Jewish leaders in Spain, in Provence, in Italy, and in other Diaspora communities for centuries to come. (See Reading 4-2.)

Hasdai's political and cultural aspirations help to explain his wish to establish contact with the Jewish king of the Khazars. In his Hebrew correspondence to King Joseph, Hasdai portrays himself as the king's equal in rank. He represents himself as the Jewish monarch of the west, striving to communicate with his Jewish counterpart in the east. Hasdai's letter demonstrates his assertion of Jewish political power, comparable in his own estimation to that of the Christians and Muslims. Yet despite the security and material benefits of his position in Cordova, he also reveals an impulse so characteristic of later generations of Spanish Jews, the yearning for messianic redemption. Hasdai's letter, apparently crafted by his secretary, Menahem, borrows freely from the language of a ninth-century Jewish messianic adventure story, written by one Eldad of "the lost tribe of Dan." Hasdai's outward success in initiating a wide-ranging program of Jewish cultural and political autonomy in Spain appears in his letter somewhat tempered by an anxious expression of hope for Israel's ultimate salvation, a hope triggered by the romantic notion of Jewish political sovereignty in a land so remote from Andalusia and the palace of Cordova.

By the beginning of the eleventh century, the Umayyad caliphate at Cordova collapsed, followed by the splintering of the Muslim state into numerous petty kingdoms. The smaller governments vied with each other to recapture the glory once associated with Cordova. Talented Jewish courtiers found their skills in great demand and took advantage of the new opportunities for government service. The most powerful of Jewish courtiers of the eleventh century was Samuel ibn Naghrela (993–1055 or 1056) of the Berber kingdom of Granada, who referred to himself by the title of *nagid*, or prince. (**See Reading 4-3.**)

According to the Spanish Jewish chronicler Abraham ibn Daud (ca. 1110–1180), Samuel successfully rose from rags to riches to assume the viziership of the state and the leadership of an army of Muslims. Never lacking in self-confidence, Samuel was well aware of his multiple administrative, martial, and literary talents. He lavishly documented his dramatic accomplishments on the battlefield through his Hebrew poems, demonstrating as well his brilliant mastery of the Hebrew language. Samuel's considerable abilities also included Talmudic scholarship, which he never relinquished in favor of his more secular pursuits. His flashy career, his inflated ego, as well as his national chauvinism, so flagrant in his writings, vividly exemplify the aristocratic delusions of grandeur which characterized the cultural attitudes of some of the elite Jewish class of that time. Certainly so ostentatious an expression of Jewish elitism did not go unnoticed by Samuel's Muslim contemporaries. A number of Muslim writers openly criticized what they considered to be Jewish pretentiousness and even disrespect of Islam. Literary skirmishes were also translated into physical assault. Samuel's son and successor, Joseph, was assassinated by a hostile mob that ransacked the Jewish quarter of Granada in 1066. (**See Reading 4-4.**)

The period of these petty states abruptly ended, however, with their conquest by two fanatical Muslim tribes—first the Almoravides, who established their rule in 1090, and then by the Almohades, who had terrorized most of Islamic Spain by the middle of the twelfth century. The end of the eleventh century also marked the disintegration of exclusive Muslim control of the Iberian peninsula and the beginning of the *reconquista*, the new offensive of the Christians to reassert their control over Spain. In 1085 the Christians succeeded in conquering the city of Toledo, a vital stronghold in the center of the peninsula. Jewish subjects of a Muslim society gradually discovered that they now lived in a potentially more hostile Christian environment. The Almohade invasion of the twelfth century proved, however, to be an even more excruciating blow to Jewish continuity in Muslim Spain. The Almohades ruthlessly carried out a policy of forced conversion of Jews and Christians, eroding further the stability of the Jewish community and precipitating the mass exodus of Jews to the north and to the east. (See **Reading 4-6.**)

Ironically, the twilight of Jewish communal fortunes in Muslim Spain, its dislocation and decline, coincided with the attainment of new heights of cultural creativity among Spanish Jewry. In the area of Talmudic interpretation and codification, Isaac Alfasi (1013–1103) and Joseph ibn Migash (1077–1141) established the preeminence of the Spanish rabbinic academies. Judah ha-Levi (ca. 1075–1141), who witnessed the Christian advance in Toledo and the subsequent Almoravid victories, brilliantly surpassed the literary virtuosity of earlier Jewish poets in Spain. Yet living in an environment ridden with anxiety and uncertainty regarding the future welfare of the Jewish community, ha-Levi writes in sharp contrast to the bold self-confidence and complacency shown in Samuel ha-nagid's earlier works. Ha-Levi exhibits most pointedly a sense of growing impatience and disillusionment with the pretensions of Spain's Jewish courtier class and their already shaky edifice of political power and cultural *élan*, dramatically crumbling by the early twelfth century.

Judah ha-Levi's major work, other than his Hebrew poetry, was the *Book of the Khazars (Sefer ha-Kuzari)*. Composed initially in Arabic, it later was translated into Hebrew and would become a classic of medieval Hebrew literature. Ha-Levi's work, cast in the mold of a philosophical dialogue, is essentially a critique of the priority given to Greek philosophy within Spanish Jewish civilization. But more than a philosophical polemic, it addresses Judaism's traditional adversaries, Christianity and Islam, and even attacks the Karaite sect as well. Above all, it is "a defense of the despised faith" (as its title indicates) against the intellectual assaults of the two major religions from without and the spiritual erosion from within at the hand of philosophy. It is a social critique also, a repudiation of the smugness and self-delusion of Spanish Jewry's aristocracy and its integration into Spanish society. (See **Reading 4-7.**)

Ha-Levi constructed an imaginary discussion between the Khazar king (the subject of Ḥasdai ibn Shaprut's earlier correspondence) and representatives of the three major faiths, plus a philosopher, each summoned by the king to present his respective position. Ha-Levi has the king reject the views of the philosopher, the Muslim, and the Christian before turning reluctantly to his last invited guest, the rabbi. The latter proceeds to articulate the author's understanding of Judaism:

> We believe in the God of Abraham, Isaac, and Jacob, who led the children Israel from Egypt with signs and miracles, who fed them in the desert; and having guided them through the Sea and the Jordan, gave them the land of Canaan for an inheritance. We believe in the God who sent Moses with his Torah, and many thousands of prophets after him, exhorting the Jews to keep the Torah, promising high reward to the observant and severe punishment to the disobedient.
>
> (*Ha-Kuzari*, opening)

For ha-Levi, Judaism was translatable in historical, not theological, terms. The existence of God is proved by the collective historical experience of the Jewish people. Jewish history constitutes evidence of the divine law for all individuals and nations. History thus discloses God's continuous revelation to Jews and provides a rationale for their special vocation as a community. Their lack of power and sovereignty does not detract from their virtue and spirituality. On the contrary, Jewish powerlessness and suffering testify to their steadfastness and the purity of their faith.

Ha-Levi's greatest contribution in understanding Jewish spirituality was his concept of the religious ideal of Judaism and its view of prophecy. He did not object to philosophy in itself; rather he denounced the fusion of Judaism and philosophy; the reduction of knowing God to knowing a philosophical "idea" of God; and the argument that Jewish prophecy is synonymous with Jewish philosophy. To know God in Jewish terms is to experience him through revelation, never through reason. Prophecy, the highest actualization of Jewish spirituality, is not intellectual perfection. Rather, perfection is the realization of total commitment to Jewish law and its observance, and, especially, immigration to the Land of Israel.

In this last point, ha-Levi shifts his critique from the intellectual to the social level. In the *Sefer ha-Kuzari*, he makes the rabbi depart from Khazaria and return to Israel. His odes to Zion, a collection of Hebrew poems which highlight his infatuation with the Holy Land, reinforce the same theme. Moreover, his own personal decision to leave Spain in favor of *aliyah* (ascent) to the land of Israel is certainly his most powerful statement in this regard. Israel, not Spain, is the only geographical location where Jews can totally fulfill their spiritual ideals and religious obligations. In Israel, not Spain, prophecy can be realized, and from Israel, not Spain, the Messiah will appear. Ha-Levi's life and thought thus constitute a ringing denunciation of the integration of Judaism with Spanish society and thought, of the ideals of the Jewish courtier class, and the dominant self-image of Spanish Jewry since Hasdai's day. For future generations of Jews, ha-Levi's work would become the ideological underpinning for promoting continued Jewish intellectual and social distance from non-Jewish civilization and for resisting the cultural encroachment of the majority upon the Jewish minority.

Ha-Levi's position, however, clearly remained that of a small minority in Spain which had become disenchanted with the promises of Spanish Jewish culture. For the overwhelming majority of the Jewish leadership, the old aristocratic ideals of social and intellectual liaison with the Muslim world continued to hold their fascination. At the time ha-Levi was contemplating his imminent departure from Spain, Moses Maimonides was born (1135–1204). The life and thought of this dominant figure of Spanish Jewry, who lived much of his adult life in Egypt, gave eloquent expression, indeed vindication, to the educational program and cultural priorities to which ha-Levi had objected.

Maimonides' youthful years in Spain bore little resemblance to the tranquility and stability of former generations of Jewish courtiers. The Almohade invasion of the mid-twelfth century brought to an abrupt end any hope of material and spiritual security in his native Cordova. Uprooting himself from Cordova, Maimonides spent many years wandering through Spain, North Africa, and Palestine before settling in Cairo, where eventually he was appointed house physician of the vizier of Egypt. Despite the turbulence of his life and career, Maimonides, unlike ha-Levi, never soured in his commitment to the life-style and intellectual goals earlier advanced by Hasdai ibn Shaprut and Samuel ha-Nagid. Maimonides' prolonged exposure to Muslim hostility and the personal hardship it imposed never altered his perception of the central place of external intellectual stimulation in defining and enhancing Jewish culture. (See Readings 4-8 and 4-9.)

Maimonides' writings reflect a three-pronged intellectual commitment which became totally integrated in his life and thought. His professional career was that of a physician; he devoted himself to patient care and composed scientific treatises on various aspects of medicine. He was also a distinguished student of Jewish law. At a youthful age, he composed a commentary on the *Mishnah*; he later wrote the *Sefer ha-Mizvot* (Book of Commandments) and finally completed the awesome undertaking of a code of Jewish law called the *Mishneh Torah* (The Repetition of the Law, also known as *Yad ha-Hazakah*, The Strong Hand). He also wrote hundreds of rabbinic *responsa* (questions and answers) which, together with his major *halakhic* (legal) writings, established his preeminence as the foremost Jewish legal authority of his age. Alongside his *halakhic* achievement was his philosophical masterpiece, the *Guide of the Perplexed*, originally written in Arabic, which soon achieved an exalted status within the Jewish, Muslim, and Christian intellectual worlds. Maimonides' study of physics and metaphysics naturally flowed from his study of the divine law and vice versa; Maimonides, the codifier, and Maimonides, the physician and metaphysician, constituted one integrated personality and thinker.

In contrast to ha-Levi, Maimonides strove to realize in his writings the overall unity of learning, a unity of the practical and theoretical, of divine law and Aristotelian philosophy. Maimonides' systematic compilation of the law was grounded in rational and theological principles. Alternatively, his philosophical work provided the intellectual foundation for the viability of Jewish faith and practice. Attacking the simplistic and naive rationalism of the *Kalam*, Maimonides strove for a more honest and sophisticated confrontation between revelation and philosophy. He was aware of the pitfalls of philosophical discourse, the possibility of the corrosive effects that intellectual elitism might have on Jewish belief and commitment. Yet he remained eager to meet head on the challenges of philosophy and universal intellectual debate. Judaism could not insulate itself from the larger intellectual community. It needed to project to that community a profile of an intellectually alive "wise and understanding people" (Deuteronomy 4:7). Moreover, Judaism itself demanded of its adherents a religious faith which was neither literalistic nor uninformed. As in the case of Saadia, philosophy and intellectual attainment became the supreme religious ideal for Maimonides. Judaism's spiritual maturation as a religious civilization was dependent on its dialogue and interaction with the outside world.

Maimonides' death in 1204 precipitated a major debate within the Jewish community over the place of philosophy, rationalism, and the study of alien cultures in Judaism, a controversy whose ramifications are still felt in contemporary Jewish life. The so-called Maimonidean controversy engaged the attention of Jewish scholars in Spain, Provence, northern France, and Germany, and even reached as far as Yemen. The entire debate ultimately involved the juxtaposition of two models of Jewish spirituality and two cultural postures: an "innerdirected" one and an "outerdirected" one vis-à-vis Judaism's relationship to the outside world. While Judah ha-Levi asserted the opposition between divine revelation and philosophical wisdom, Maimonides found the dialogue between revelation and human rationalism to be a virtue, indeed a necessity for Judaism's continued vitality and relevance. The ha-Levi–Maimonides controversy constitutes the major dialectical tension of all subsequent Jewish intellectual and cultural history. It provides the ideological framework and intellectual justification for the two absolute poles of Jewish response to cultural interaction with western civilization—a call for either total isolation, or integration, or some relative response between the two. As the major representatives of medieval Jewish civilization in Spain, ha-Levi and Maimonides vividly demonstrate the formative influence of Spanish Jewish culture on later Jewish thought and society.

## THE RISE OF MEDIEVAL ANTI-JUDAISM IN NORTHERN EUROPE

The beginning of the Christian insurgence into north-central Spain at the end of the eleventh century represented only the opening round of a major offensive against the Islamic world. Some eleven years after Toledo's fall, the papacy launched its boldest attack against the Muslims, this time at the eastern front in the direction of the land of Israel. Proclaiming the objective of liberating the Holy Land from the "polluted" hands of the "infidel," the Pope called together a massive army of crusaders from varying nationalities, cultures, and economic backgrounds. Undisciplined and theologically unsophisticated, thousands of Europeans gathered to "atone" for

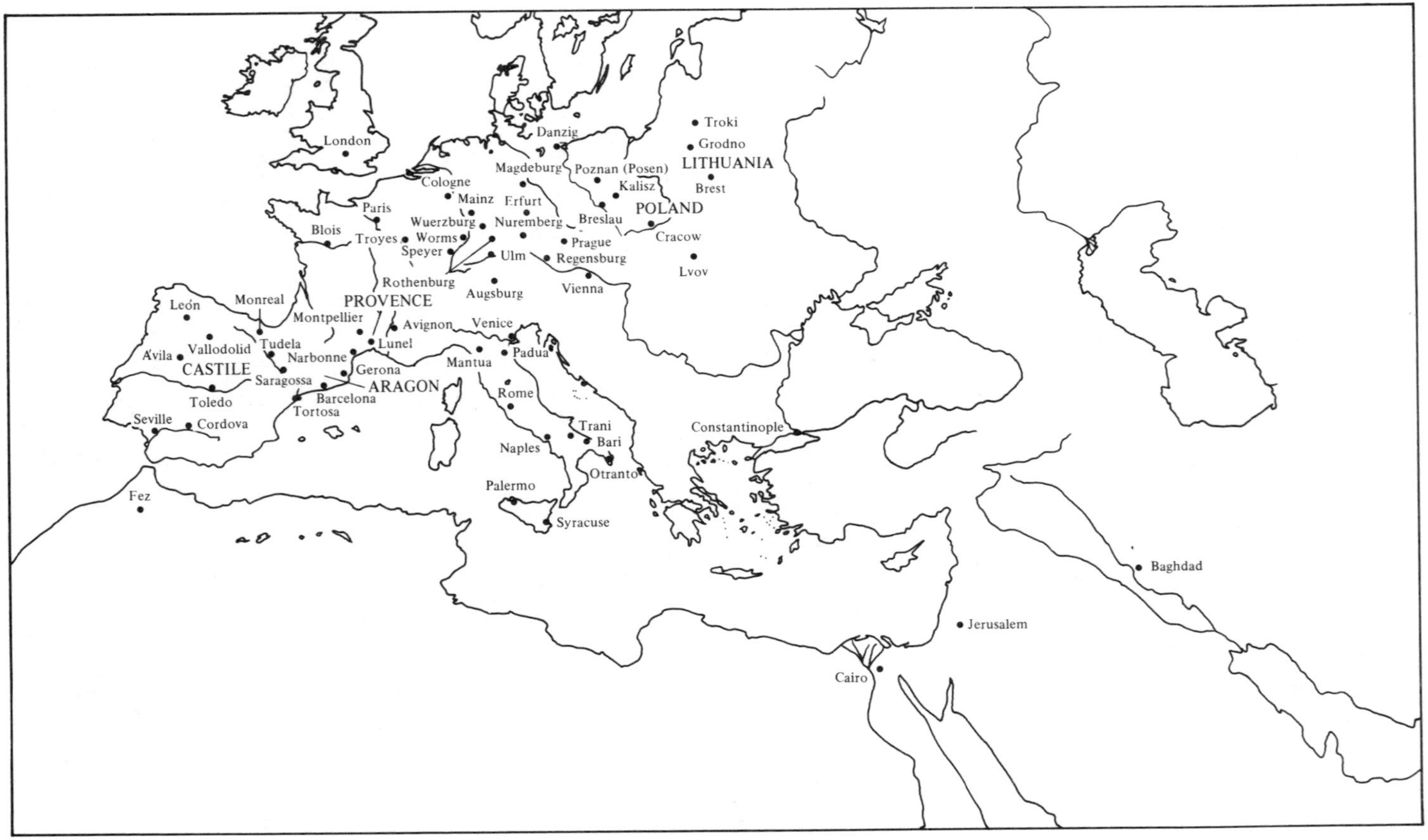

**Map 6  Jewish Population Centers, Eleventh to Mid-Fifteenth Centuries**

their sins by doing battle for Christ. The concentration of crusading hordes dangerously swarming across the European continent constituted a major threat to the welfare and security of peoples and communities in their path. To European Jews, especially those living in Germany's Rhineland area, the crusader presence proved to be particularly alarming. (See Reading 4-10.)

In the minds of hysterical, hungry, and ignorant crusaders, inflamed by popular religious fanatics, the fine points of the Church's theory of the Jews were beyond comprehension. The Church preached that salvation would be assured for anyone who took the cross and destroyed the Muslim enemies of Christ, who had usurped the Christian holy places. Such religious hatred had never before been directed at Jews living in northern Europe. To many crusaders, however, it seemed preposterous to set out on a long journey to kill God's enemies while his worst adversaries, those who seemingly had murdered him, the Jews, were dwelling in the midst of the Christian world. The Augustinian doctrine, which held that although the Jews were damnable, they ought to be preserved until the end of time, also eluded them. The distinction between social degradation and physical assault on Jewish victims who had committed the most heinous crime of all—deicide—made sense to only the few theologically astute. Neither the Church nor the secular princes empowered to protect the Jews were prepared to offer formidable resistance to the crusaders. Both were caught by surprise; both proved impotent to control the unruly crowds who burst upon defenseless Jewish communities, acting out a hatred nurtured by years of church teaching and fueled by infectious crowd hysteria. (See Reading 4-12.)

Some five thousand Jews lost their lives during the first crusade of 1096, either massacred by Christians or having taken their own lives as religious martyrs. Several hundred more also died during the subsequent crusades of the twelfth century. The loss of lives was accompanied by a cultural and spiritual loss. Already by the tenth century, the Rhineland Jewish communities, especially Mainz, Speyer, and Worms, had emerged as nascent centers of Jewish communal life, attracting individual Jews in search of economic prosperity and physical security. Under the leadership of Rabbenu Gershom b. Judah ("the Light of the Diaspora," 950–1028), these communities, especially Mainz, established distinguished institutions of rabbinic learning. They reformulated and adapted Talmudic law to the new conditions of the miniscule Jewish communities scattered throughout the Rhineland. These German (Ashkenazic) communities suffered the greatest losses at the hands of the crusaders. In the wake of the catastrophe, rabbinic learning underwent a major decline and a major shift westward. R. Solomon b. Isaac (Rashi, 1040–1105), a former student at the German academies, established his own academy in Troyes, northern France, which soon eclipsed the Rhineland schools. (See Reading 4-11.)

The memory of the crusade massacres is preserved in three major Hebrew chronicles, in various Hebrew liturgical poems and in some shorter Christian notices. The chronicles, in particular, provide not only a relatively accurate picture of the Christian atrocities but also a lucid indicator of Jewish responses to the new Christian aggressiveness. In contrast to previous centuries of relative stability in Jewish-Christian relations, Christian verbal assault now had exploded into physical violence. The Jewish survivors were forced accordingly to reevaluate their attitudes about Christians, their own religious faith and their own self-image as a consequence of this dramatic crisis. The chronicles thus document both particular historical events and emerging theological and social attitudes.

The authors or compilers of the Hebrew crusade accounts wished to memorialize the dead and to glorify the sanctity of their lives and the manner of their deaths. The narratives faithfully describe the various actions taken by the leadership of each Jewish community to elude their hostile oppressors. They demanded protection as part of their legal contractual relationship with the secular rulers. When moral suasion proved insufficient, they offered monetary compensation. Some even defended themselves physically while others made every effort to escape. When all worldly means failed them, the victims prepared to meet their end through spiritual resistance: they prayed, they put on sackcloth and ashes and, ultimately and tragically, they assembled to murder themselves rather than be brutalized by their adversaries or be obliged to approach the baptismal font.

The Jewish victims and their chroniclers shared a common perspective. God was testing his people bound to him in holy covenant. As the biblical Abraham had been tested by making ready the offering of his son Isaac on Mount Moriah, these martyrs similarly conceived this as their own special vocation. Yet they considered themselves far greater in sacrifice and conviction than Abraham. He ultimately had been restrained from butchering his child; but they, the martyrs of 1096, did not hesitate to carry out the final act. The chronicles capture poignantly the metamorphosed behavior of the Jewish martyrs: the futile mood of political action is replaced by a growing acceptance of death as a spiritual vindication and transcendence. The martyrs conceived of themselves as the Holy Temple, never to be violated by the filth of their enemies' faith. In the moment of violent confrontation with the crusaders, the Jewish victims revealed openly their revulsion toward Christianity, their readiness to choose death over Christian life and their willingness to testify to the truth of their own faith by repudiating that of the Christian.

In the piercing moments of religious confrontation with the crusaders, the Jewish victims elected religious martyrdom in a manner patently different from other Jewish victims in other lands and in other times. The quietistic martyrological ideal of Ashkenazic Jewry, as delineated in the chronicles, stands in sharp contrast to the emphatic warnings of Maimonides and other Spanish rabbis, who counseled escape or feigned conversion rather than suicide to Jews in similar circumstances. Perhaps influenced by a Christian martyrological ideal, accentuated under conditions of extreme psychological stress, these Jewish martyrs came to epitomize the singular response of a beleaguered Jewish minority striving to make religious sense out of the tyranny of the Christian majority. Through the crusade narratives and through liturgical hymns recited in Ashkenazic synagogues, the martyrs of Germany and their horrific acts were ennobled and romanticized by succeeding generations.

From the twelfth century on Jewish life throughout Christian Europe—in England, in France, in Germany, and eventually in reconquered Spain—steadily began to erode. Whether the crusades represented the major cause of this deterioration remains unproven. What is clear is that the events of 1096 undoubtedly contributed to an atmosphere of growing intolerance and antagonism toward Jews and Judaism in Christian society. One of the most perceptible signs of this decline can be detected in the changing definition of the legal status of Jews in Christian lands. As we have already seen, from the Carolingian period until the end of the eleventh century, individual Jews and, later, entire Jewish communities had been granted special charters with privileges of protection and relative legal autonomy. By the beginning of the twelfth century, however, their status in Germany was altered under the new imperial land peace legislation. While their former privileges remained, Jews were excluded from holding arms. The result was a further diminution of their honor and an enhanced dependence on their lords.

Already, in England in 1135, the so-called "Laws of Edward the Confessor" had described the king's right to possess Jews by defining their status as serfs. In Germany, the term *servi camerae nostrae* (the serfs of our chamber) was first used in relation to Jews in 1236. Removing any ambiguity in describing their social position in Christian society, Frederick II, the Holy Roman emperor, made explicit the total dependence of "his" Jews on his good graces. Frederick perhaps was objecting to papal demands that the Church had the ultimate right to supervise the status of Jews in the Christian world. Thomas Aquinas had so stated: "Since the Jews are the Church's serfs, it can do as it wishes with their wealth." In reaction to what he considered the usurpation of power by the papacy, Frederick offered his own imperial formulation of Jewish status. By so doing, the emperor defined the subservient and dependent social standing of Jews living within his regime as a general principle of law and provided a clear example for other Christian rulers to follow.

In the economic sphere, Jewish life also was transformed during the same period. In the twelfth and thirteenth centuries, because of the insecurity following the crusade massacres, but more significantly because of the development of Christian commercial organizations, Jews turned increasingly to money-lending. Prior to this period, Jewish economic life was more diversified and unrestricted; some Jews still owned land and earned their living from agriculture. Yet in this era, first in England, then in France, and eventually in Germany, the Jews were excluded from commerce and were obliged to lend money on interest. Their activity in this area undoubtedly was facilitated by the stigma attached to usury by the Church regarding Christian money-lending. Since money-lending was critical to an emerging commercial economy, Jews uncomfortably assumed a distasteful although necessary occupation within medieval Europe. The Jews were never as predominant in usurious operations as their popular economic image seemed to project. Most often they were subjected to damaging losses and even physical abuse because of their unpopular profession.

No doubt, the proliferation of Jewish money-lenders was encouraged and tightly controlled by royal authorities who used the Jews for their own profit and financial advantage. The royal governments, especially in England, were particularly skillful in appropriating funds collected by Jews, taxing them heavily, treating them harshly and isolating them socially, all under the guise of religious piety and Christian anti-Judaism. The ultimate step in exploiting their Jewish subjects by expropriating their entire wealth and property was expulsion. It is no coincidence that the royal government of England was the first to expel its Jews in 1290. France imitated the English example in 1306 and later in 1380. The principalities of Germany and later Italy, as well as the united monarchy of Spain, followed suit from the fourteenth through the sixteenth centuries. (See Reading 4-14.)

The image of the Jew as usurer and economic exploiter represented only one dimension of a composite stereotypical portrait of the Jew in Christian society that emerged with alarming intensity in the aftermath of the crusades. Appearing first in the town of Norwich, in England, in 1144 the infamous blood libel against Jews rapidly spread to the continent, becoming a recurrent feature of Jewish-Christian relations even until the twentieth century. Despite the patent falsity of such charges, Jews were accused of capturing an innocent Christian child and performing a ritual murder in order to utilize his blood for the production of unleavened Passover bread. One of the most publicized of these accusations took place in the town of Blois, in northern France in 1171. Here a Jew was accused of killing a child whose corpse was never found. Theobald V, the count of Blois, by officially acknowledging the accusation as true without evidence, was responsible for the death of thirty-one Jews held accountable for the alleged murder.

In the same period Jews were also accused falsely of desecrating the host, that is, of using the wafer of the Eucharist ceremony for diabolical schemes. As with the blood libel, their Christian accusers could visualize Jews acting out their enmity toward Jesus by mutilating his bodily representation, as their ancestors supposedly had done in the first century. In times of mass anxiety during the Black Death, Jews also were convenient scapegoats, accused of poisoning wells and of serving as the primary carriers of the dreaded disease. (See Reading 4-13.)

From ballads, poetry, songs, plays, spectacles, and especially artwork, there emerges a composite portrait of Jewish civilization far worse than the official view of either the Church or the secular governments of Europe. At their most basic level, the popular charges leveled against Jews in the later Middle Ages centered around a diabolical image. The Jew was considered an enemy of mankind, closely associated with the devil. He also was portrayed as the Antichrist, the Jewish messiah who was to be vanquished ultimately by Christ himself. He possessed horns like the devil, wore a horned hat and sported a goatee, all items associated with the devil's favorite animal. He also exuded the *foetor Judaicus*, a Jewish odor, distinctively smelling like Satan.

The Jew was considered to be a sorcerer as well. His magical powers allowed him to perform ritual murder and poison the water supply. He was also conceived as a heretic, despite the fact that he was never a part of the Christian community of believers. In the popular mind he was responsible, nevertheless, for the Judaizing heresy, for causing other Christians to lose their own orthodoxy. All these themes together with that of the pitiless creditor, the shylock, served to conjure up a horrific portrait of European Jewry in popular Christian culture. They allow us to understand the popular support Church and state most decidedly received when carrying out their anti-Jewish policies.

The twelfth and thirteenth centuries also mark a reevaluation of and departure from previous official Church policy regarding the Jews. In this period, a new polemical offensive emerged within the Church to cancel the right of Judaism to exist as a religious faith distinct from Christianity. The prevalent Augustinian tolerance of Jews was displaced by a more aggressive policy of vilifying Judaism and missionizing among Jews. No doubt Dominican and Franciscan friars were in the forefront of this new intolerance, but especially prominent was a group of Jews themselves who converted to the Christian faith and assumed central roles in the new campaign to undermine Jewish identity and facilitate Jewish conversion to Christianity.

A critical feature of the new Christian strategy was the public disputation, a staged spectacle in which Jews were forced to participate. The disputation was not an open debate between two equal partners; it was rather a demonstration of Christian intellectual superiority contrived in advance. In just such a forced disputation, held in Paris in 1239, Nicholas Donin, a recent convert, accused his former coreligionists of establishing an alien, secret tradition within their Talmudic literature with the express purpose of blaspheming Christianity. The *Talmud* was the primary cause of their diabolical behavior, their perfidiousness, and their antipathy toward Christianity, so he claimed, and thus the *Talmud* became the primary target of this apostate's indictment. The final outcome of this public denunciation of postbiblical Judaism was the incineration of Talmudic tomes throughout France. (**See Reading 4-15.**)

In 1263, in the city of Barcelona, Pablo Christiani (d. 1274), also a former Jew, employed another tactic in attempting to defeat his Jewish opponent, the distinguished rabbi Moses b. Naḥman (Naḥmanides, 1194–1270). He argued that rabbinic literature itself could be used to demonstrate Christian truth. Christiani's method was essentially an extension of the manner former Christian apologists had "discovered" in *testimonia* of their faith in Old Testament passages. This apostate now combed rabbinic homiletical literature for the same purpose—to uncover an authentic Christian faith within rabbinic Judaism itself in order to persuade Jews to realize the veracity of the Christian position. His method of using rabbinic literature as testimony for Christianity was followed and embellished by other churchmen, most notably Raymond Martinus (1220–85) in his massive *Pugio Fidei* (The Dagger of Faith, ca. 1280). That both strategies—denigrating rabbinic literature while using it at the same time to prove the truth of Christian dogma—directly contradicted each other apparently proved to be no obstacle for these clerics. Both tactics could be employed in the service of the "higher Christian mission" where consistency surely represented no special virtue.

The new emphasis in Church policy toward the Jews was also reflected in discriminatory legislation further segregating and humiliating Jews living among Christians. The fourth Lateran Council of 1215 reaffirmed the Church's regulations concerning the Jews, stemming back to the Theodosian and Justinian codes. It prohibited Jews from taking "excessive" usury, leaving ambiguous the meaning of what constituted excessive interest. It insisted that the Jews wear special costumes—a conical hat and a Jewish badge—all to serve as public reminders of their inferior status. Although not uniformly enforced, the new regulations contributed to the growing social isolation of the Jews. The special marks on Jewish clothing were displayed prominently in contemporary iconographic portraits of Jews, thus serving to reinforce their negative image in European popular culture.

The profound deterioration of Jewish life in Christian Europe—politically, socially, economically, and religiously—is thus easily documented from the twelfth century on. What is more difficult to assess, however, is the issue of responsibility for this overall decline.

Some historians have attributed general Jewish abasement to the Church, yet such a facile approach misses the complexity of the phenomenon of anti-Judaism in the Christian Middle Ages. In the first place, if the Church was the primary agent of aggressiveness toward the Jews, how might one explain the relatively tranquil period of Jewish-Christian relations for some 1,000 years prior to the crusades? And secondly, such an assumption misses the obvious distinction between basic Christian beliefs and the use to which such beliefs were put by particular individuals in specific contexts. So simplistic a view that the Church alone was responsible for anti-Judaism fails to take into account the huge range of conduct of individuals and institutions with their basic fears and motivations, who purported to act in the name of Christian values.

No doubt the Church's teachings on the Jews, formulated as we have seen in a period of intense rivalry between the two faiths, was bound to be exploited by those who wished to degrade the Jewish community and its religious beliefs. All the materials—the scriptural passages, the homiletical flourishes, the iconographic images—were conspicuously available in the Church's arsenal of anti-Judaic weapons. Church doctrine always remained a standing provocation for mistreating Jews. But doctrines themselves do not sufficiently explain why individuals act to brutalize other human beings. Furthermore, by the later Middle Ages the growing involvement of the Church in secular affairs and the increasing intervention of secular princes in Church affairs blurred the distinction between the secular and religious in medieval Europe. Who actually spoke for authentic Christian values? Was it the papacy, or the secular princes, or the lay clergy in various parishes and national settings? Did the churchmen or princes promote anti-Judaic attitudes or did they merely support and play upon fears and passions about Jews already current among the many segments of the populations they represented?

The actual changes in European society in the twelfth and thirteenth centuries appear to provide a more promising explanation of the causes of medieval anti-Judaism than does Church doctrine alone. The crusades and their destructiveness were symptomatic of a deeper anxiety that plagued European society—a fear of the impotence of Christian civilization, of Muslim domination from without, and of heresy and inner dissolution from within. The hatred of the Jew should be seen in the larger context of irrational fears, deeply felt insecurity, and growing intolerance of individual variation and of nonconformity in European culture. It should also be linked to the increasing urbanization and social stratification of medieval society, of an increasingly more complex social and political organization, and of a more differentiated economic order. The emergence of town life and commercial guilds, which excluded Jews, the strengthening of central government, which took advantage of Jews for its own special purposes, and the growing separation between rich and poor vying for shrinking economic resources, all might help to explain anti-Jewish prejudice as well. In short, the intense forms of medieval anti-Judaism emerging in the later Middle Ages represent more than the result of religious antagonism between Judaism and Christianity alone. They constitute a sensitive barometer of wider and deeper social, economic, and political strains affecting all levels of Christian society within the same period. They also serve to lay the solid foundations of the enduring theory and practice of anti-Judaism in Europe and beyond throughout modern times.

## PATTERNS OF JEWISH CULTURE IN MEDIEVAL EUROPE

Jewish life in Christian Europe, from the crusades until the beginning of the fifteenth century, was much more than just this well-known series of Christian atrocities and Jewish responses. Despite the incessant pressures exerted by Christian society on the Jewish minority, Jewish communities endured and Jewish culture continued to flourish and respond to the challenges of its surroundings. Like their Jewish counterparts living in Muslim lands, the Jews living under Christian rule inherited the Talmudic tradition of their ancestors in Palestine and Babylonia, reshaped it, and expanded it in the context of their own requirements and values. (See Reading 4-16.)

The crusades themselves provided a major impetus in the crystallization of Jewish culture in northern Europe. With the destruction of the Rhineland centers of rabbinic learning, Talmudic scholarship shifted geographically to northern France. Moreover, in an effort to preserve the rich legacy of Ashkenazic rabbinic culture, oral traditions soon were committed to writing. R. Solomon b. Isaac (Rashi) of Troyes undertook the prodigious task of recording these interpretive traditions indigenous to northern European Jewry. His accomplishments included the writing of a commentary on the entire Hebrew Bible and a parallel one on almost the entire Babylonian *Talmud*.

Almost immediately, the sheer quality of his work was universally recognized by all sectors of the Jewish community. His biblical commentary, drawing heavily from *Midrashic* sources, became an indispensable guide to the elementary students of scriptures, providing simple, literal meaning for the text. Not only Jewish students mastered the Hebrew Bible with Rashi's commentary; Christian biblical scholars like Nicholas de Lyra (ca. 1270–1349) freely consulted Rashi's interpretive insights and translated them into Latin.

Rashi's *Talmud* commentary proved to be an even more significant achievement. It became the most important critical introduction to the language and logical arguments of the *Talmud*; its clarity and insight enabled the Talmudic student to comprehend the most impenetrable passage. After Rashi's death, students of the *Talmud* always approached it with Rashi's commentary in hand.

Rashi also wrote rabbinical *responsa*, pioneering for northern European Jewry an independent legal tradition which gave ample consideration to local custom. Moreover, he surrounded himself with able students of the law, many from his own family, who established their own school of critical Talmudic scholarship. These scholars, of whom Rashi's grandson Rabbenu Tam (ca. 1100–1171) was the most distinguished, were called the *ba'alei tosafot* (literally "masters of additions," referring to their comments on the *Talmud* text). The focus of the *tosafot* usually was Rashi's commentary; they discussed it, refined it, and even refuted it. In so doing, they introduced into *Talmud* study a new level of critical insight and logical deduction. Their dialogue with Rashi, their master, continued the mode of interaction between the *Gemara* and the *Mishnah*, between rabbis of one generation and the next. Their tendency was to expand and open the text to higher ranges of understanding, to the multitude of nuances stored up in its pages. Debate and critical questioning led in their minds to more penetrating insight. In contrast to the rabbis of Spain, the *ba'alei tosafot* were less interested in the codification and summary of Jewish law; they were also less inclined to study philosophy and the sciences. More like the canon lawyers of northern Europe, they shared a commitment to a scholastic methodology of question and answer; every linguistic obstacle, every convoluted passage, every concealed textual subtlety became for them an invitation to greater awareness and understanding of the divine will. In their relatively insulated cultural settings, the scholars of northern France were stimulated more by their own indigenous traditions and revered texts than from a dynamic cultural universe surrounding them. (See Reading 4-17.)

Talmudic scholarship, the hallmark of northern French Jewish culture, also constituted a central component of Spanish and Provençal Jewish culture. By the thirteenth century, Spanish rabbis were thoroughly familiar with the *tosafot*. In the fourteenth century in Spain, Jacob ben Asher, the son of an Ashkenazic Jew, compiled the *Arba'ah Turim* (Four Columns), one of the major codes of Jewish law. Yet rabbinic learning still represented only one mode of Jewish piety in Christian Europe. In Muslim and later in Christian Spain and in Provence, the Maimonidean school of philosophy continued to dominate the intellectual and spiritual life of Jewish elite circles. In these same regions philosophy and rabbinic scholarship also were challenged by further dimensions of Jewish spirituality, the pietistic and mystical modes.

The *kabbalah*, the collective traditions of Jewish mystical contemplations of the divine, can be traced to early rabbinic times in Palestine and in Babylonia, where it was stimulated by contact with parallel ancient ideas. The ideal of spiritual ascent, of escaping the material and mundane human existence, of striving to touch and participate in the world of God, found ample expression in rabbinic circles. In the Islamic world, in Baghdad and North Africa, Jewish descriptions of mystical journeys to the heavenly and divine realms are not infrequent in Hebrew and Aramaic literature. Most representative of the earliest texts of the *kabbalah* were mystical scenarios, based on the vision of the celestial chariot (called the *merkabah*) described in the Book of Ezekiel with depictions of an ascent through the seven heavenly palaces of the divine king (called *hekhalot*). In each case the Jewish mystic sought to unlock the mysteries of the divine realm and to reveal them to the rest of Israel.

European Jews under medieval Christendom were equally receptive to such spiritual pursuits. By the twelfth and thirteenth centuries in Provence and in Spain circles of Jewish kabbalists produced an extensive literature purporting to describe the mysterious workings of the divinity. In Germany, roughly between 1150 and 1250, a small community of Jews introduced a unique social philosophy and set of religious practices called German pietism (*Hasidut Ashkenaz*).

The German phenomenon centered around one particular family, known as the Kalonimides, who traced their origin to Italy. The dominating figure of this family was Judah he-Hasid (the pious) (d.

1217), who was the primary author of the classic text of this circle of kabbalists, entitled *Sefer ha-Ḥasidim* (the Book of the Pious). Maintaining no clear doctrinal unity, the pietists preached self-denial and renunciation of the material concerns of this world, striving for complete serenity of mind, humility, restraint, and social equality. They emphasized especially a higher religious demand, a heavenly ordinance that transcended the strict requirements of Jewish law itself. They formulated an elaborate theory of penitence which they practiced assiduously. They viewed their self-appointed mission "of laying bare the will of God" with a sense of *noblesse oblige* and moral arrogance. It is difficult to establish the specific context of this pietistic revival. Perhaps it grew out of a spiritualized reaction to the crusade massacres on the part of a community of survivors. Perhaps it was influenced by ascetic and pietistic tendencies within Christian society that were developing particularly in Franciscan monasteries. Perhaps it constituted a negative and alienated response to the French school of *tosafists* on the part of a displaced German Jewish aristocracy disdainful of the *tosafists'* intellectual accomplishments and frustrated in their efforts to regain the center stage of Ashkenazic Jewish culture. Whatever its precise background, German pietism left its imprint on Jewish culture in later ages, particularly in its colorful folklore and in its moral literature.

Kabbalistic writing first appeared in Provence in the twelfth century in an anonymous book called *Sefer Bahir* (the Book of Brightness). The speculations of this work, along with later Jewish writings of this type, constitute a form of complex interpretations of biblical and rabbinic materials, attempting to penetrate the concealed meaning of the divine realm made accessible through God's revelation. Although the kabbalists occasionally give personal mystical testimonies in their writings, they brooded especially on the sacred texts of Judaism and the symbolic reinterpretation of these writings. Kabbalistic texts often appear to be discursive, ponderous, and intellectualistic. Kabbalists never divorced their mystical activity from other modes of Jewish piety, especially the study of Jewish law. To unravel the divine mysteries embedded in God's revealed texts constituted their primary concern, a goal both rooted in Jewish tradition and at the same time transcending it.

In the thirteenth century kabbalistic activity shifted from Provence to Gerona in northern Spain where an influential circle of Jewish scholars, including the celebrated Naḥmanides, produced an extensive literature of mystical speculation. The most significant kabbalist writing, called *Sefer ha-Zohar* (the Book of Splendor), appeared in Spain by the end of the century. Attributed by its real author to Rabbi Simeon bar Yoḥai, an important second-century rabbi, it was actually written by Moses de Leon (ca. 1240–1305). The *Sefer ha-Zohar* is a mystical interpretation, written in Aramaic, of the Pentateuch, Song of Songs, and Ruth. But it is more than a conventional interpretation of the scriptures. Rather, it attempts to disclose a deeper level of mystical reality within the words and letters of God's revealed message to the Jewish people.

The most significant and enduring feature of this work is its perception of the divine realm available to man. Since most kabbalists had accepted the basic premise that God's entire essence was unknowable to men and thus a total mystical union with God was virtually impossible, they sought a strategy whereby the mystic could at least become familiar with a part of God's being. They called that infinite unknowable part of God the *ein sof* (literally, the infinite). That part of God revealed to man—aspects of the divine mystery emanating from the *ein sof*—they called *sefirot*. The *sefirot*, ten in number, were given the names of positive attributes found in earlier Jewish writing—*ḥokhmah* (wisdom), *binah* (understanding), *din* (judgment) and so forth. De Leon thus described a dynamic process of interrelationships between each of the *sefirot*, symbolic representations of God's identity, alternatively conceived as instruments or vessels or actual parts of God's essence. Although they appear as separate entities, they are in fact one unity, thus preserving at least theoretically the Jewish belief in monotheism. The kabbalist enters into relations with the *sefirot* in order to elevate his own soul but also to affect the health and harmony of God and the entire cosmos. (**See Reading 4-18.**)

The *kabbalah's* proliferation in the thirteenth century was, to a great extent, a negative reaction to the influence of philosophy and rationalism on the Jewish community. The kabbalists saw little value in reconciling Jewish and non-Jewish cultures. The sacred texts of Judaism did not require allegorical interpretation in order to demonstrate their harmony with reason. On the contrary, the kabbalists were intrigued with the most irrational, mysterious, impenetrable aspects of Jewish revelation. They believed that Judaism's secret tradition both preceded and was superior to all other national cultures; it was inconceivable that it be compared to or translated into terms compatible with those of other civilizations. Judaism's mystery, its irreducibility, defined its unique spirituality and vocation.

The *kabbalah* of Provence and Spain, together with German pietism, were clearly responses to an environment with shrinking opportunities for cultural openness and religious dialogue. It, like the rabbinic learning pursued in northern Europe, offered Jewish intellectuals spiritual replenishment and a focus for their creative energies in a world increasingly unsympathetic and hostile to Jews and their cultural legacy. That the Jews never relinquished their involvement in western European culture is indicated by the enduring achievements of Jewish philosophers and scientists, especially those living in the relatively more tolerant surroundings of Provence and Spain. Jewish mystics, legal scholars, and pietists also were never oblivious to the larger cultural landscape of Christian Europe. Nevertheless, Christian hostility toward the Jewish minority had taken its toll; the modes of Jewish cultural creativity and spirituality that endured from the twelfth century on were reflections of that somber fact of life.

## THE DECLINE AND EXPULSION OF SPANISH JEWRY

Of all the medieval Jewish communities living within the Christian orbit, Spanish Jewry was the oldest and the largest. Uniquely situated between the Muslim and Christian worlds, it was stimulated simultaneously by elements of both civilizations. In Spain, until 1492, Jews, Christians, and Muslims lived together. Until the end of the fourteenth century, Jewish community life in both Castile and Aragon, the two major Christian kingdoms, generally remained intact. Despite the gradual penetration of Christianity southward, Jewish neighborhoods usually remained unviolated. The Christian offensive of the thirteenth century, most apparent in the forced disputation at Barcelona, had a limited long-term impact on Jewish community welfare. In Spain, Jewish economic life was diversified; the tradition of Jewish courtiers who participated in affairs of state was never relinquished. The kings of Castile and Aragon generally were pragmatic in taking advantage of Jewish administrative and commercial abilities as well as in utilizing the Jews' general familiarity with Muslim culture. (**See Reading 4-19.**)

The year 1391 marked a turning point, however, in Jewish-Christian relations in Spain. Aggravated by economic instability, class hatred, and religious fanaticism, anti-Jewish violence erupted throughout all the major cities of Castile and Aragon. This dramatic display of physical assault against Jewish life and property followed similar patterns of anti-Judaic aggression throughout northern Europe. To Spain's credit, its Jewish population previously had suffered less than other Jewish communities brutalized during the period of the Black Plague at mid-century. What was unique about the massacres of 1391 was not that they had finally erupted, but rather the reaction of the victims. For the first time in Jewish history, thousands of Jews converted en masse to Christianity in order to save their lives and property.

Examples of individual cases of apostasy are easily documented throughout the long history of Jewish life in Christian lands. It is worth recalling the special role of apostates in anti-Jewish activity, religious disputation, and proselytization of Jews. However, entire families and neighborhoods of Jews had never openly repudiated their ancestral heritage in order to avert Christian hostility. On the contrary, as we have seen, a number of Ashkenazic Jews of the crusade period willingly took their own lives rather than succumb to Christian baptism. The mass conversion of Spanish Jews at the end of the fourteenth and throughout the fifteenth centuries offers telling testimony of a major spiritual crisis within this Jewish community. Until this time conversion was never a viable option for most Jews; it constituted a passage from one familiar secure world to one totally alien and repulsive. In this period the barriers appear to have eroded. It was then possible to elect the option of becoming a Christian. Baptism might mean total allegiance to the newly adopted faith, or secretly professing Judaism while living only externally as a Christian, or considering one's conversion as only a temporary stage before exiting Spain and rejoining the Jewish fold. Whatever the motivation—religious, economic, social, or fear of physical persecution—and whatever the rationalization for converting, the converts of 1391 and those who came after had initiated a dramatic break with past Jewish experience, a break whose repercussions would be felt for centuries to come. (See Reading 4-20.)

After a period of relative stability and quiet in the aftermath of the 1391 riots, Christian hostility against Spanish Jews again surfaced in 1412. This time the focus of the new pressure was in the town of Tortosa, where a forced public disputation was staged by a group of converted Jews. The debate was prolonged painfully for a period of almost two years. Despite valiant attempts of individual Jewish spokesmen to defend the honor and integrity of Judaism, the Jews who participated in and witnessed this sorrowful spectacle came out as losers. They could no longer withstand the pressure to surrender their Jewish faith. Thousands more willingly chose the Christian religion throughout the fifteenth century. By 1450 one-third to one-half of a Jewish population numbering in the hundreds of thousands had abandoned the Jewish religion.

The waves of conversion to Christianity eventually resulted in the presence of a new socioeconomic group called New Christians or *conversos* (the term *marrano*, "swine," a derisive expression coined by enemies of the *conversos*, is frequently employed in referring to this group). Yesterday's political restrictions against Jews no longer applied to these eager and conscientious new members of the Christian community. New opportunities in municipal and state administration, in commerce, and even in the Church were seemingly made available to them. By mid-century, however, much of the *conversos'* new enthusiasm in becoming Christians had dissipated. They still encountered discrimination and outright contempt even in their new Christian garb. A Christian society which had encouraged, indeed pressured, Jews to join its ranks ironically was unwilling to accept them as equal members.

Resentment toward the New Christians was accompanied by the oft-repeated charge of backsliding. The *conversos* were insincere in their conversion, so it was claimed; they practiced Judaism in secret and continued to identify with the Jewish community. In the 1480's, after the union of Castile and Aragon under Ferdinand and Isabella, the Spanish Inquisition was established in various communities to investigate the charges of insincerity leveled at the *conversos* and to take appropriate action to punish proven heretics of the Christian faith. Under the leadership of Tomás de Torquemada, the Inquisition immediately went to work, gathering evidence, extracting confessions, and trying thousands of *conversos* who were accused of hiding their secret Jewish loyalties.

The phenomenon of *conversos* in fifteenth-century Spain, their loyalty to Judaism, and the objectives of the Inquisition to try and punish them are not easy problems for the modern historian to disentangle. He is faced with the complex issues of determining how many converts over the course of the fifteenth century actually converted under duress and how many voluntarily; how many, after converting, identified fully as Christians and how many tenaciously held on in some form to their Jewish faith; and finally, what was the real motivation of the Inquisition: was it a purely religious institution acting solely to root out heresy or did it mask its true motives—social and economic jealousy and resentment to the *conversos* as a group—in the guise of religious ideology?

The answers to these questions are not unanimous; they depend, to a considerable extent, on what credence the historian gives to the evidence of inquisitional testimony itself. The general impression of those historians who have studied intensively the rich, detailed dossiers of inquisitional testimony is that such detailed documentation hardly could be fabricated. Whatever the fanatic perversity of the inquisitors who tortured (and burned at the stake) thousands of victims, their basic motivation appears to have been sincerely religious. They saw themselves exclusively as a religious court sanctioned by the Pope himself to destroy heresy. The collected testimonies were not for public consumption; rather, they were guarded zealously in locked archives. No doubt *conversos* were hated in Spain for reasons other than their clandestine allegiance to their former faith. Nevertheless, their unfortunate fate at the hands of the inquisitors appears to stem from a genuine desire on the part of many *conversos* to preserve some bond with Judaism and the Jewish people.

In early 1492 Ferdinand and Isabella conquered Granada, the last Muslim stronghold on the Iberian peninsula. Soon after, on March 31, 1492, in the city of Granada the king and queen signed the edict of expulsion for all Jews living under the crowns of Castile and Aragon. The monarchs explicitly stated that they had issued the decree in order to prevent the Jews from contaminating the Christian faith through their ongoing contacts with the *conversos*. The language of the edict suggests the direct influence of the Inquisition. From the perspective of the Spanish crown and Inquisitor General, the link between *conversos* and Jews was indeed real and constituted the major obstacle to the successful integration of New Christians into Spanish society. Economic gains also may have been a factor in the decision. Jews were forced to sell their properties cheaply, they were forbidden to take away gold or silver, and their public institutions were confiscated. For some Jews, the edict provided sufficient reason to convert. But the majority of them, numbering around 100,000, accepted the expulsion edict and departed. Of this number, the overwhelming majority chose to immigrate to Portugal, where, only five years later, they tragically were forced to convert to Christianity. The remainder sailed to Italy, North Africa, or Turkey. On July 31, 1492, three months after the edict, the last Jew left the soil of Spain. (See Reading 4-21.)

The expulsion of the Jews from Spain represented more than an isolated national tragedy. It was not only more massive than any previous expulsion; it was also the only instance, with the exception of the relatively small English Jewish community, where all the Jews of one nation simultaneously had been banished. Beyond the physical suffering and upheaval it engendered, its symbolism did not go unnoticed by those of the exiled generation. Spain was not just another nation of the Jewish Diaspora; it held the largest, the most dynamic and the proudest of Jewish communities. It had been the home of Ḥasdai ibn Shaprut, Samuel ha-Nagid, Maimonides, and recently Don Isaac Abravanel (1437–1508), the last of Spanish Jewry's great courtiers. Of all the states of medieval Europe, it had offered the Jews so many opportunities, and they willingly had contributed much in return for over five centuries.

The tragedy of 1492 was compounded by the fact that the Spanish eviction represented the culmination of Jewish expulsions from Christian lands, signaling the retreat of the Jewish presence from most of the European continent. By 1500 no Jew lived legally in England, France, Spain, or Portugal, and only a small Jewish community remained in Germany. Indeed, from the vantage point of the last Spanish Jews, their departure marked a low point in the history of their people. The sanguine hopes of their ancestors, who had placed their innocent trust firmly in the goodwill of Spanish monarchical authority for some five hundred years, ultimately were dashed by a royal edict of two sovereigns named Ferdinand and Isabella.

---

*Editor's Questions*
AFTER VIEWING AND READING

- Who were Hasdai ibn Shaprut and Samuel ibn Naghrela? How did both courtiers contribute to Jewish culture in Muslim Spain? Were they influenced by their Muslim surroundings?
- Both Maimonides and Judah ha-Levi were Jewish writers and philosophers. Did they agree on a definition of Judaism?

- Evaluate the Jews' response to the first crusade in 1096.
- What was the image of the Jew in the medieval mind? How did the rise of medieval anti-Judaism affect Church and governmental policies toward the Jewish minority?
- What were the contributions of Rashi and the *ba'alei tosafot* to Talmudic scholarship?
- What are the *sefirot*? How was the idea of *sefirot* integral to medieval Jewish mystical thought?
- How and when did the *converso* class come into existence? Did this group's fortune become connected with the ultimate fate of Spanish Jewry?

SUGGESTED READINGS

Israel Abrahams, *Jewish Life in the Middle Ages* (Atheneum, 1969)

Eliyahu Ashtor, *The Jews of Moslem Spain* (2 vols.) trans. from the Hebrew by Aaron Klein & Jenny Machlowitz-Klein (Jewish Publication Society of America, 1973, 1979)

Yitzkhak Baer, *A History of the Jews of Christian Spain*; (2 vols.) trans. by Louis Lerensohn, Hillel Halkin, S. Nardi, and H. Fishman (Jewish Publication Society of America, 1962)

Jacob Katz, *Exclusiveness and Tolerance: Studies in Jewish-Gentile Relations in Medieval and Modern Times* (Schocken, 1962)

Joshua Trachtenberg, *The Devil and the Jews: The Medieval Conception of the Jews and Its Relation to Modern Anti-Semitism* (Meridian, 1961)

Isadore Twersky, "Aspects of the Social and Cultural History of Provençal Jewry," Haim Hillel Ben-Sasson, "The 'Northern' European Jewish Community and its Ideals," and Haim Beinart, "Hispano-Jewish Society," in H. H. Ben-Sasson and S. Ettinger, eds., *Jewish Society through the Ages* (Schocken, 1971)

Isadore Twersky, ed., *A Maimonides Reader* (Behrman House, 1972)

# 5

## The Search for Deliverance
## (1492 to 1789)

### David B. Ruderman

*Editor's Suggestions*
BEFORE VIEWING THE SHOW

Examine Map 7 in the *Study Guide* and note where Jews resided after the expulsions from Western Europe.

*Overview of the TV Program*

The Jews who were expelled from the Iberian peninsula settled throughout the Mediterranean world in North Africa, Italy, and later in the Ottoman Empire. The Jews returned in numbers to the Holy Land where a thriving community was created in Safed and new mystical concepts were developed. In Italy there was much economic and intellectual change, and the ideas of the Renaissance influenced many Jews. New forms of religious thought emerged at this time, and Luther set the groundwork for the rise of Protestantism. The Church at Rome, threatened by these developments, attacked those who held different religious ideas, mainly Protestants and Jews. The Jews were separated from Christian society and in some cities forced to live in ghettos. In the Netherlands the Spanish yoke, with its dreaded Inquisition, was overthrown. The Spanish and Portuguese Jews who had converted to Catholicism but retained their Jewish identity migrated there. New ideas circulating in Holland also prompted the Jews, Spinoza among them, to challenge traditionally held beliefs.

The Ashkenazim, the Jews of Central and Eastern Europe, developed a more inward religious cultural tradition and played an important economic role in their society. Employed as middlemen by the Polish nobility and standing between the nobility and the peasants, they incurred the wrath of the people. Many Jews were killed in the Chmelnitzki revolt of 1648.

Meanwhile in the Ottoman Empire, a man named Shabbetai Zevi declared himself the Messiah and many Jews were attracted to his banner. Later on, he converted to Islam and Jewry was demoralized. In Eastern Europe, though, an itinerant miracle worker, Rabbi Israel, called the *Ba'al Shem Tov*, preached of the joy to be found in the observance of Judaism and in attempting to become closer to God. Rabbi Israel brought much-needed moral and religious support to a beleaguered populace.

In Western Europe the Jews contributed to the growing economy, and ideas slowly circulated that all people were to be treated equally. Some Jews looked forward to their integration into European society and began, as did Moses Mendelssohn, to study the philosophy and science propounded by the Enlightenment. These ideas were translated into politically revolutionary movements, such as the French and American Revolutions, and a new age appeared to be dawning for the Jews.

*Watch for . . . and Think about*

Note the many Sephardic and Ashkenazic synagogues and their variety of architectural styles. Do these buildings evoke contrasting moods?

Observe the beautiful city of Venice and the ghetto, the separate quarter where the Jews were ordered to live. How might it feel living in such a closed neighborhood?

Watch for the excerpt of a Lessing play that appears at the end of the show. What do you think is the main point of the scene?

WHILE READING THE *STUDY GUIDE* AND *SOURCE READER*

Look for the following:

- How the Jews responded to the tragedy of the Spanish expulsion. How did they interpret their historical experiences?
- The Jews' interaction with Italian Renaissance culture. How did the exchange of ideas affect Jewish and Christian thought?
- How and why Jewish life declined in Renaissance Italy. Trace the change in Martin Luther's attitude toward the Jews.
- The areas within the Ottoman Empire which the Spanish exiles settled. Safed in Israel was known for its scholars and mystics. How did the Safed resident, Isaac Luria, view the

world? See how Luria's ideas led to the Shabbetean and Frankist movements.

- How Polish Jewry was economically, communally, and culturally distinguished. What brought about the disaster that befell this most populous Jewish community? Note Israel the *Ba'al Shem Tov*'s prescription for this troubled Jewry. Identify Hasidim, *mitnagdim*, and Zaddik.
- The difficulties *conversos* encountered upon returning to Judaism, even when they lived in tolerant Amsterdam.
- The court Jews and Moses Mendelssohn. Were these people the vanguard of Jewish integration into Western European society?

## IN THE WAKE OF THE SPANISH EXPULSION

Don Isaac Abravanel, Spanish Jewry's most illustrious exile, poignantly described the emotional state of his community upon learning of the decree of expulsion:\* "When the dreadful news reached the people, they mourned their fate; and wherever the report of the decree spread, Jews wept bitterly. The terror and lamentation were greater than at any time since the expulsion of our forefathers from their own soil in Judah to foreign lands."

The writings of the other exiles similarly resonate with the anguish and despair of separation and defeat. The finality of the expulsion forced them to reflect on the ultimate meaning of Jewish existence and Jewish belief. Why had their generation been singled out for suffering? Had their faith in divine providence been misguided? Where was God in their hour of need and what future could they expect as wandering, unwanted castoffs?

It was a time for self-appraisal and deliberative response. As Abravanel wrote in his introduction to his commentary on the Book of Kings: "It was a time to recall the destruction of our Holy Temple and the Exile of our people. . . . It was a time to remember our glories and our misfortunes." Abravanel, more than others, sensed the widening gap between past expectations and present realities. In the

---

\*Abravanel, "Introduction to Commentary on Book of Kings," trans. Leo W. Schwarz, *Memoirs of My People.* New York and Toronto: Farrar & Rinehart, 1943, pp. 46–7.

light of the liquidation of Iberian Jewry, Abravanel attempted to offer comfort and consolation by placing the tragedy within a historical and theological perspective. God had not deserted his people, so Abravanel claimed. Nor should their history and current predicament be judged by the standards of other nations. Echoing his ancestor, Judah ha-Levi, Abravanel distinguished between the supernatural course of Jewish history and the natural careers of other nations. History reflects a divine pattern for Jews, one of exile and redemption. The expulsion constitutes a low point in Jewish history, a blatant indicator of the era immediately preceding history's ultimate consummation.

In a trilogy of compositions on the messiah, written in the aftermath of 1492, Abravanel, the statesman, economist, and philosopher, seemed to repudiate his former secular life by looking within himself and to the inner spiritual resources of his religious tradition. Refuting the Christian contentions that the messiah already had come, he set out to affirm the imminent arrival of the Jewish messiah and to calculate precisely the time of his public revelation. For Abravanel, the expulsion represented the surest sign that the redemption of Israel was near at hand. (See Reading 5-1.)

Some decades later, a work written in Portuguese by a former *converso* named Samuel Usque (sixteenth century) was published in Ferrara, Italy. The book, called *A Consolation for the Tribulations of Israel*, related the same message to its readers as that of Abravanel: a plea to the disillusioned among the Jewish community to restore their faithful hope in the destiny of their people. Israel had suffered because of its own sins, but at this juncture, its misfortunes were about to end.

Usque's innovation was his use of the historical argument. By holding the mirror of the past up to the present, he hoped that his readers, especially those *conversos* still clinging to their Christian garb in Spain and Portugal, might recognize that their situation was no different from that of former generations and thus would find comfort and return to the Jewish fold. Setting his narrative in the framework of a pastoral dialogue between three shepherds—Ycabo (Jacob, the personification of the Jewish people), Numeo (Nahum, "the comforter") and Zicario (Zachariah, "the remembrancer"), Usque sought to review all of Jewish history from the biblical period to the present. By looking at the contemporary vicissitudes in context, the sufferers might take comfort that divine intercession was soon forthcoming;

the Messiah was about to appear. Moreover, the astute observer of contemporary politics could draw consolation from other unmistakable signs of God's intervention: the opening of borders of the Ottoman Empire to Spanish Jewish emigrés, the discovery of the New World, the welcome haven offered by Italian city-states, and the threatened status of Christian Europe at the hands of the Turks. Through the artistry of Usque's narrative, the tragedy of his era was transformed into a triumph of the Jewish spirit to survive.

Usque's use of history to explore the meaning of Jewish collective suffering was part of a sixteenth-century resurgence of Jewish historical writing stimulated for the most part by the existential issues raised by the Spanish expulsion. Aside from Usque's work, Solomon ibn Verga's Hebrew composition *Shevet Yehudah* (The Scepter of Judah) was the most original. Like the *Consolation*, ibn Verga's work constitutes a series of imaginary dialogues, interspersed within a comprehensive history of persecutions, which serve as a backdrop for exploring contemporary tribulations. But unlike Usque, ibn Verga used his dialogues to probe more deeply into the sociological and psychological causes of Christian persecution of Jews before resorting to a more traditional theological response. (**See Reading 5-2.**)

In a discussion between a typical Hispanic king, whom he called Alphonso, and his trusted royal adviser, Thomas, ibn Verga treated directly what he considered to be the real causes of Spanish antipathy toward Jews. Through the device of his imaginary characters, he charged that arrogance, conspicuous consumption, social standoffishness, and usury were all factors in contributing to the expulsion. He viewed the kings as the most natural protectors of Jews; the clergy and the masses who follow them, the most natural enemy. He implied that Jews lacked military prowess because of their excessive reliance on supernatural intervention. He recalled the story of the father and his three sons made famous by Boccaccio and later by Lessing: each son receives a precious stone, which he conceives to be authentic, although there is only one. Ibn Verga's parable, alluding to the three great religions, transparently conveyed his sentiment that "religions are only based upon imagination" and thus are all essentially equal in worth.

Yet for all his incipient modernism, ibn Verga persistently clung to traditional Jewish pieties, both theological and political. Thomas' arguments notwithstanding, ibn Verga still understood the tragedy of Jewish existence within the conventional framework of exile and redemption. And despite the manifest actions of the Spanish and Portuguese crowns ruthlessly to undermine Hispanic Jewish life, he reasserted blindly, in the face of all somber historical experience, that, until a final redemption, only royal authority protected Jews. Notwithstanding its provocative reflections, ibn Verga's work failed to offer his readers a novel political and social program for restructuring Jewish society. Nevertheless, his fascination with history offered a fresh, though ultimately unsatisfying, antidote for discerning the stark realities of sixteenth-century Jewish life.

Historiography, with all its promise, still constituted no more than a transient outlet for grappling with the spiritual anxieties generated by the exile. By the end of the sixteenth century, Jews, who sought the meaning of history, ironically looked beyond history for an answer. Usque's work, written in Portuguese with the intent of a wide readership, soon became for the vast majority of Jewish readers an anachronism consulted by only a small audience of *converso* emigrés. Ibn Verga's book also proved incapable of yielding a satisfactory religious answer for most Jews. The historians were replaced by a circle of mystics who offered a key to understanding history in a myth which declared that Jewish suffering was rooted in an event which had occurred before history had begun. Even before the rapid dissemination of the *kabbalah* of Isaac Luria (1534–72), with its grandiose interpretation of the exile (to be discussed below), the writing of history as Jewish consolation had proved itself a languid spiritual palliative.

## CHRISTIAN-JEWISH DIALOGUE IN THE SETTING OF RENAISSANCE ITALY

Despite its seminal importance, the fate of Spanish Jewry, its exodus, and dispersion throughout the Mediterranean regions, still constituted only one dimension in the unfolding of Jewish history in the post-1492 era. Alongside the decline of Hispanic Jewish life, Jewish communities began to flourish in Italy and in Eastern Europe as well as throughout the Ottoman Empire. The late-fourteenth through sixteenth centuries also marked in Western civilization as a whole the emergence of rapid social, cultural, and political changes which profoundly influenced the identity and cultural priorities of European Jews. The Renaissance and the Reformation, the discovery and colonization of the New World, the uninterrupted religious wars,

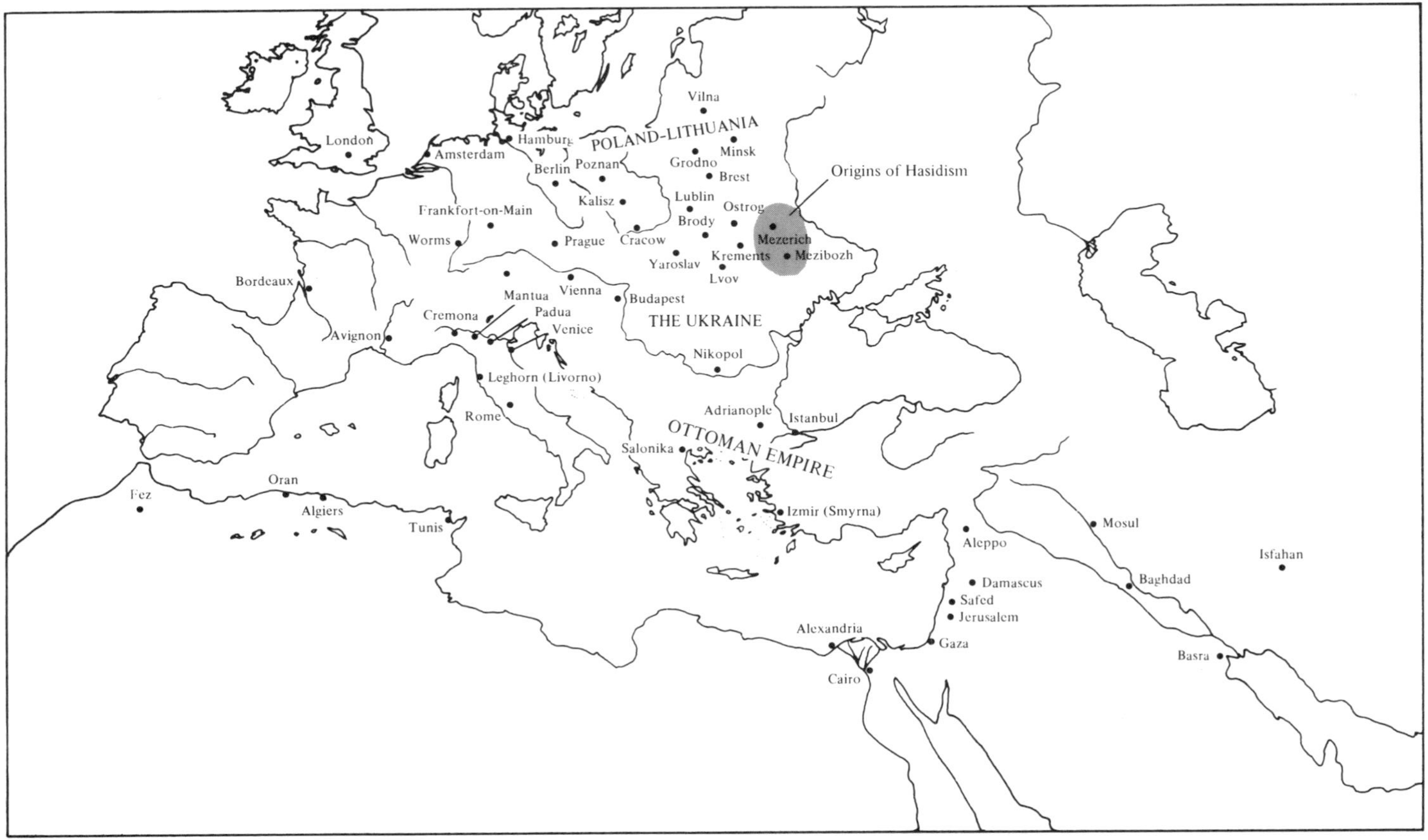

**Map 7  Jewish Population Centers, 1500–1780**

sharp economic fluctuation, and widespread disease and impoverishment accounted for some of the cataclysmic changes affecting European life in this period. The Jews were hardly oblivious to so dynamic
and fast-changing a political and cultural climate.

The Italian city-states of the fourteenth through sixteenth centuries provided the initial setting for a momentous transformation in
European civilization designated as the Renaissance. Jews had lived
within the borders of Italy since ancient times, especially in the environs of Rome. By the second half of the fourteenth century, however,
the Italian Jewish community underwent major changes in its size
and social composition. In this era, nascent Jewish communities
appeared throughout the northern half of the Italian peninsula.
These were composed of Jews who had migrated from southern and
central Italy, from Germany and France, and later from Spain, all of
whom found their new environment more secure and attractive than
the Christian regions they had left behind. With the prevalence of
relatively favorable conditions for the Jews, especially money-
lenders who were able to gain favorable lending arrangements from
local authorities, these small Jewish settlements flourished. A relatively open social and economic environment, reminiscent of the earlier settings of Muslim Spain and Provence, assured as well the rapid
dissemination of Renaissance culture within Jewish society in such
cities as Venice, Mantua, Ferrara, Padua, and Florence. Exposed to
new currents of thought, a limited but noticeable number of Italian
Jews participated in the intellectual pursuits of Renaissance culture
while maintaining an intense awareness of their own specific
identity.

An illuminating example of the interaction between Renaissance
and Jewish culture is the case of Judah Messer Leon, a Jewish doctor,
rabbinic scholar, and master of Aristotelian philosophy, who lived in
a number of cities in north-central Italy in the second half of the fifteenth century. Sometime before 1480, Messer Leon composed a
Hebrew work entitled *Nofet Zufim* (The Book of the Honeycomb's
Flow) in which he introduced to his Jewish readers a new genre of
rhetorical writing, placing himself squarely in the center of a new
and ultimately dominant expression of Renaissance cultural life, that
of Italian humanism. Already by the fourteenth century with the
revival and imitation of classical antiquity the humanists reclaimed
rhetoric as a significant and independent part of the new *studia
humanitatis*, which also included grammar, poetry, history, and

moral philosophy. As a reaction to the more technical philosophical interests of Aristotelian scholars, the humanists revived the ideal of the ancient Latinists Cicero and Quintilian. They believed that the integration of rhetoric with philosophy would shape a new breed of educated persons endowed with both wisdom and eloquence. (See **Reading 5-3.**)

Messer Leon's rhetorical compendium similarly projected to its readers the ideal of a good and righteous man, gifted in the oratorical art, who thus combined his knowledge and noble character to produce a new and effective leadership for the Jewish community. Moreover, in grafting the Ciceronian ideal onto Judaism, Messer Leon boldly attempted to portray his new image of leadership as an intrinsic part of Jewish tradition in the first place. He designated his new Jewish leader the *ḥakham kolel* (a direct Hebrew translation of the expression *homo universalis*), a person obliged to lead his community by right of a unique combination of broad and substantive learning together with good character. As Messer Leon Judaized the civic orator, so too did he treat the entire field of rhetoric. The model of classical oratory initially was conceived not in Greece or Rome but in Israel itself, so he claimed. If indeed the entire Hebrew Bible, and especially its prophetic orations, were the font and exemplar of the rhetorical art, it followed not only that rhetoric was a subject worthy for Jews but also that it was incumbent upon them to appreciate and to master a discipline that had been theirs in the first place. Furthermore, the idea that rhetoric had been perfected first by the Hebrews offered to Jews a satisfying reassurance regarding the intrinsic worth of their own cultural legacy.

The influence of the *Nofet Ẓufim* on subsequent Jewish writing has never been systematically investigated, but it is apparent nevertheless that Judah's effort served to inspire Jewish humanist interests well into the sixteenth century. Printed before the beginning of the sixteenth century, it was studied as a handbook of rhetorical art by Jewish students and helped to inspire the writings of Hebrew rhetorical compositions, letters, and sermons for a number of generations. Especially in the sixteenth century, Italian rabbis such as Azariah Figo (1579–1647), Judah Moscato (ca. 1530–93), and Leone Modena (1571–1648) imbibed directly the Ciceronian ideal by perfecting the art of oratory in both their Italian and Hebrew sermons. Wisdom combined with style became a prominent goal of Italian Jewish educators and orators even after the general decline of the humanist curriculum in Italy.

Even more decisive than the impact of humanism on Italian Jewish culture was that of the encounter between Giovanni Pico della Mirandola (1460–93), the famous Florentine philosopher, and a number of contemporary Jews. Out of a mutually stimulating interaction and prolonged study of Jewish texts between Pico and his Jewish associates at the end of the fifteenth century, there emerged one of the most unusual and obscure currents in the intellectual history of the Renaissance, the Christian *kabbalah*. While in the case of humanism the interaction between Renaissance and Jewish culture was generally one-sided, wherein Jews were primarily recipients of cultural forms which they absorbed from Renaissance culture, the encounter with Pico and his circle was substantially different; the interaction was mutual. In a relatively unprecedented manner, a select but influential group of Christian scholars actively desired to understand the Jewish religion, its culture, and its texts in order to penetrate their own spiritual roots more deeply. They didn't conceive Judaism to be negative, irrelevant, or peripheral to their culture; on the contrary, it held intrinsic worth and represented a significant dimension of the human experience for them. Such a major reevaluation of contemporary Jewish culture by Christians would also leave a noticeable mark on thinking and Jewish self-consciousness during the period.

Pico and his colleagues were drawn to Jewish study partially out of a sincere devotion to missionary activity, as had earlier Christians before them, especially in Spain. But Pico's attraction to Jewish texts in general and to the *kabbalah* in particular had more to do with the philosophical and theological assumptions of his contemporaries in Florence. From Marsilio Ficino (1433–99), the leading contemporary student of the ancient philosopher Plato in Florence, Pico derived the vital concept of ancient theology, that is, that a single truth pervades all historical periods. In the ancient authors, pagan and Christian alike, a unity and harmony of religious insight can be discovered. Every philosophy and every religion thus possesses a common nucleus of universal truth. By universalizing all religious knowledge, Ficino and Pico fashioned an open and more tolerant theology of Christianity; in searching for the source of truth in ancient cultural and religious settings distant from their own, they came to appreciate the centrality and priority of Hebrew culture in Western civilization.

While ancient theology led Pico back to the beginnings of Jewish civilization, another concept he employed, called "poetic theology," stimulated his concentration on the *kabbalah*. For Pico, the ancient pagan religions had concealed their secret truths through a kind of "hieroglyphic" imagery of myths and fables; so too Moses had addressed the Hebrews in a veiled manner called the *kabbalah*. The *kabbalah*, therefore, constituted that part of the Jewish tradition where the essential divine truths could be located; it was the key to lay bare the secrets of Judaism, to reconcile them with the mysteries of other religions and cultures, and thus to universalize them. To Pico *kabbalah* also represented power, a means of enhancing man's ability to control his destiny. It was a higher form of licit magic, superior to the magical procedures of pagan texts, establishing a direct link between heaven and earth, enabling man to assert his true nobility as a true "magus" (magician). (**See Reading 5-4.**)

In order to study Jewish sources systematically, Pico engaged three notable Jewish scholars, among others: Elijah Delmedigo (1460–93), an authority on Averroes; a Sicilian convert called Flavius Mithridates (fifteenth century), who succeeded in translating some forty kabbalistic works for Pico; and an erudite and prolific Jewish writer and doctor named Yoḥanan Alemanno (ca. 1535–1605). Through the influence of these teachers and through his own synthetic powers, Pico became the pioneer figure in the gradual penetration of contemporary Jewish thought into fifteenth- and sixteenth-century European culture. Pico's Christianization of kabbalistic techniques and his amalgamation of magic and Jewish mysticism, while officially condemned by the Church, were enthusiastically received by a notable number of Christian thinkers in Italy, France, Germany, and England, well into the eighteenth century. Through Pico Christian *kabbalah* left its mark on Renaissance culture through its integration with Florentine philosophy; it also influenced both the Catholic and Protestant reformations through its impact on such thinkers as Egidio of Viterbo, Cornelius Agrippa, and Johannes Reuchlin, to name only a few. Its remarkable persistence as a formative factor in post-Renaissance cultural developments—in art, in literature, and even in scientific thought—is only now fully coming to light.

Pico's unique theology also noticeably affected contemporary Jewish thought. Yoḥanan Alemanno, like Pico, recast the *kabbalah* in a fashion reminiscent of Pico. Judah, the son of Isaac Abravanel, better known as Leone Ebreo (ca. 1460–after 1523), wrote a work in the spirit of Plato called the *Dialoghi d'amore* (Dialogues of Love), which was well noticed by Italian writers. Other Jews in the sixteenth century displayed the marked influence of the Florentine school; some Jews even followed Flavius Mithridates in accepting Pico's universal faith through conversion to Christianity. (**See Reading 5-5.**)

The interaction between Pico's circle and Italian Jews is significant because Pico offered a novel challenge to Jewish national existence. He introduced the Jews for the first time to the image of a universal culture transcending either Christianity in its present form or Judaism. Pico argued that a human cultural experience, albeit still clothed in Christian guise, consisting of the best of all previous religious and national cultures, was infinitely superior to Jewish culture. Pico's religious syncretism ushered in a new dimension to Jewish-Christian relations, one which anticipated to a considerable degree the modern Western world's challenge to Jewish particularity. Humanism, too, presented the Jews with a universal cultural experience open to all mankind, one which challenged Judaism in a similar way.

Renaissance culture, of course, still was pervaded by religious values; it was neither as secular nor as rational as some modern historians have conceived it to be. Jewish communal life was not radically altered from what it had been throughout the Middle Ages. Christians still attacked Jews; they still held public disputations with them, and they still preoccupied themselves with converting them. But perhaps in one respect, the dialogue between Judaism and Christianity was different in the Renaissance. The Renaissance offered certain Jews a preview of the intellectual and cultural challenges their descendants would face with growing regularity and intensity in the modern world. In sensing a greater urgency to justify their own particularity before an intellectual community that was increasingly ecumenical and cosmopolitan in spirit if not in practice, Renaissance Jews had entered the modern age.

## THE DETERIORATION OF JEWISH LIFE IN THE LATE SIXTEENTH CENTURY

The relatively tolerant climate Italy had offered its small Jewish community was short-lived. As a result of the oppressive policy of Pope Paul IV (1476–1559) and his successors, the Italian Jewish community experienced a radical deterioration of its legal status and physical state, a predicament which stood in sharp contrast to the earlier Jewish-Christian relationship of the Renaissance. The Italian Jews suddenly faced a major offensive against their community and its religious heritage, culminating in the public burning of the *Talmud* in 1553 and in restrictive legislation leading to increased impoverishment, ghettoization, and expulsion. The situation was aggravated further by severe conversionary pressures, including compulsory appearance at Christian preaching in synagogues and the establishment of houses for potential new converts which were designed to facilitate large-scale conversion to Christianity. Whether motivated primarily by the need to fortify Catholic hegemony against all dissidence, Christian and non-Christian alike, or driven by a renewed missionary zeal for immediate and massive conversion, the papacy acted resolutely to undermine the previous status of this small Jewish community in the heart of western Christendom. (See Reading 5-8.)

The ghettoization of Italian Jewry gradually eroded the liaisons between Christian and Jewish savants of previous years. Even before the papal bull of Paul IV, the internalization of Jewish culture had begun, precipitated in part by the increasing presence of the Spanish Jews who had settled in Italy. The emergence of pious confraternities (*ḥevrot*) in every major Italian town were not mere imitations of similar Christian organizations; they also constituted a communal response to Jewish fears and anxieties in the wake of an increasingly hostile Christian environment. The confraternities provided men and women an opportunity for charity, the care of the sick, and burial of the dead. They also provided an outlet for prayer, public devotion, and intense spiritual fellowship. They were particularly receptive settings to the new pietistic and mystical trends which swept the Italian Jewish community by the second half of the sixteenth century. (See Reading 5-9.)

But despite the "turning in" which marked this era, Renaissance tendencies among the Italian Jews remained perceptible even through the beginning of the seventeenth century. Jewish authors of the late sixteenth century and thereafter reveal their understandably diminished confidence and increased insecurity in the future stability of their communal life. Nevertheless, they remain committed to the study of Greek and Latin, history and rhetoric, and especially medicine and science. Modern history textbooks usually offer the erudite Azariah dei Rossi (ca. 1511–78) or the prodigious Leone Modena as the most typical exemplars of Renaissance Jewish culture. The first composed a work called the *Me'or Einayim* (Enlightenment to the Eyes), a critical historical evaluation of Talmudic chronology correlated with non-Jewish sources of late antiquity. The second was a prolific writer, preacher, and polemicist who served as the Rabbi of Venice in the early seventeenth century. Yet both produced their "Renaissance" scholarship in a post-Renaissance age relatively inhospitable to Jews. Similarly, Salomone de' Rossi (late sixteenth to seventeenth centuries) composed his famous "Renaissance" madrigals within the confines of the Mantuan ghetto of the early seventeenth century. Moreover, the increasing intolerance toward Jews did not inhibit them from attending Italian universities, especially Padua, in unprecedented numbers from the sixteenth through eighteenth centuries. Despite the external barriers of Catholic counterreformation policies and the growing internal diffusion of the *kabbalah*, some Italian Jews continued to nurture cultural bridges with enlightened sectors of Christian society.

Yet such pockets of enlightened Christian tolerance toward Jews were becoming harder to locate within Catholic societies under the direct influence of the Roman *curia*. And despite initial Jewish expectations to the contrary, Jews living to the north in the Protestant German principalities unfortunately fared no better. German Jewry already had experienced oppression, impoverishment, and decline years before Luther's schism. Large numbers of Jewish immigrants already had migrated eastward to the more tolerable surroundings of Eastern Europe. Those who remained had been expelled from most German cities. Their only recourse was to live in villages or rural areas owned by petty German princes where they were heavily taxed and periodically persecuted.

Martin Luther's challenge to the hegemony of the Catholic Church, initiating the Protestant reformation in 1517, was first viewed by several Jewish witnesses as a positive development, signaling the dismemberment of western Christendom. Writing from Jerusalem, the Spanish kabbalist and messianic enthusiast Abraham Eliezer ha-Levi (ca. 1460–after 1528) portrayed Luther as a kind of secret Jew, rebelling not only against papal authority but against the essence of Christianity itself. Ha-Levi believed Luther clearly signified the beginning of a process whereby Christians would begin to draw close to Judaism in the advent of the messianic age. Indeed Luther's initial statement about the Jews seemed to confirm ha-Levi's judgment. In a work written as early as 1523, *That Jesus Christ*

*Was Born a Jew*, Luther evinced a sympathetic posture toward the Jews; however, contrary to ha-Levi's expectation, Luther hoped that Jews would embrace his version of Christianity, not that Christians would embrace Judiasm.

The Jews did not flock to the Protestant camp; nor did Protestants seek out their Jewish brethren. Both ha-Levi's and Luther's expectations remained unfulfilled. Ha-Levi and his coreligionists gradually came to realize that with regard to the Jews, German Protestants and Catholics were very much alike. No doubt there were notable exceptions to the general rule in both camps. The Protestant reformer and Christian kabbalist Johannes Reuchlin (1455–1522), for example, earlier had defended the value of rabbinic writings. But at least in Germany and throughout most of Europe (Dutch Calvinism being the major exception) the political, social, and economic standing of the Jews under Protestant rule remained unchanged.

Luther, however, proved himself a less capable judge of realistic Jewish-Christian relations than most contemporary Jews. He became increasingly bitter and disillusioned by the fact that the Jews remained indifferent to him and his cause. Exactly twenty years after his first pronouncement, he composed a revised statement, entitled *Concerning Jews and Their Lies*. His anti-Jewish remarks rivaled those of the most vociferous anti-Jewish antagonists within the Catholic camp both in their tone and substance. Ironically, Luther's distasteful pamphlet was read and quoted frequently by later anti-Jews. (**See Reading 5-10.**)

There remained, however, a few islands of refuge for German Jews in the sixteenth century. Despite the successive upheavals of Jewish life in Central Europe, which followed familiar patterns established elsewhere, Jews still founded important communities in Worms, Vienna, and Frankfurt, and especially in the adjacent Bohemian capital of Prague. From the end of the sixteenth through the early seventeenth centuries, particularly during the reign of Rudolph II and his successor, Matthias, Prague emerged as a Renaissance center, importing art and literature from Italy and Germany; attracting astronomers, alchemists, and magicians from all over Europe; and recreating much of the former *élan* that had marked the earlier Renaissance in Italy. In such an atmosphere, Jewish society and culture also flourished. Jews distinguished themselves particularly in science, mathematics, history, and theology. The two most outstanding cultural luminaries of this era were David Gans (1541–1613) and

Judah Loew ben Bezalel (Maharal) (ca. 1525–1609). Gans wrote an important historical work in the tradition of Spanish Jewish writing of the earlier sixteenth century called *Zemah David* (offspring of David). His most original Hebrew composition, entitled *Nehmad ve Na'im* (Delightful and Pleasant), focused on the latest geographical and astronomical discoveries of his day. At the end of the work he even described in inspired tones his visit to the astronomical observatory of the Dutch scientist Tycho Brahe at the castle of Benatek outside Prague. The Maharal, also an enthusiastic follower of science, wrote numerous works on Jewish theology, ethics, and education; he also assumed the leadership role within the Jewish community, and interpreted in a most original way the fundamental issues of Jewish existence in the context of sixteenth-century realities. As in post-Renaissance Italy, a precarious social and political situation for Jews did not necessarily silence a creative dialogue between the Jews and Christians or obstruct the intense stimulation of the outside environment upon various modes of Jewish creativity. (**See Reading 5-11.**)

## JEWISH CULTURAL DEVELOPMENTS IN THE OTTOMAN EMPIRE

One of the brightest signs of God's continual care and help for the Jewish people, so thought Samuel Usque, had been the welcome accorded the Spanish Jews and *conversos* in the lands of the Ottoman Turks. By the mid-sixteenth century, the Turks had succeeded in establishing a vast empire that extended across southeastern Europe, the Middle East, and most of North Africa. The Ottoman government, as previous Muslim governments had done, relied heavily on religious minorities like the Jews to enhance its economic welfare. Jewish, Greek Orthodox, and Armenian merchants were offered favorable trading opportunities in exchange for much-needed tax revenue. The availability of large numbers of Spanish refugees, educated and highly skilled in trade, various crafts, and medicine, constituted a rich opportunity which the Ottoman state could ill afford to ignore.

The thousands of Spanish Jews and *conversos* fleeing the Inquisition in the sixteenth century were united with older Jewish communities which had lived in the former Byzantine regions and throughout the Middle East. Initially, certain frictions developed between the older and the more recent Jewish residents in the Balkans, in Greece, and in towns of the Middle East. Yet because of the sheer number and the formidable talents of the new immigrants, the Spanish element soon came to dominate the Jewish communities in their newly adopted territories. By the end of the sixteenth century, important Jewish centers were thriving in Salonika, Constantinople, Cairo, Damascus, Izmir, and other cities. Spanish Jews also were attracted to the towns in the Land of Israel, settling chiefly in Jerusalem and in the hill town of Safed.

The Spanish immigration also infused new vitality into Jewish cultural and religious life in Ottoman lands. New centers of rabbinic and kabbalistic scholarship emerged in Salonika, Cairo, and Constantinople. Jewish doctors were employed at the highest levels of society, including the Ottoman court at Constantinople. Open cultural and commercial bridges existed between Italy and the Turkish empire, allowing considerable cross-fertilization between the two communities. Italian Jews were visited regularly by representatives of the burgeoning communities of Israel, and Italian Jews regularly took pilgrimages to Jerusalem and to the other holy cities. Nor were the boundaries between Central and Eastern European Jewry and Ottoman Jews sealed off either economically or culturally. Jewish books printed in Prague, Cracow, or Venice easily made their way to Salonika and Constantinople; the printing presses of the Turkish Jewish centers also were accessible to far-off Jewish settlements. Spanish Jews, many university-educated, also provided a direct link between western Christian and eastern Muslim learning. Indeed, the new and dynamic Jewish communities of the Mediterranean regions of the sixteenth century resembled in many ways their active and ambitious ancestors of the *genizah* period whose intersecting networks of economic and social communication often transcended all existing political and religious borders.

Of all the new communities of this vast region, the modest town of Safed in the northern Galilee seemed unlikely to emerge as a major religious center for the Jews. Yet the Jewish population of Safed reached some 10,000 inhabitants by the end of the sixteenth century, many earning a living from the manufacture and trade of cloth. More importantly, Safed attracted some of the most distinguished rabbinic and kabbalistic scholars of the sixteenth century to its academies of learning, even eclipsing the venerable academies of Jerusalem. R. Joseph Caro (1488–1575), the most influential rabbinic scholar and codifier of the period, settled in Safed in the 1530's. Prior to his immigration to Israel, Caro had written a detailed commentary to Jacob ben Asher's earlier code, the *Arba'ah Turim*. Upon completing this lengthy commentary, which he called the *Bet Yosef* (House of Joseph), he incorporated his rulings into a briefer work called the *Shulḥan Arukh* (Prepared Table). This latter work became the definitive code for traditional Jewish practice for centuries to come. Caro, the legal scholar as well, was also a mystic and was attracted to Safed because of its unique spiritual climate. His student R. Moses Cordovero (1522–70) also lived in Safed, where he became the major expositor and systematizer of Spanish *kabbalah*, working the sundry speculations of earlier Jewish mystics into a more integrated philosophical framework.

The spiritual revival of Safed was fed especially by Spanish emigrés who, throughout the sixteenth century, painfully ruminated over the Spanish catastrophe and incessantly yearned for the coming of the messianic age. In the aftermath of the expulsion, messianic speculation and activity were particularly widespread among Jewish and *converso* groups. Inquisitional testimony reveals numerous instances of highly charged messianic anticipation among accused *conversos*. The aforementioned Abraham Eliezer ha-Levi, a Spanish refugee who eventually settled in Jerusalem, devoted most of his creative energies to messianic prognostication. (**See Reading 5-6.**)

In 1524 David Reuveni (d. 1538?), a dark-skinned Jew claiming to be a representative of the ten lost tribes, having arrived from Israel, appeared in Italy and was even granted an audience with the pope concerning his effort to organize a joint Jewish-Christian force to overthrow the Turks and regain the Holy Land. Despite some detractors, Reuveni was able to muster considerable support from Christian and Jewish messianic enthusiasts alike. Continuing his mission in Portugal, he found there an eager following of *conversos* who mistook his coming for the imminence of the messianic age. In Lisbon he attracted one young follower who took the name Solomon Molkho (ca. 1500–32), circumcized himself, and left Portugal with his newly discovered spiritual mentor. Molkho, in contrast to Reuveni, had few inhibitions about declaring himself the messiah. Arriving in Salonika he attracted the attention of some of the most illustrious rabbis of the city; he published a book of electrifying sermons he apparently had delivered there. He visited Italy, where he received considerable attention from both the Jews and Christians. While in Italy, he and Reuveni enjoyed the complete protection of the papacy. However, when visiting the Holy Roman emperor, in anticipation of further support for their cause, both were imprisoned. Molkho was tried by the Inquisition and burned at the stake; Reuveni was imprisoned for the rest of his life. The Reuveni-Molkho episode dramatically discloses the deeply rooted and persistent messianic thoughts in the consciousness of sixteenth-century Jewry some three decades after the Spanish expulsion. (See Reading 5-7.)

Yet this upsurge of messianic activity among Jews was not based on their emotional response to the expulsion of 1492 alone. The sixteenth century was also an age replete with Christian millennial stirrings. Living within the larger cultural landscape of the Mediterranean lands, Christian apocalyptics undoubtedly were influenced by stimuli that similarly may have affected some Jews as well. Astrological events, political and military upheavals, the Reformation and Counter-Reformation, as well as the discovery of new lands and new peoples were tabulated by Christian and Jewish messianic prognosticators alike. Some Christians also took note of Reuveni and Molkho; they envisioned the Spanish expulsion as the beginning of the universal flagellation of Christ's enemies preceding the renovation of his kingdom on earth. Christian kabbalists pored over Jewish messianic prophecies, and *conversos* like Molkho were obsessed with messianic visions colored in part by their own previous Christian backgrounds and associations. In an age of intense social and cultural liaison between the Jews and non-Jews, such shared messianic visions should hardly come as a surprise. (See Reading 5-13.)

The messianic fever of Safed's residents was stirred up by their intense religious practices too: midnight prayer vigils, public fasting and ablutions, and prayers at the graves of ancient sages. Meetings of worship and spiritual meditation helped to reinforce a deeply felt sense of spiritual ecstacy and religious mission among Safed's congregations. (See Reading 5-14.)

Such was the ideological and psychological climate of Safed in the mid-sixteenth century. To such a climate the youthful Isaac Luria (1534–72) was drawn in 1569, three years before his death. In his short lifetime Luria never reached the scholarly stature of Safed's giants, Caro and Cordovero, or even that of Cordovero's major disciple, Hayyim Vital (1542–1620). In fact, with the exception of a few short writings, Luria composed nothing at all, neither in the areas of *halakhah* or *kabbalah*. Yet through the careful transmission of his ideas by his students and their eventual dissemination throughout the

European continent, he became a cultural hero to his generation and to those after him. Much of Luria's mythic system had been anticipated by earlier kabbalists; what was novel about his approach was its dramatic focus on the end of creation rather than its beginning and its emphasis on national redemption within the context of the entire universe. Lurianic *kabbalah* also was unique in its ability to transform itself from secret to popular lore, from opaque symbolism to a series of code words transparently familiar to large numbers of sixteenth-century Jews. Thus the history of Lurianic ideas is first the genesis of a daring mystical imagery that responded directly to the spiritual needs of a community in turmoil; it also presents the history of the diffusion and percolation of arcane mysteries to larger communities of Jews throughout the Diaspora.

In the simplest of terms, Luria's theosophy can be explained in three stages, defined by the Hebrew terms *zimzum* (contraction), *shevirat ha-kelim* (the breaking of the vessels) and *tikkun* (restoration). In order to create the world, Luria imagined that the first act of God was to remove a part of himself from himself, since he was spatially everywhere. His paradoxical withdrawal or self-diminution represented an act of genuine beneficence on his part in offering to create the world; at the same time, it opened up the possibility of imperfection (i.e., evil) in a system that previously had been perfect.

Following the divine retreat, God sent out from himself a ray of light into the vacuum he had formed, giving rise to the figure of a primordial man (*adam kadmon*). From the eyes, mouth, ears, and nose of this figure, the lights of the *sefirot* burst forth. The light that emerged from the eyes took the form of "atomized" points which required that they be caught and preserved in special bowls or vessels (*kelim*). At a critical moment, however, these bowls were incapable of withstanding the pressure of the rays they were holding and shattered.

The "breaking of the vessels" constituted the most dramatic stage of the cosmic process. Most of the scattered lights returned to their source but some remained attached or "captured" by the shards of the broken vessels. Those that did not return to God "fell" from the divine source and found themselves in the realm of the shards, now called *kelippot* (husks), which personified the forces of evil in the world. Whether the breaking stemmed from a technical mishap in the structure of the cosmos or from the residue of God's essence left over in the original space, this breaking came to symbolize the Lurianic explanation of evil in the world, of the emergence of a flaw or deficiency within the divine realm. The Lurianic myth of evil rationally was no more satisfying than any other theological explanation of evil, but it offered a moment of suspense and high drama, of nervous anticipation and disquietude in the daring metaphor that part of the divine creation had been shattered.

With the emergence and diffusion of evil into the world, the final stage of Luria's system began—the restoration of the divine sparks, the cosmic mending process called *tikkun*. By separating the divine sparks from their captors, the evil *kelippot*, the divine harmony which was present prior to the moment of "breaking" was to be restored.

Luria's three stages were to be understood in a three-dimensional way: cosmically, nationally, and personally. They described a cosmic process; yet they also referred to the history of the Jewish people scattered like divine sparks among the evil husks in the Diaspora. They defined as well the fate of each individual Jewish soul who, because of Adam's sin, had been dispersed throughout the universe. *Tikkun* accordingly was a restoration of the soul of every member of Israel's household; it was also the national redemption of the Jewish people to their homeland; and finally it was the cosmic repair of a divine system, indeed of God himself, deficient and "in exile" because of the shattering of the vessels.

Lurianic *kabbalah* powerfully captured the experience of exile for every Jew. Exile was no longer the aberration of one peculiar nation; it was rather a condition of cosmic significance. Subsequently, "getting out" of exile signified much more than a Jewish obsession. It meant no less than the universal restitution of God and his entire universe.

Luria's system also underscored the singular vocation of the Jewish people and of each individual person within the community. Jews were the divine cleansers of the world and entrusted by God to gather sparks. Only by their human efforts could *tikkun* be effectuated. Although for the kabbalists of Safed, human activity meant primarily prayer, spiritual meditation, and performing the divine commandments with mystical concentration, Luria's system was humanistic at its core. God required human beings to "reform" a world flawed by a deformity which God himself had engendered. The messiah would not come by divine intervention; he would only appear when Jews had released him through their own activities, as divine confirmation of their own accomplishments. Lurianic *kabbalah* ultimately provided the Jewish community a vigorous response to the expulsion and the subsequent tribulations of exile. It represented a movement of mystical reform embedded in a vision of national and cosmic regeneration. By projecting onto the entire universe their own tragedy of exile, the disciples of Luria reassured themselves of their own spiritual worth and their own unique religious purpose.

Some one hundred years after Isaac Luria died, the Jewish community experienced an explosion of millenarian fervor unparalleled in its history since the first century C.E. The focus of this frenzied behavior was a self-proclaimed messiah named Shabbetai Zevi (1626–76). Figures with messianic delusions were not uncommon in Jewish history, as we already have seen. What was unusual about Shabbetai Zevi was his wide appeal, even after he seemingly had acknowledged himself a pretender, and the subterranean following who persisted in believing in his messiahship well into the next century. Shabbetai's movement also revealed the revolutionary and nihilistic potentialities within Jewish messianic ideology. (**See Reading 5-15.**)

There seemed little in Shabbetai Zevi's background to indicate exceptional intellectual or spiritual abilities. Born in Izmir in Turkey, he possessed an ordinary training in rabbinics and *kabbalah*. Apparently emotionally unstable, he occasionally was induced to violate some marginal Jewish laws. He wandered through various cities in Greece, Egypt, and Israel until in 1665 meeting his soon-to-be chief prophet, Nathan of Gaza (1643–80). Nathan was shortly convinced of Shabbetai's messiahship and proclaimed his coming soon afterward. Upon gaining additional support during the next year, Shabbetai aroused the suspicion of the Turkish authorities and was arrested by order of the grand vizier, who had him incarcerated in the fortress of Gallipoli in 1666. Later that year he was brought before the sultan, who offered him conversion to Islam or death. Shabbetai chose Islam, for which he was awarded an honorific title and a government pension.

The matter seemingly was over for many of his followers, but for his most ardent disciples the paradox of his apostasy could not simply be attributed to Shabbetai's insincerity. Nathan and some of the other architects of his messianic movement provided an ideology to explain why Shabbetai Zevi had converted and why the redemption of the

Jewish people had been postponed. Their explanation was in-
capsulated into the following slogan: *ha-miẓvah ha-ba'ah be-
averah* (the commandment which comes out of sin). Utilizing the
ideological framework of Lurianic *kabbalah*, they argued that
Shabbetai converted so they might descend to the realm of the evil
*kelippot* in order to draw out the captive divine sparks. By immersing
himself in evil, the messiah eventually would accomplish a greater
good.

This new rationale for the conversion provided the opening for a
blatant repudiation of Jewish law on the part of some of Shabbetai's
followers. Their belief was now based on a contradiction which
affirmed that evil is actually good; the destruction of the *Torah* equals
its affirmation. A new messianic ideology was constructed in the language of older Jewish texts and experiences. Shabbetai was likened to
the "suffering servant" of the book of Isaiah (Chapter 53); to Esther,
who saved her people by marrying a non-Jew; or to Moses, who, like
Shabbetai, lived in the house of a "caliph" for many years.

The appeal of so paradoxical and dangerous an ideology is difficult to understand. Jewish suffering may have been a factor; only
some twenty years earlier thousands of Jews had been massacred by
the Cossacks in the Ukraine and Poland. Yet hostility to the Jews had
been present in other periods and other localities. Furthermore,
Shabbetai Ẓevi first appealed to the Jews in Israel, not in Eastern
Europe. No doubt the wide diffusion of Lurianic *kabbalah* helped
prepare the ideological and psychological grounding for Shabbetai's
followers to translate their historical reality into religious terms. Nor
was it a coincidence that the new ideology was particularly suited for
a *converso* mentality. *Conversos*, so accustomed to living in two paradoxical worlds—an external one and an internal one—especially
were attracted to the new movement. The fact that the years 1665–
66 were also years of Christian millennial awakening throughout
Europe also may have contributed to Shabbetai Ẓevi's credibility.
Whatever the cause, the movement clearly responded to certain
deep-seated anxieties and nihilistic tendencies within the Jewish community in the Ottoman Empire and in Western and Eastern
Europe.

Many of the movement's followers attempted to keep a low profile after the apostasy. They adhered to Jewish law and saw
Shabbetai's conversion as no example to others. Yet even their moderate stance had within it the seeds of an inner spiritual crisis. The

secret of a new faith had been revealed privately and soon would be divulged in full.

There was also a more radical, anarchist branch associated with Shabbetai's ideology. It preached the holiness of sin; it affirmed that Shabbetai Zevi's behavior was to be emulated by others by breaking Jewish laws on behalf of a supposed higher ideal. The two most extreme groups within this faction were the Donmeh in Turkey and the Frankists in Poland. The first group was prominent toward the end of the seventeenth and into the eighteenth centuries. They converted to Islam as their redeemer had done, and they considered the most heinous crimes against Jewish law to be positive commandments. They viewed Shabbetai Zevi as the incarnation of the deity and believed in the continuous reincarnation of the redeemer in the person of their own leaders in subsequent generations. (**See Reading 5-16.**)

The Frankists, named after the diabolical figure of Jacob Frank (1726–71), saw themselves as a direct continuation of the Donmeh. Frank spent several years in Turkey before returning to Poland to declare himself the reincarnation of Shabbetai Zevi and to preach the nullification of Jewish law. He dreamed of an army of disciples "to follow their leader step by step," a territory of his own, and total freedom from the bondage of rabbinical authority. In 1759 he openly converted to Christianity with one thousand of his followers. He soon was caught by the Inquisition who incarcerated him until his death. As in the case of Shabbetai Zevi, some of Frank's followers, forced to go underground out of fear of governmental harassment, continued to cling to their delusional beliefs well into the next century. Whatever the actual number of adherents, the Donmeh and Frankist sects sent shock waves through the established Jewish communities of Turkey and Eastern Europe. Their nihilistic state of mind had precipitated an inner crisis in the Jewish soul, unrelated directly to social and political changes in the larger Christian or Muslim environments. The traditional Jewish community eventually recovered, especially in Eastern Europe, but not before a prolonged period of acrimonious debate, public recrimination, and agonizing inner turmoil.

## THE JEWISH EXPERIENCE IN EASTERN EUROPE

The Frankist schism had erupted within a Jewish community in Poland and Lithuania whose total population numbered some

200,000 by the beginning of the eighteenth century and already had surpassed the Ottoman Jewish community in its institutional and cultural achievements. Because of the existing strengths of its overall communal structure, it experienced a noticeable revitalization by the end of the eighteenth century, the Frankist controversy notwithstanding. No such fate awaited Ottoman Jewry, which declined concomitantly with the deterioration of the Ottoman state.

Individual Jews had migrated to Poland as early as the eleventh century, but the real influx from German lands began only in the fourteenth and fifteenth centuries. The Polish region was a virtual frontier, offering new economic opportunities for enterprising Jews and a relative absence of governmental interference in their internal religious life. By the end of the fifteenth century the Jewish population of Poland had reached almost 15,000; in the next century and a half, the number increased tenfold. With fewer economic restrictions, Jews assumed diversified economic roles for the Polish nobility and kings in leasing lands, tax farming, trade, and manufacturing. More importantly, taking advantage of the relatively less developed political institutions of Eastern Europe, they established their own autonomous communities based on the Ashkenazic model of Jewish communal life in the Middle Ages.

In Eastern Europe, the size, sophisticated structure, and political effectiveness of Jewish self-government surpassed all previous Diaspora Jewish communities. From the microcosmic level of the local congregation with its educational, social, and judicial services, to the macrocosmic level of the supercommunity, comprising all of Polish-Lithuanian Jewry, the Jewish community represented, in its heyday in the early seventeenth century, a functioning government within a government. The national body of Eastern European Jewry, called the Council of Four Lands (including Great Poland, Little Poland, Podolia-Galicia and Volhynia, as well as Lithuania until 1623), was responsible for collecting taxes, representing all Jewish interests before the Polish government, as well as handling all internal religious and cultural matters.

The traditions of northern European rabbinical scholarship reached unsurpassed heights in the receptive political and social climate of Eastern Europe. Major academies of Jewish law were founded in every major Polish town; commentaries and codes, kabbalistic and ethical tracts, sermons and biblical exegesis, were all products of the Polish effervescence of Judaic learning. Nor were humanistic and scientific ideas originating from Italy and the west unknown to Poland's rabbinic scholars. Although Eastern European Jews lived in an environment relatively less culturally developed than that of Jews living to the west and the south, the bridges of communication with these cultural centers still remained open. Polish Jews traveled regularly to Italy; Jewish and *converso* physicians settled throughout the farthermost regions of Poland; and Polish rabbis like Moses Isserles (ca. 1520–72), Solomon Luria (ca. 1510–73), and Mordecai Yaffe (ca. 1535–1612) exhibited a remarkable awareness of non-Jewish culture in their Talmudic and theological writing. (**See Reading 5-12.**)

Polish Jewry experienced a major setback, however, when in 1648 the Cossacks of the Ukraine revolted against the Polish crown and nobility. The Jews were conspicuously associated with the Roman Catholic Polish nobility in their economic activities. When the Cossacks, along with Crimean Tartars and Greek Orthodox Ukrainian peasants, went on a rampage from city to city, the Jews became prime targets for brutality. During the initial bloodshed and throughout a subsequent period of almost twenty years, thousands of Jews were slaughtered, died from famine or the plague, or expired as martyrs. The Cossack pogroms wiped out almost a quarter of the Jewish population. Although the community made every effort to recover its losses and rebuild, the steady political and economic decline of Poland nevertheless weighed heavily on its Jewish population.

Polish Jewry never fully recovered from the debacle of the seventeenth century. A population explosion, economic impoverishment—particularly in the provinces of Podolia and Volhynia—and political disintegration from within (the abolishment of the Council of Four Lands in 1764) and without (the Polish partitions of 1772, 1793, and 1795) further impaired the weakened political and cultural state of Polish Jewry in the eighteenth century. Internal tensions also were exacerbated by the deepening division between oligarchies of wealthy families in positions of authority and the majority of Jews who increasingly found themselves in the ranks of the poor. The glaring dichotomy between the relatively prosperous regions of the north (Lithuania and especially its major town of Vilna) and the poverty-stricken regions of the south and west also served to magnify resentment and jealousy between the two populations. And finally, Jacob Frank and his followers caused increasing bitterness and mutual recrimination among all sectors of the community.

Under these circumstances a new pietistic movement called Hasidism (unrelated to the medieval German movement of the same name) arose in the poorest regions of Podolia and Volhynia in the last decades of the eighteenth century. It was founded by an itinerant wonder worker named Israel ben Eliezer (1700–60) of Medzibozh in Podolia, who called himself the *Ba'al Shem Tov* (master of the good (divine) name, known as the Besht). The term *ba'al shem* refers generally to a group of folk healers; the Besht distinguished himself from this group by the additional adjective *"tov"* (good). The Besht, like Luria, committed little to writing; his teachings were transmitted through the works of his followers, especially his major disciple Jacob Joseph of Polonnoye (d. ca. 1782). The followers of the Besht were the poor and disenfranchised of the neglected regions from which he himself came. His understanding of Judaism was ideally suited to meet the needs and aspirations of the common semi-illiterate Jews who had become alienated from both the rich and the educated. (**See Reading 5-17A and B.**)

It is difficult to isolate the basic features of the Hasidic movement, given the diversity of views and emphases of its early leaders after the Besht. Nevertheless, at least three key elements especially stand out in assessing the genesis of this major movement of Eastern European Jewry and its unusual popularity. In the first place, Hasidism represented a social movement for the common Jews, articulating an ideology of Judaism that heightened their human dignity and creative function. It gave higher priority to prayer over study, to joy and inner peace over melancholy and self-denial, to spontaneity and social equality over formalism and social elitism. It strove for the full participation of every member of the community and for the fostering of a sense of brotherhood between all participants. It sought to celebrate every mundane feature of human life as aspects of holiness and spirituality.

Secondly, Hasidism constituted a clear reaction to the excesses of Frankist messianism and the wounds engendered to the Jewish community by the followers of Shabbetai Zevi. It sought to purify Lurianic *kabbalah* of its anti-rabbinic accretions and to utilize its rich spiritual symbols to reinforce traditional values. In the literature of Hasidic parables, Frank and Shabbetai Zevi were characterized in the most negative terms. More substantially, Hasidism consciously utilized Lurianic kabbalistic terminology and even the liturgy of Luria while steering clear of the instability of revolutionary messianic tensions. While references to national redemption still remained in Hasidic thought, the movement sought to draw attention to the fate of the individual along with that of the nation, his communion with God, and his personal redemption through his acts of personal piety. (See Reading 5-17C.)

Thirdly and most importantly, Hasidism introduced within the Jewish community a new image of the religious leader called the *zaddik* (the righteous one). Hasidism bitterly denounced the traditional leadership of the community for its lack of concern and involvement with the ordinary Jew and for its constant deprecation of the image and life-style of that individual. Hasidism offered instead the ideal of a mystic sage with social concern; a leader who descends to the level of his constituency in order to raise them to his level (a re-interpretation of the dangerous concept of descending into the evil *kelipah* to extract the divine spark); and a leader who inspires others by extolling their virtues and by providing an example to them through his own behavior.

In the early years of the movement, Hasidism engaged in acrimonious controversy with its opponents (called *mitnagdim*). The latter were drawn essentially from two groups. The first was primarily a lay leadership who saw Hasidism as a threat to the social cohesion of the Jewish community and to their own hegemony over the community. The second group objected to Hasidism on ideological grounds. Their spiritual leader was the most prominent rabbinic authority of his day, Elijah, the *gaon* of Vilna (1720–79). A man of immense learning and deep intellectual commitment, he objected most strongly to the vacuous spirituality of Hasidism, bereft of *Torah* learning, unearned through scholarly diligence and concentration. His own blueprint of Jewish life placed the study of the *Torah*, intellectual ingenuity, and rabbinic and secular learning on a higher scale than prayer or pious sentiment.

Despite the apparent chasm between the postures of the Besht and the Vilna *gaon*, however, their views did not prove to be irreconcilable in the long run. Elijah was not adverse to kabbalistic visions, as long as they "were filled with Torah." More significantly, the next generation of Hasidic leadership, following the Maggid Dov Baer (1710–72) of Mezeritch and his disciples, had little taste for prolonged debate and schism. On the contrary, they worked for a rapprochement with traditional authorities. They saw it as their role to reinforce and strengthen traditional values and to foster communal harmony. In Lithuania, one dynasty called Ḥabad Hasidism sought to engender a fusion between rabbinic intellectualism and Hasidic piety. By the beginning of the nineteenth century, both camps found that they were capable of living side by side with each other. Both discovered an enemy more formidable than either of their distinctive ideologies, an enemy whose challenge to traditional institutions and values required of them a united front. This new enemy was the enlightenment and modern secularism.

## THE *CONVERSO* DIASPORA IN AMSTERDAM

The effects of enlightenment and modern secularism on Jewish society and culture at first were felt more profoundly in the West than in the East, long before the beginning of the nineteenth century. For the Jews, one of the earliest encounters between Jewish culture and modern secularist tendencies took place in the receptive setting of seventeenth-century Amsterdam. Thousands of former *conversos* fleeing Spain and Portugal chose to settle in the Dutch city as a welcome haven in which to return to their former faith. By the end of the century Amsterdam's Jewish community could claim some 10,000 inhabitants, making it the largest Jewish community in western Europe. (See Reading 5-18.)

When Portugal's Jewish community had been forcibly converted to Christianity in 1497, a secret Jewish life instantly became a reality for the majority of these new converts. While Spain's *converso* problem substantially diminished by the sixteenth century, Portugal soon discovered it now had inherited Spain's problem. By 1536 the first inquisitorial trial was held in Portugal; by 1540 a regularized inquisitorial structure was established in Lisbon. In 1580, however, when Spain annexed Portugal, Spain faced again its *converso* problem. Thousands of Portuguese *conversos* migrated back to Spain in search of relief from religious persecution and better economic opportunities.

Spain proved as unwelcoming an environment for them as had Portugal. Fears of inquisitional punishment; discriminatory exclusion from governmental service, social brotherhoods and military orders; and shrinking economic opportunities all induced thousands of *conversos* to exit the Iberian peninsula throughout the seventeenth century.

For *converso* refugees, however, communities willing to receive them were still limited. Venice and Leghorn both took advantage of the *conversos'* proven economic skills by extending invitations to some of them. Others found refuge in southern France where they were forced to live a rather clandestine existence; others settled in Hamburg; still others eventually settled in England and the New World. But in Amsterdam the opportunities for *converso* immigrants were surely the most beneficial. After 1590 the Dutch had asserted their independence from Spain; they clearly had no inhibition in inviting former victims of Spanish persecution to settle within their boundaries and to enjoy religious freedom.

Amsterdam's open borders quickly provided a boon to the city's burgeoning capitalistic economy. The former *conversos*, now reintegrated in a powerful Jewish community, were active in international trade, in manufacturing, in banking, in stock speculation, and in printing. Amsterdam became the leading commercial center of Europe in the seventeenth century, owing, to a considerable extent, to Jewish participation.

Commercial interchange was accompanied by intellectual and religious interaction between the Jews and Dutch Protestants. Amsterdam's Jews, the majority of whom were former *conversos*, constituted a most atypical Jewish community. Highly educated, originally reared as Christians, literate in Latin and conversant in Spanish and Portuguese, they chose to return to Judaism as adults and to enter a traditional social and religious milieu totally alien to their previous identity and background. Migration from Catholicism to Judaism involved both an intellectual and a psychological passage from one world to another, and their reemergence within the Jewish community was not without painful emotional, religious, and educational stress for which their former Christian lives hardly had prepared them. (**See Reading 5-19.**)

For the majority of returning *conversos*, the transition to traditional rabbinic Judaism was formidable but not insurmountable. They educated themselves in Jewish sources; they familiarized themselves with traditional Jewish practice, and even became enthusiastic apologists for the rabbinic faith. The most outstanding representative of this type was the physician and theologian Isaac Orobio de Castro (1617–87) who, after living a secret life in Portugal and Spain, fled the Inquisition, reclaimed his birthright as a Jew, and became an eloquent spokesman for the Jewish community. Orobio's career and writings vividly depict the complicated spiritual and cultural world of his contemporaries: their love-hate relationship with their Spanish heritage, their feelings of guilt and bitterness about their past, and their obsession with rehabilitating other *conversos* sinking in the "mud" of Catholicism, or in deistic and secularistic philosophies.

Not all returning *conversos* chose to follow the path of Orobio, that led directly back to traditional rabbinic Judaism. Some became ardent followers of Shabbetai Zevi's messianic movement, as we have seen. Others remained convinced Catholics, while still others opportunistically elected what was easiest for them—remaining indifferent to all religious or ideological issues. The career of Manasseh ben Israel (1604–57), his writing and publishing career, his fascination with the discoveries of the New World, and his obsession to win entrance to England for the Jews, offers still another illustration of creative response by a former *converso* to the dynamic cultural setting that Amsterdam offered. (See Reading 5-20.)

Amsterdam's social and intellectual environment also provided the seeds of heresy and desertion from this same community of returning *conversos*. Individuals like Juan de Prado (ca. 1615–ca.70) and Uriel da Costa (1585–1640) ultimately were incapable of reconciling what they had hoped and dreamed Judaism might mean with what they eventually found it to be. They had imagined the Jewish culture to be essentially biblical yet spiritually tolerant of individual diversity; they discovered it to be something quite different in its rabbinical mode. They objected especially to the idea of a rabbinic oral law which supplemented and superseded the written one. They found contemporary Jewish life intellectually stifling, socially isolating, and morally bankrupt. These negative feelings were reinforced by the hostile and uncompromising responses of the faithful within their own community. The final outcome was often heated polemics, widening polarization between the two camps, hardening positions between orthodoxy and heterodoxy—even excommunication. (See Reading 5-21.)

This intellectual and religious climate helps to explain the genesis of the thinking of Amsterdam's most original and creative thinker, Barukh Spinoza (1632–77). Born in Amsterdam to a family of former *conversos*, Spinoza gradually ceased his Jewish observance, withdrew from the community, and devoted his life to a philosophical system ultimately antithetical to Jewish culture and faith. His devastating critique of Judaism is found in his *Tractatus Theologico-*

*Politicus* published in 1670. In this work he polemicized especially with the rationalist philosophy of Maimonides, not out of an antiphilosophic stance, but in the name of rationalism. He objected to the arbitrariness, artificiality, and downright cynicism of Maimonides' allegorical interpretation of the Bible, his identification of prophecy with philosophy, and his ideal of the state grounded in divine law. For Spinoza, scripture was to be studied and evaluated on its own terms. It was not synonymous with philosophy but inferior to it. The prophets evoked belief in the souls of people incapable of knowing the truth through rational perception. Their belief in miracles, in the chosenness of the Jewish people, and in material rather than spiritual salvation in no way could be reconciled with philosophical truth. The theocratic state under Mosaic law, once appropriate for a citizenry of former slaves, no longer was desirable or compatible with a society where the separation between religious belief and political sovereignty, as conceived within the Protestant state, represented the highest ideal.

In Spinoza's view reason had come to judge biblical and Jewish faith on its own assumptions and had found them lacking. For the philosopher "the human mind must be allowed to search for truth, unhampered by dogma, for the free activity of mind is the highest form of piety." Spinoza's scathing formulation placed Jewish (and Christian) religious authority in direct opposition to the views of western philosophical thinking. In offering a religious experience based exclusively on personal autonomy whose only guide was reason, Spinoza had presented a formidable challenge to every subsequent thinker hoping to legitimate and justify Jewish particularity, rabbinic law, and traditional Jewish faith in the modern era.

## THE ROAD TO EMANCIPATION

By the beginning of the eighteenth century Jewish life in Western and Eastern Europe had undergone radical political, economic, and cultural transformations since the medieval period, but it still remained essentially unchanged. Despite the major migratory shifts from the West to the East and slowly back to the West, the intellectual attraction of the Renaissance and seventeenth-century philosophies, the fermentation of kabbalistic messianism and its anarchic tendencies, and the cultural and spiritual reawakening of Eastern European Jewry, traditional Jewish society was still intact.

Jews still lacked equal political status with other citizens; the Jewish community still functioned essentially as its medieval counterpart had. Jews were still limited occupationally; their cultural habits, religious outlook, and behavior had not been significantly altered.

Yet portents of change affecting Jewish life also were more highly visible than at any other previous time. The experience of the Amsterdam community prefigured the corrosive impact modern rationalistic tendencies would have on increasingly larger segments of the Jewish community. Spinoza had become the archetype of the Jewish intellectual who chooses to desert the Jewish community in the name of a higher personal ideal; his example would be followed by many others in subsequent generations. (See Reading 5-22.)

Germany in the seventeenth and eighteenth centuries also had experienced a new phenomenon—an emerging stratum of court Jews (*Hofjuden*) who, like their medieval ancestors, accumulated considerable power and wealth through their close financial and social contacts with secular rulers. Unlike the earlier court Jews, however, these individuals wielded greater influence and participated in more numerous business undertakings in return for which they were rewarded exceptional rights and privileges. Together with individual *converso* businessmen in Amsterdam and in other European and American localities, these German Jewish financiers reveal the conspicuous though limited economic power of some of the Jews during the era of the rise of modern capitalism in Western Europe. Nevertheless, the individual gains of the "exceptional" Jews were constricted and marginal. Their personal advancement in non-Jewish society had either minimal or no impact at all on the status of the overwhelming majority of their coreligionists.

Other winds of change were encountered faintly during the same era. Within an increasingly vocal sector of elite Western European society, ideas of religious tolerance, universal suffrage, and the separation of the powers of church and state were gaining widespread legitimacy and currency. John Locke and John Toland in England openly expressed enlightened views regarding the moral self-sufficiency of the secular state and the elimination of Christianity as a political factor in governmental policy. Such views still indicated only a possibility rather than an expression of reality in restructuring the social and political status of most of the European Jews, but nevertheless they represented a possibility articulated with increasing regularity and moral cogency by the eighteenth century. (**See Reading 5-23.**)

A further indication of the possibility of future Jewish integration and equality within non-Jewish society was the entrance of the German Jewish philosopher Moses Mendelssohn (1729–86) into Berlin salon society in the 1760's and 1770's. Mendelssohn's significant literary and philosophical accomplishments and social contacts with German intellectuals like Gotthold Ephraim Lessing (1729–81) and Wilhelm Christian von Dohm (1751–1820) gave vivid expression to an intellectual journey from an exclusively Jewish environment to a European one. Yet Mendelssohn's status, like that of his fellow countrymen, the *Hofjuden*, was still the exception rather than the rule. Furthermore, his integration was not granted without significant concessions on his part. In the minds of his contemporaries, full citizenship for Jews like him was conditional on his ability to emphasize what was human and universal at the expense of what was particularly Jewish about himself. They assumed that enlightened Jews like Mendelssohn eventually would see the light and, like Spinoza, abandon their Jewishness. Mendelssohn's insistence that Judaism and rational enlightenment were compatible with each other (articulated in his book called *Jerusalem*) failed to convince most Christians or even many Jewish intellectuals of the integrity or relevancy of his theological position.

The edict of tolerance of Joseph II of Austria in 1782 and the edicts of universal suffrage in France in 1790–91 marked the culmination of a process of political and cultural integration of the Jews into western civilization which gradually had been set in motion centuries earlier. An entire Jewish community now was radically inserted by legal fiat into areas of European society previously available only sporadically and fragmentedly to a small minority of its members. The Jews no longer were denied political and economic rights available to all other citizens. They now could mix freely with other peoples and cultures; they were considered equal in the eyes of the law.

Yet few within Jewish society were fully capable of anticipating what might happen to Jewish identity and faith, previously nurtured by an insulated and authoritative Jewish communal structure, under the new circumstances now afforded them. Without an effective rabbinate able to assert its authority through Jewish religious law, would individual Jews retain their loyalty to Jewish faith and practice? With the Jewish community transformed into a voluntary association, could it retain its former powerful hold over its adherents? And with the Jews suddenly pushed into more intimate and conspicuous encounters with non-Jews, would the ubiquitous traditions of anti-Jewish hostility in European society and culture continue to persist and even intensify? An event of such great promise as that of the political emancipation of the Jews in European society would also sow the seeds of their anxiety and despair.

---

*Editor's Questions*
AFTER VIEWING AND READING

- Identify Samuel Usque and Solomon ibn Verga. How were their writings an attempt to console the Spanish and Portuguese Jews who now found themselves in exile?
- Who was Pico della Mirandola? How did his relationship with Jews and Jewish texts reflect the contribution of the Jews to Renaissance civilization?
- How would you compare the attitudes of sixteenth century popes and Luther toward the Jews?
- What effect did Shabbetai Zevi and the ideas of his followers have on the Jews of the seventeenth and eighteenth centuries?
- Why did the 1648 Cossack revolt lead to the murder of thousands of Jews?
- What were the attitudes of Uriel da Costa and Barukh Spinoza toward Judaism? How did the Amsterdam authorities respond to these challenges?

---

SUGGESTED READINGS

Jacob Katz, *Tradition and Crisis: Jewish Society at the End of the Middle Ages* (Free Press, 1961)

Cecil Roth, *A History of the Marranos* (Jewish Publication Society of America, 1932)

Cecil Roth, *The Jews in the Renaissance* (Jewish Publication Society of America, 1950)

Solomon Schecter, "Safed in the Sixteenth Century: A City of Legists and Mystics," and Isadore Twersky, "The Shulhan Aruk: Enduring Code of Jewish Law" in Judah Goldin, ed., *The Jewish Expression* (Yale University Press, 1976)

Gershom Scholem, *Major Trends in Jewish Mysticism*, 3rd ed. (Schocken, 1954)

Gershom Scholem, *Sabbatai Ṣevi: The Mystical Messiah 1626–76*, trans. by R. J. Zwi Werblowsky (Princeton University Press, 1973)

Bernard Weinryb, *The Jews of Poland: A Social and Economic History of the Jewish Community in Poland from 1100–1800* (Jewish Publication Society of America, 1973)

# 6

# Roads from the Ghetto
# (1789 to 1914)

## Michael Stanislawski

*Editor's Suggestions*
BEFORE VIEWING THE SHOW

Examine Map 8 in the *Study Guide* which will aid in understanding the end of the program.

### Overview of the TV Program

It was the era of the industrial and French revolutions, of economic and political change. Aristocrats and monarchs were deposed and the middle class came to the fore. Napoleon's conquests brought French revolutionary ideals to Western Europe and with them the concept that all men were equal. Ghetto walls that surrounded the Jews came tumbling down and the Jews were faced with a dilemma. They had to determine how much of their Jewish identity they would have to compromise in order to integrate themselves fully into Western society.

Napoleon was defeated, liberalism suffered a setback, and the promises of equality were postponed. Some of the Jews felt that only through baptism could they be accepted in the European world. Previously, Moses Mendelssohn had argued that a Jew could embrace Western ideas while maintaining his own culture. Now, some Jews argued that Judaism needed to be reformed before they would be accepted by their countrymen. Traditionalist Jews disagreed with them on the amount of accommodation needed.

The Jews rose to new political heights but there were obstacles. Lionel Rothschild of the famous banking family was prevented from taking his seat in the English Parliament because he refused to take the requisite oath of allegiance to the Christian faith. Finally he was permitted his seat.

In Eastern Europe, Enlightenment ideas did not gain currency and the Jews' places of residence were restricted. The area permitted within Russia was called the Pale of Settlement. Most of the Jews continued their traditional life, though some sought to integrate Western ideas with Jewish practices. Under Tzar Alexander II hope arose for the reform of Russian society, but in 1881 he was assassinated and later that year riots broke out against the Jews. Anti-Semitism was fueled by economic competition and traditional Church hatred of the Jews.

The Jews faced prejudice in Western Europe but did not suffer violent attacks. Anti-Semites exploited people's difficulties in modern society and blamed the Jews for all their dislocation. Conservatives and liberals alike saw the Jews as destructive to the fabric of society.

In response to the Dreyfus affair, where a French Jew was wrongly accused of treason, many Frenchmen were inflamed with anti-Semitic sentiment. For one acculturated Jew, Theodor Herzl, it meant that the Jews had to build their life in a land separate from Europe. Under his leadership the Zionist movement emerged as a response to the rising prejudice. But not all Jews were interested in rebuilding a Jewish homeland in Palestine. Many sought other ways to express their Jewish nationality, such as the Jewish socialist movement.

In Western Europe prior to World War I, the Jews had entered Western society but were perceived as separate. During the war Jews fought alongside their countrymen on both sides of the front. After the war hope for a Jewish state received an unexpected boost. The British, who now controlled Palestine, offered the Jews the right to establish a national homeland in Palestine.

*Watch for . . . and Think about*

The Industrial Revolution began in Western Europe in the late eighteenth century. Glimpse the tremendously powerful machines and think about how they were able to produce extraordinary quantities of manufactured materials.

Look for the black-and-white photographs of Jewish society in Eastern Europe. Was their life comparable to that of Western Jews?

Observe the anti-Semitic drawings and the cartoons of the Jews and Jewish life. How were these artists portraying the Jewish people?

WHILE READING THE *STUDY GUIDE* AND *SOURCE READER*

Look for the following:

- The innovations of modern society and see, in turn, how they affected the Jews living in Western Europe.
- Some of the ideas espoused by the French Revolution. How did these ideals generate a movement for the emancipation of the Jews? Identify emancipation, Enlightenment.
- The differences in Jewish legal status in Western European countries.
- Why some Jews tried to reform their religion. What were they trying to achieve? Did all the Jews agree with their first efforts? Identify *Wissenschaft des Judentums*, Positive Historical Judaism, and Neo-Orthodoxy.
- How the political and economic situation in Eastern Europe differed from that in France and Germany. What options were open to the Jews of Russia?
- The nature of anti-Semitism in Eastern and Western Europe. Was it the same? Who were its spokesmen? Why were many people receptive to anti-Semitic ideas? How did Jews across Europe respond to these attacks? Identify Zionism, Diaspora Nationalism, Bundism.

---

## THE CHALLENGES OF MODERNITY

The modern age presented the Jews with new challenges and opportunities that would remake Jewish history as well as the role of Jews in western civilization. The period since the French Revolution witnessed at one and the same time the most successful integration of the Jews into non-Jewish society and the most extensive slaughter of Jews since their origin. Thriving Jewish communities were created in vital parts of the world at the same time that ancient Jewish centers were forcibly abolished. A shattering crisis of identity and faith tore many Jews away from their ancestral moorings, while new compelling philosophies and ideologies emerged to guide other Jews through the unprecedented maze of the modern world.

The complex, often paradoxical, history of the Jews in the last two centuries has revolved around their relationship to the three major revolutions that have defined modern life—what might be called the intellectual, political, and social revolutions.

The intellectual revolution resulted from the spread of the ideas of the Enlightenment. First and foremost this meant the acceptance of a new conception of the primacy of the individual: each human being was deemed to hold the same natural rights, to deserve equal treatment regardless of station in life, family, or origin. All philosophies or religious traditions that were based on inequality or claimed unique divine inspiration were strongly attacked. No one religion had a monopoly on the truth, proclaimed the Enlightenment. Rather, all religions shared the same philosophical and spiritual premises, clothed in different garb. Religion, therefore, was to be a matter of the individual conscience and to be relegated to the private sphere where it could not perpetuate restrictions on individual liberty. Any such limitations were artificial, irrational, and anachronistic. In sharp contrast to the ancient view that the past was glorious or holy, and ancestors were wiser and thus ought to be emulated, the Enlightenment proclaimed that the world was now better than it had ever been before and was getting better all the time. By relying on reason and cooperation, mankind was moving inevitably to a glorious future of boundless promise and liberty for all.

Some of the Jews were involved in the elaboration of these new ideas. Moses Mendelssohn was the first and most famous Jewish Enlightenment philosopher, and as such, has been called the first modern Jew. But the participation of Jews in the Enlightenment did not diminish the dilemmas that the intellectual revolution laid on the doorstep of the Jewish world. Along with Roman Catholicism and the various Protestant denominations, Judaism was forced to defend itself against this new way of thinking or to respond to the profound criticism leveled against it. For the Jews, moreover, the Enlightenment's relegation of religion to the private domain raised another quite different problem: the definition of a Jew. Until this time everyone agreed that the Jews were both a nation and a religious group. But now that the two categories were separated, the question was posed: Are the Jews simply adherents of a faith parallel to all other faiths, or are they members of a distinct national group? (**See Reading 6-1.**)

This quandary was closely intertwined with the issues raised by the second modern revolution—the political revolution. In the late eighteenth century, age-old rules and institutions of statecraft were cast aside as new forms of government and political organization were invented, implemented, and refined. Perhaps most dramatically, the monarch ceased to be the natural ruler of the state: kings and queens were deposed, and often executed, in the name of the new supreme authority—the people. Nobilities and aristocracies were either abolished or substantially weakened. What replaced these hallowed hierarchies differed from place to place, but in general a radical transformation occurred in the basic way in which political life was organized: in premodern society, the individual had no direct connection to the state or its centers of authority. He or she was simply a member of a distinct group—the peasantry, the merchants, the clergy. Now, each person was to have a direct relationship to the state, each individual was to become a distinct political entity—a citizen. As a result, previously inescapable group ties increasingly became voluntary, and the former leaders of social groupings either lost their power or had to find a new basis for exercising their authority.

For the Jews, the implications of this new political order were clear-cut. As a minority subject to religious and ethnic tension, the Jews over the centuries had evolved a rather sophisticated strategy for coping with kings, nobles, and other ruling bodies. The success of this strategy varied from country to country, but on the whole the political status of the Jews—where they were allowed to live at all—was stable, well-defined, and arguably better than that of the vast majority of the population, the peasants. But both this status and this strategy were predicated on the Jews' constituting a distinct and separate community. Where would the Jews fit in the emerging new society, based on the individual citizen? The new political order had to face the question of whether to allow the Jews to become citizens, to hold equal rights with all other individuals. The Jews who fought for emancipation had to face the question of how to maintain their group identity and institutions on a voluntary basis, how to organize their community in this novel political context.

Not only were the intellectual and political environments radically transformed at this time: the social and economic order was also revolutionized. The Industrial Revolution spread from England to the rest of Europe and across the seas, changing the ways most people earned their daily keep. The old world, in which the vast majority of the population worked the land, was slowly but persistently giving way to the new "modern" economy. Advances in technology and science made agriculture more efficient and led to the creation of new enterprises, predominantly in cities, that employed former farmers in factories and plants. Alongside the traditional classes of peasants and landlords, there were now industrial workers and factory owners. To serve these new social groupings, trade and commerce had to be reorganized, and the liberal professions such as law, medicine, and education had to respond to significantly new audiences and problems. Thus a new kind of middle class also came into being.

While a small number of the Jews were involved in these economic changes from the start, it was clear that the new phenomena were bound to have serious ramifications for the lives of most of the Jews, who had survived the centuries by shaping and honing economic skills that served the traditional economy but were shunned by the majority of people. As trade and commerce became more respectable and more profitable, the Jews would have to face new and stronger competitors in these realms. How would they adapt to the disruption of the traditional economy, the emergence of the factory system, the transformation of the liberal professions? How would the Jews be affected by the increasing attraction of their primary terrain, the cities?

In short, the revolutions that created the modern world challenged the Jews to respond to a new economy, a new political order, a new type of society, and a new intellectual universe. The story of how the Jews reacted to these challenges and played a vital role in the creation of modern civilization is the essence of modern Jewish history— an intricate web of grand success and dismal disillusionment.

## THE FRENCH REVOLUTION AND THE EMANCIPATION OF THE JEWS

The opening act of this drama unfolded in Paris in the spring and summer of 1789, as the ideas of the Enlightenment were realized in the French Revolution. The old monarchical regime was toppled and replaced by a revolutionary government dedicated to the principles of "liberty, equality, and fraternity." The king and nobles lost most of their rights and privileges as power was seized by the National Assembly—the representatives of the French people as a whole. On August 27, 1789, the basic premise of the new society was articulated by the Assembly in its Declaration of the Rights of Man: "All men are born, and remain, free and equal in rights. . . . No person shall be molested for his opinions, even such as are religious. . . ."

What did this declaration mean for the Jews of France? It seems clear that they, too, were included in the category of men born free and equal, and their right to freedom of religion and thought was guaranteed. But were the Jews to be citizens in the new French state? This question soon began to be debated on the floor of the National Assembly. The opponents of granting citizenship to the Jews—or "emancipating" them—claimed that the very nature of Jewish life and tradition precluded their equal participation in the state. Jews were indeed men, but they were not Frenchmen. They belonged to the Jewish nation, which insisted on its separateness, hoped for an eventual return to their ancestral home in Palestine, and had religious laws, such as the prohibition of work on the Sabbath, which made it impossible for them to bear equally the responsibilities of citizenship. Thus, the Jews could be tolerated but not called equal citizens.

The supporters of the emancipation of the Jews agreed that the traditional Jewish community and way of life were incompatible with the demands of the new French state, but firmly argued that the Jews would change if granted equal rights. After all, they insisted, the Jews are men just like all men and differ only in respect to their idiosyncratic religion, which is as irrelevant to the new state as is Catholicism. Grant the Jews equal rights as individuals, but deny them any rights as a group. (See Reading 6-2.)

The arguments went back and forth without either side convincing the other. By the beginning of the new year, 1790, an interim compromise was agreed upon: the small Sephardic Jewish community of southern France was to be emancipated. These Jews, mostly of Portuguese and Spanish origin, were already highly integrated into French commerce, culture, and society. They seemed, in fact, to differ from other Frenchmen only in regard to their religious affiliation, which they appeared not to take very seriously. Although over a third of the Assembly was still not convinced, the three thousand Sephardic Jews of France were emancipated on January 28, 1790. For the first time in history, a parliamentary institution had formally declared that Jews were legally citizens, part and parcel of the body politic, equal in all respects to all other citizens of the realm. (See Reading 6-3.)

Such a status, however, was not so easily granted to the much larger community of Ashkenazic Jews in France. These thirty-odd thousand Jews, living in the northern territories that periodically belonged to Germany, spoke Yiddish, dressed in the traditional Jewish garb of Central Europe, strictly adhered to the religious and cultural teachings of Judaism, and practiced the traditional Jewish economic pursuits of petty commerce, trade, and moneylending. The National Assembly could not agree on the civil status of these Jews. So another debate went on for more than a year, with the same arguments and attacks, but no resolution. Meanwhile, the Assembly had agreed on a question far more central to the new state—its Constitution. On September 3, 1791, the French Constitution declared the abolition of all vestiges of the old regime and guaranteed national, civil, and religious rights to all citizens of France. When the Assembly later returned to the question of the Jews, one deputy pointed out that any debate of the emancipation of the Jews was now out of order, for it would implicitly deny the very bases of the Constitution. Without settling the disagreement over the possibility of integrating the Jews into the new society, the Assembly followed the logic of its Constitution and emancipated the Ashkenazic Jews of France on September 28, 1791. In the new French state, there could be no vestiges of the medieval estate structure; a collective Jewish legal entity was impossible in a society based on the absolute integrity of the individual. The Jews of France were no longer legally distinct from their Christian neighbors; they were equal citizens of a modern nation-state. (See Readings 6-4 and 6-5.)

Although some traditional Jews feared the effect that the new freedom might have on their religious and communal ties, most French Jews viewed the emancipation as an unmitigated blessing. Indicative of this enthusiastic response was a letter written by a prominent Jewish businessman and politician, Berr Isaac Berr, the day after the emancipation. Berr effusively thanked the National Assembly for doing God's will, restoring to the Jews the rights taken from them eighteen hundred years earlier with the destruction of the Jewish commonwealth in Judaea. With boundless optimism he declared, "We are now, thanks to the Supreme Being, and to the sovereignty of the nation, not only Men and Citizens, but we are Frenchmen." He continued, however, to draw the implicit lesson of emancipation. The Jews, he argued, must prove themselves worthy of this godly trust by improving themselves morally, culturally, and economically. They must reject their previous behavior and be guided solely by patriotism and civic duty. In his letter Berr not only voiced the emotions of his contemporaries but also defined the essential terms of the contract that the Jews had entered into—perhaps unconsciously—

with their legal enfranchisement: in exchange for equal rights, the Jews had to renounce their previous group solidarity and possibly many aspects of their distinctive way of life. But how much, and in what ways, the Jews had to change in response to their emancipation was a question they would continue to confront in the years to come. (See Reading 6-6.)

In the meantime, to be sure, the outside world was engulfed by enormous changes. The Revolution was extended beyond the borders of France as the French army cascaded through neighboring countries abolishing old forms of government, nobilities, and traditions and creating mini-states based on the principles of liberty, equality, and fraternity. Part of the package of the Revolution was the emancipation of the Jews, and ghetto walls came tumbling down in many parts of Western and Central Europe as a result of French military victories. On the other hand, in France itself liberty was quickly turning into unbridled license, and freedom was reduced to chaos. In January 1793, King Louis XVI was executed; three months later a dictatorial board called the Committee of Public Safety was established to take control of the country. Soon thereafter the Reign of Terror began with various factions attacking and assassinating one another in an orgy of senseless violence that seemed to many in France and abroad either to betray the principles of the Revolution or to prove their dangerousness. All the while, the military conquests of the French army continued, and as so often happens in similar chaotic circumstances, a leading military commander built upon his successes on the battlefield to assume more and more political power. By the end of the century Napoleon Bonaparte emerged as the virtual dictator of France and all its conquered territories. (See Readings 6-7 and 6-8.)

Napoleon brilliantly manipulated his popular support and his immense personal talents to implement what he believed to be the lessons of the Revolution. He reorganized the French army, political system, tax collection, and education; he entered into a remarkable arrangement with the Pope that gave the French government extensive control over the Catholic Church. In 1804 Napoleon declared himself Emperor of France. At this time and for a decade to come he continued to lead his troops in battle after battle against the major armies of Europe, extending French control over large parts of Western and Central Europe.

In the process of establishing order and control over French society, Napoleon confronted the question of the Jews. Particularly troublesome was the continued economic tension between non-Jews and Jews in the northeast provinces of France. Napoleon issued a series of laws intended to solve these problems. More important than the specific content of these laws was their context: a decade and a half after the emancipation, special laws were being passed to treat the Jews as a distinct and separate community. This contradiction of emancipation was even more explicit in the most dramatic measure Napoleon took in regard to the Jews. In 1806 he called together an Assembly of Jewish Notables and charged them with answering basic questions about the relations between the Jews and France: Do Jews born in France regard France as their fatherland? Do they pledge themselves to obeying its laws? What role do the rabbis have in Jewish legal and communal life? Can a Jew marry a non-Jew? Can a Jew have more than one wife? In the eyes of Jews, are Frenchmen considered brethren or strangers?

The very phrasing of these questions speaks volumes about the incomplete nature of the integration of the Jews in France in the period after their emancipation. Jews were still distinct from Frenchmen—but precisely in what ways? The Jewish deputies to the Assembly struggled with these difficult issues and subtly defended their position: the Jews of France unilaterally regard France as their country and all French citizens as their brothers. The Jews remain committed to Jewish law—but that law does not in the least require anything incompatible with French citizenship. On the contrary, all the political aspects of Jewish communal autonomy were superseded by the Revolution. The Jews are now simply a religious denomination in France like all other denominations.

This patriotic consensus was accepted by Napoleon, who then organized a spiritual assembly to ratify the declarations of the lay leaders. Napoleon called the new meeting the Sanhedrin—the name of the ancient Jewish supreme court, the highest authority in Jewish law. His use of this term was deliberate. He was invoking the prime source for his challenge to the Jews: if you truly want to be Frenchmen, you can no longer have any outstanding Jewish national aspirations; you must subordinate yourselves entirely to the authority of French law, customs, and institutions, except insofar as they touch upon matters of individual religious conscience.

Clearly, then, even in France the gaining of political emancipation was only one step toward the integration of Jews into modern society. Legal equality had to be fought for, but even where it was achieved, much depended on the degree of tolerance and pluralism afforded by society at large, and the spiritual and cultural concessions required of the Jews themselves. In other words, along with legal emancipation, the Jews would have to face the challenges and opportunities of social emancipation.

## THE FATE OF EMANCIPATION, 1815-1858

In France, the legal equality of the Jews was secure and remained unchallenged even after Napoleon's defeat in 1815 and the subsequent reaction against many aspects of his rule and the revolutionary tradition as a whole. Indeed, in the decades to come Jews were accepted slowly but steadily into more and more realms of French life and began to play an active role in the creation of new forms of French culture and politics.

In the rest of Western and Central Europe, however, the period of reaction after 1815 created a more complicated context for Jewish rights and Jewish participation in society. Dismayed by the excesses of the Reign of Terror and outraged by the aggressive foreign policy of Napoleon, many governments sought to combat all ideologies and innovations that smacked of the French Revolution. The victorious powers that met at the Congress of Vienna in 1815 decided to reinstitute much of the status quo that had been in effect before the upheavals—former rulers, borders, hierarchies, and laws were restored. Reinstated, too, was the prerevolutionary position of the Jews. In most of the German, Italian, and Austrian states, along with the other features of egalitarian society, the emancipation of the Jews was rescinded in the name of order and social peace.

The Jews, of course, were quite distressed by this retrenchment of their status, and they began a strenuous campaign for emancipation. Because this battle was closely connected with the overall fight for the ideals of the French Revolution, Jewish politics became inextricably linked with liberal, and in some measure, radical causes. Thus Jewish leaders in Berlin, Vienna, and Rome became more and more involved in the political life of their countries, and Jewish emancipation became a cardinal doctrine of the platforms and ideologies of many non-Jewish parties and politicians. This trend came to the fore in the Revolutions of 1848 when, for a brief time, the ideals and practices of 1789 were once more brought to life throughout Western and Central Europe. Jews were active participants in all the movements that fought for reform, and wherever liberal and radical forces seized power, the Jews were emancipated. But once more, the gains of the revolution were reversed with its demise. By the end of 1848 the old regimes were again back in control and the old forms of government, including their Jewish policies, back in place. Only in France were the Jews still enfranchised as free and equal citizens.

Matters took a different course in England where the fight against Napoleon and the French Revolution did not result in reactionary politics. Instead, the middle decades of the nineteenth century witnessed an age of reform in English life and politics. The impact of this reform on the Jews was somewhat complex: in England, the Jews had never been emancipated, but this had little to do with the European debates over this issue. The nature of English law and government precluded the necessity of a formal act proclaiming the Jews as citizens. England had no constitution; its law was based more on informal custom and precedent than on radical pronouncements and innovations. In short, law tended to follow life, rather than the reverse. In keeping with this unique setting, the Jews never were formally readmitted to Britain. They just came, and once they were there they needed no formal law permitting them to share the rights, liberties, and obligations of all other subjects of the Crown. The only limitations on the Jews—and other nonconformist religious groups—were access to the Bar and universities, service on juries, and most political offices that required an oath to be sworn in conformity with the rite of the Church of England.

From the late 1820's on, these restrictions began to fall, as the movement for social and political reform spread through England. First Roman Catholics, then dissident Protestants, and finally Jews were admitted to the Bar, juries, and the University of London. In 1837 Moses Montefiore, a prominent Jewish banker, became Sheriff of London and was knighted by the Queen. Soon the last barrier would be breached: Parliament itself. In 1847 Lionel de Rothschild was elected to the House of Commons, but he could not take his seat because he refused to take the Anglican oath. His supporters argued that the oath be rescinded, but they were in the minority. Lionel continued his noble campaign, winning election after election, suffering refusal after refusal in Parliament. Finally, on the fourteenth vote, in 1858, the oath was lifted and Lionel de Rothschild took his proper place in the House of Commons. (See Reading 6-9.)

However offensive the obstacles to political office-holding, they did not affect the basic civil rights and freedoms of the vast majority of the Jews in England. The English Jews, like their French counterparts, entered more and more into all realms of non-Jewish society. To be sure, in a society still based on clear demarcations of class and accent, social barriers continued to limit Jewish access to the top rungs of the social ladder. But the Jews continued to enjoy upward mobility in England. The rise of a baptized Jew, Benjamin Disraeli, to the position of prime minister was not directly related to the civic advance of the Jews, but Disraeli's idiosyncratic flaunting of his Jewish origins and his extravagant claims about aristocratic Jewish lineage could not have been possible without a substantial integration of Jews in British society.

## SOCIAL AND INTELLECTUAL CHANGES

The English experience was only an extreme indication of the complex, paradoxical nature of Jewish emancipation: on the continent as well, Jews discovered that social advancement and some measure of integration were possible without formal legal enfranchisement. Even where political advances lagged, the social and intellectual revolutions of modernity affected the Jews in remarkable ways. In the first half of the nineteenth century large numbers of Jews in Germany, Austria, Italy, and England, just as in France, abandoned the traditional modes of Jewish life. Perhaps the first changes took place in the external realm: Yiddish (or its Sephardic equivalent, Ladino) was increasingly abandoned in favor of the language of the country in which the Jews lived; typical Jewish styles of dress were replaced by new modern fashion; men began to shave their beards; social graces began to be modeled on European rules of etiquette. More significantly, Jews began to keep their children away from the *heder*—the traditional elementary school whose curriculum was based on the Bible and *Talmud*—and the *yeshivah*, the advanced Talmudic academy. Instead, parents began to send their sons, and their daughters, either to modernized Jewish schools which taught more secular subjects, or to public schools and ultimately to universities. Within a few decades throughout Central and Western Europe the traditional Jewish school virtually disappeared, and Jews began to be represented in huge numbers in every non-Jewish school system.

A good part of the attraction of the modern schools was their practicality, their usefulness for business. With the expansion of the middle class and the changes in trade and commerce occasioned by the Industrial Revolution, the Jews could no longer expect to make a living without knowing how to read, write, and keep accounts in the language of society at large. They also began to appreciate the utility of a knowledge of geography, history, basic sciences, and mathematics—all subjects largely neglected in the old Jewish schools. Where they could, the Jews streamed into the rising civil services, and throughout Western Europe they entered en masse into the liberal professions, particularly medicine and law, that required a university degree. Not all the Jews successfully made the move from their old economic roles to the new middle class but most did. A small number rose to positions of great wealth and economic power at this time: the Rothschilds were the richest and most famous but not the only Jewish family of this rank wielding substantial clout both inside and outside the Jewish community.

These social and economic transformations were most intense in countries where the Jews enjoyed the greatest political freedom: the fewer the limitations on their activities, the more they could achieve. But the opposite relationship between freedom and change seems to have been the case in the intellectual sphere. The revolutionary transformations in Jewish self-perception—the ways in which they thought about themselves, their religion, their past, and their future—found the most fertile soil precisely in those areas in which they had to struggle for their civil rights.

The first rounds of the intense battle over Jewish minds took place in Germany. Here, the disciples of Moses Mendelssohn carried on his search for a means of reconciling Judaism to the modern era. But very soon after Mendelssohn's death his specific approach lost its attractiveness. The next generation was not satisfied with the Jewish Enlightenment's rather optimistic assertion that Judaism and modernity could coexist in easy harmony. Why retain the specific customs and rituals of Judaism if all religions were essentially the same? Why study and pray in Hebrew if language was universal and German the model of culture and civilization? Why congregate in a synagogue, so foreign to German concepts of dignity and order?

Many of the Jews, particularly the young and better educated, could not provide convincing answers to these questions, so they proceeded to leave the Jewish community. Some merely ceased to view themselves as Jews and took no special measures in this regard. In France and England and to some measure also in Italy there had emerged a large enough neutral realm of society where one could fit in without being either a Christian or a Jew. Therefore, the Jews in these lands who no longer wanted to live as Jews could do so without a formal renunciation of Judaism. But this was not so easy in Germany: here the political inequities and barriers to employment made simple assimilation virtually impossible. And so in the early decades of the nineteenth century a large number of German Jews rushed to convert to Christianity. The most famous of these converts was the great poet Heinrich Heine, who sarcastically referred to his baptismal certificate as his "ticket of admission to European culture."

Yet most Jews, however disenchanted with traditional Judaism, would not take this radical step of conversion. Emotional ties, family connections, vague feelings of allegiance all played a part in this reluctance. For many, a basic religious skepticism applied equally to the tenets of Christianity and thus made baptism seem dishonorable. German Jews no longer satisfied by the Judaism of their parents, but wishing to remain Jewish, invented a variety of new ideologies and movements dedicated to a synthesis between Judaism and modernity, or between Jewishness and Germanness.

The first such attempt was the Reform movement, which arose at the beginning of the nineteenth century. The early Reformers argued that Judaism's uniqueness consisted in its essential religious truths, its teachings of ethical monotheism, and not in its specific rituals or laws. These were merely guides to the core truths, necessary for previous generations but largely superfluous in the modern age. To be a good Jew meant to live according to Judaism's moral and ethical precepts, and the task of the Jews as a group was to spread these lessons to the world at large. This new type of Judaism had no national boundaries or implications; Jews in Germany were simply "Germans of the Mosaic persuasion" parallel to "Germans of the Christian persuasion." Any vestiges of national exclusiveness to be found in Jewish liturgy or theology had to be expunged: the messianic hope was transformed from a belief in a personal messiah, who would lead the Jews back to Palestine, to a commitment to universal brotherhood and freedom; all references to the Land of Israel were to be deleted; German, or any vernacular language, was acceptable as the language of prayer.

In line with these theoretical dictates Jewish practices were reformed. The synagogue, now renamed the temple—like the Temple in Jerusalem—was rearranged to look more like a Protestant church. The service was to take place facing the congregation; organ music was introduced; the rabbis dressed in Lutheran clerical garb and preached in German; strict decorum was enforced. (**See Reading 6-10.**)

These innovations deeply offended the traditional Jews, who tried to have the new temples closed as dens of radical nonconformity. But the Reform movement proved to be more popular than its opposition. Throughout the first decades of the century Reform spread slowly but steadily to all major German-Jewish communities and would later count among its supporters the majority of the Jews in Germany.

The Reform ideology insisted that it was restoring Judaism to its original essence, removing only the anachronistic outer shell that had crusted over the pure Mosaic faith. In order to discern what was essential and what peripheral, the leading Reformers undertook far-reaching research into various phases of Jewish history and culture. Transferring to Jewish subjects the techniques of the new disciplines they had learned at German universities—history, philology, philosophy—Reformers such as Abraham Geiger and Leopold Zunz created a new phenomenon: a secular Jewish scholarship. Known by its German name as *Wissenschaft des Judentums* (Science of Judaism), this rigorous approach to the Jewish past differed radically from the age-old traditions of Jewish learning and established the fields of Jewish scholarship that continue to this day. In Germany another incentive to the scientific study of the Jewish past was the political need to explain Jews and Judaism to the outside world. It was felt that if only an accurate picture were drawn of who the Jews really were and what they believed, all enmity toward them would cease, and true emancipation would be forthcoming.

Despite the close connection between the Science of Judaism and the Reform movement, not all modern Jewish scholars shared the same religious orientation. Very soon the Wissenschaft movement became religiously neutral, and adherents of non-Reform tendencies in German-Jewish life became central figures in the scholarly enterprise. Prominent among these were a group of rabbis and scholars who at first aligned themselves with the Reform movement, but in the course of the 1840's and 1850's felt that the Reformers had gone too far in their abandonment of Jewish traditions and beliefs. Led by Rabbi Zecharias Frankel, this group began to advocate "Positive Historical Judaism"—a moderate approach to the reform of Judaism, based on sensitive historical research and insistent on the emancipation of the Jews, but equally dedicated to the preservation of Hebrew as the vehicle of Jewish prayer and to the centrality of the hope of returning to the Land of Israel. In sharp contrast to the Reform celebration of biblical Judaism as the true essence of the faith, Frankel and his colleagues believed that Judaism was a continuously evolving tradition. For them, the *Talmud* and rabbinic literature, as well as the Bible, were authentic expressions of Judaism and the building blocks of a modern, historically appropriate Jewish faith. (**See Reading 6-11.**)

This insistence on historical context and moderate reforms clearly separated Frankel and his colleagues from the third new force in German-Jewish life, the Orthodox movement. This group insisted on the eternal veracity of all aspects of Talmudic Judaism and an uncompromising observance of Jewish law as expounded by rabbis through the ages. But the new Orthodox movement, led by Rabbi Samson Raphael Hirsch, was committed as well to a restatement of Judaism in modern terms. Perhaps most importantly, Hirsch and his disciples unflinchingly campaigned for Jewish emancipation (which the more traditional Jews had come to abhor as destructive of Judaism). Hirsch attempted to present the doctrines and teachings of Rabbinic Judaism in a vocabulary accessible to university-trained German Jews and was prepared to accept a limited number of external modifications of the liturgy and service. Hirsch's most radical step, however, was to insist that only *his* version of Judaism was authentic: Reform and Positive Historical Judaism were perversions of the true Jewish faith and thus were not to be tolerated. He therefore encouraged his disciples to separate themselves as much as possible from Jewish communities that did not conform to the new Orthodox stance. (**See Reading 6-12.**)

By the last third of the nineteenth century, then, German Jewry had produced three distinct new religious responses to the challenges of modernity—Reform, Positive-Historical Judaism, and Orthodoxy—and a new approach to Jewish scholarship, the Science of Judaism.

## CULMINATION OF EMANCIPATION IN THE WEST

The intense religious and intellectual creativity of German-Jewish life in the mid-nineteenth century was at once a response to and a part of the remarkable flowering of culture and thought in Germany in these decades. In literature, art, music, philosophy, and countless other fields, Germany set the tone for the rest of Europe. It is fascinating to note that in all of these realms, many of the stellar figures were either themselves born Jewish or had forebears who had been baptized—for example, Heinrich Heine, Felix Mendelssohn (grandson of Moses Mendelssohn), and Karl Marx. Soon the political climate would change sufficiently to allow actively professing Jews to make as much of a mark in the outside world as their converted cousins.

Political advance for Jews in Germany and the rest of Central Europe was made possible by the fruitful intersection of two movements: liberalism and nationalism. The first quite naturally looked with favor on the emancipation of the Jews for reasons already discussed; the second was far more ambivalent, but was willing to make compromises that helped the overall cause of national liberation. In Germany and Italy the drive for unification of previously fragmented territories led to broader definitions of who could be included in the new national body politic. In the vast Austrian Empire, small communities claiming the status and prerogatives of nations vied with one another for the largest possible populations and opened their ranks to all who chose to identify with them. In many of these struggles, pragmatic political calculations forced those wishing the support of liberals to accept all planks in the liberal platform including the enfranchisement of the Jews.

Several small German principalities granted the Jews emancipation in the early 1860's, but it was the four-year period from 1867 to 1871 that witnessed the most dramatic concurrence of emancipatory decrees: Austria-Hungary in 1867, Prussia in 1869, Italy in 1870, and the remaining sections of the Second German Reich in 1871. The century-long battle for equal rights for the Jews was finally victorious throughout all of Central and Western Europe; the optimistic prognoses of the Enlightenment had vanquished the gloomy predictions of the fearful and the skepticism of the nationalists. From Berlin to Birmingham and from Prague to Palermo, the Jews were free and equal citizens of confident new states. The future, they were sure, shone brightly with promise and success. (**See Readings 6-13 and 6-14.**)

# EASTERN EUROPE

The 1860's and 1870's were a time of hope and high spirits for the Jews everywhere in Europe. But the millions of Jews in Russia and Poland shared only the optimism of their coreligionists in the West, not their political liberty. Emancipation was far off for the largest Jewish community in the world, which was ensconced in a social and political context very similar to that of the rest of Europe a century or two earlier.

There were about a million and a half Jews in Poland at the end of the eighteenth century when Russia, Prussia, and Austria partitioned the once great Polish-Lithuanian Commonwealth. In the place of a united Jewry, destitute but proud, between 1772 and 1795 four different East European Jewish communities were created. The smallest of the four, inhabiting the western part of former Poland, now found itself under Prussian administration. Over the course of the next century this Jewish community was rapidly Germanized and came completely into the orbit of Berlin. Indeed, most of the Jews left this territory as soon as they were allowed to move into the richer sections of Prussia.

The second community, in the southern province of Galicia, was transferred to Austrian control but remained defiantly Eastern in its culture and economy. The Jews of Galicia were almost entirely Hasidic, overwhelmingly poor, and largely impervious to influence from Vienna. The local Jewish elite emulated the Berlin Jewish Enlightenment, at first creating artistic, polemical, and even philosophical works in Hebrew, but soon falling under the sway of the German language and culture. As subjects of the Austrian emperor, the Galician Jews were emancipated in 1867 and increasingly came under the influence of the Polish language and culture as Polish became the official language of government and culture in Galicia.

The third group of East European Jewry lived in the central provinces of the former Polish state, ruled by the Russian tsar as the semi-independent Kingdom of Poland. Here the Jews at first enjoyed somewhat greater freedom than the Jews directly under Russian command. But as the struggle for Polish independence intensified in the nineteenth century, the autonomy and coherence of the kingdom diminished, and its populations came under the immediate supervision of the Russian bureaucracy.

The Jews living in the provinces of Lithuania, Belorussia, and the Ukraine, annexed to the Russian Empire, constituted the fourth, largest, and most influential of the East European Jewish communities. The Russian state, which had never tolerated any Jews in its midst, was now faced with an enormous Jewish population—approximately one million people—growing at a rapid pace, living in autonomous communities, speaking Yiddish, practicing traditional Judaism, and engaging in the time-honored Jewish businesses of petty trade, commerce, and crafts. (See Reading 6-15.) The problem for these Jews was that although they had not moved anywhere, they had entered a realm that was vastly different from the Polish context they had known and dealt with for centuries. The Russian Empire in the late eighteenth century was politically and socially similar to Western Europe in the sixteenth or seventeenth centuries. The monarch ruled as an unlimited autocrat with no brakes on his (or her) power; the nobility, clergy, and merchant classes were strictly fixed and controlled from above; the peasants were tied to the land in a type of serfdom unheard of in the west even in the Middle Ages. In short, the social and political revolutions that transformed Western European life, and thereby the fate of the Jews, were utterly foreign to the Russian lands.

At the precise moment that the Jews came under Russian control, however, the intellectual revolution of the West was making some headway in the elite groups in St. Petersburg and Moscow. The empress herself, Catherine the Great, avidly corresponded with some of the leading lights of the French and German Enlightenment and tried to introduce some of their teachings into Russian society. In regard to the Jews, Catherine was, at first, most pragmatic: perhaps they could bring to her realm some of the rational features of the European economy that she was seeking. She therefore argued strenuously for their right to participate in whatever organs of municipal government there were in Russia and to ply their trades without obstruction. Against those who believed that the Jews had absolutely no place in Russian society, Catherine insisted that the Jews could remain in the former Polish provinces and even move to some of the new areas she was opening up for commerce on the shores of the Black Sea. To her mind, then, the establishment of the Pale of Settlement—the regions of the Russian Empire in which the Jews were permitted to reside—was not a limitation on the Jews' rights but a protection of them. (See Reading 6-16.)

After the outbreak of the French Revolution, and especially after the execution of Louis XVI, Catherine recoiled from her faith in Western models of development, and the teachings of the Enlightenment and its philosophical descendents became anathema to the rulers of Russia. Western ideas and ideologies continued to seep across the frontiers of the empire, but they were accepted only by those opposed to the political status quo. The Jews in Russia in the nineteenth century were therefore in a situation analogous to that of the Jews of the West before the rise of the modern state: they were a tolerated minority with limited rights and obligations, enjoying far greater personal liberty than the vast majority of the population—the peasants—but substantially less freedom than the nobles and other privileged groups.

The problem, of course, was that this was the nineteenth century. On the one hand, the Jews were keenly aware of the fate of their brethren in the West. The Jewish Enlightenment movement gradually made its way from Berlin to Vienna to Galicia to the Russian Jewish communities where it found extremely fertile soil. Here the striving for a modern Jewish culture expressed itself not in philosophy, scholarship, or movements for religious reform, but in literature—Hebrew and Yiddish poetry, drama, novels, short stories. The overwhelming majority of the Jews in Russia were either oblivious to this new culture or antagonistic toward it, but the seeds were sown for a remarkable explosion of Jewish creativity within the context of political repression.

On the other hand, as an avid participant in international politics, the Russian government was well aware of developments in the rest of Europe and attempted to reap the benefits of Western progress without paying the price in individual liberty. Like the new Western states, then, the tsarist state began to insert itself more and more into the lives of its individual subjects without extending citizenship to them. For the Jews this meant that the age-old isolation and insularity of their communities were abolished, as they were in the West, but without emancipation. Equal rights were not feasible in a state that had no concept of equality. Thus, in the first half of the nineteenth century the Russian government began to intervene in unprecedented ways into the internal workings of Jewish society. Beginning in 1827 the Jews were conscripted into the army, in ways specifically designed to erode Jewish unity; in 1844 the autonomous Jewish community boards were abolished, without clearly specifying how the communities were to continue to exist; in the late 1840's and 1850's the government joined hands with the Jewish Enlightenment to create new secular schools for Jewish children designed to introduce them to Russian culture and the Russian language. (**See Reading 6-17.**)

The Jewish intellectual elite was thrilled by these developments, certain that in Russia they would lead to the same ends of liberty and justice as they had in the West. This optimism was particularly acute in the 1860's when the new tsar, Alexander II, emancipated the serfs, created a modern court system on the European model, introduced new agencies of self-government, and even permitted various categories of Jews—students, rich merchants, and artisans—to move outside the Pale of Settlement to the interior of Russia.

Both inside and outside the Pale, the Jewish Enlightenment was on the rampage; new journals were founded in Hebrew, Yiddish, and Russian; books, poems, plays, pamphlets, and articles were issued at a dizzying pace. More and more Jews were learning to speak and even think in Russian. The Jews began to flock to the Russian high schools and universities and thus began to learn about the new ideologies entering Russia from the West. Some young Jews became prominent members and theoreticians of clandestine political movements dedicated to overthrowing the tsarist regime. Most Jews, though, remained loyal to Russia and its rulers, awaiting better treatment, increased opportunities, and more freedom. (**See Reading 6-18.**)

These improvements, however, were not forthcoming. Alexander II was willing to go only so far in modernizing his empire; he had indeed emancipated the serfs, but in a manner that ensured their continued dependence on the land and the peasant communes. He allowed the introduction of some modern industries into Russia but refused to support them adequately. As the opposition to his regime and to tsarism as a whole became more popular and more violent, he became increasingly alarmed and suspicious of innovation.

The Jews suffered from this retrenchment both as ordinary subjects of the state and as Jews. In the first place, their numbers were growing rapidly, producing many more mouths to feed, but the government's restrictions on where they could live and how they could earn their keep left them in a frenzied bind. Some of the most enterprising among them, hearing that German Jews had been moving westward in the last few decades, left and attempted to seek their fortune in England or America. But emigration was an isolated phenomenon at this point. Most Jews wanted to remain at home with their families, to find some way of improving their lot in Russia. Many were fearful of the effects that moving even within Eastern Europe would have on their religious and communal life. Even some of the intellectuals began to have second thoughts about their devotion to the tsar and the gradual improvement of the status of the Jews in Russia—just how long would it take?

This skepticism was born not only out of impatience and disappointment, but also out of the new notions of nationalism that were taking hold in Western Europe and were heard faintly even in Russia. In the West, as we have seen, a new kind of nationalism tempered by liberalism had made possible the extension of the emancipation of the Jews and their inclusion in the national entity. In Russia, on the other hand, nationalism never evolved along liberal lines and only made people more xenophobic and suspicious of outsiders. The Jews, intrigued by the new concepts of liberal nationalism, naturally began to think of themselves as members of a modern nation. Unlike the Reformers in the West, they had, after all, not attempted to denationalize Judaism. They believed that the Jews shared a common past, a sense of identity, a variety of Jewish languages, a hope to return to a homeland. Moreover, they were sufficiently influenced by the Enlightenment to reject traditional religious precepts and beliefs. They accepted, in fact, the Enlightenment's distinction between religion and nationality and simply chose the other side of the coin. The Jews, they argued, were not a religious group but a nation. One could be a Jew regardless of one's private faith and even in the complete absence of religion. Granted, the nationality of the Jews was different from that of most modern nations in that the Jews lacked a territory, but some solution would be found to this problem. Perhaps some answers could even be found in socialism, the other rising new movement of the time.

In the late 1870's such thoughts began to appear in the journals that were the mainstay of Jewish ideological activity in Russia. Still hazy and unformulated, the ideas created no great waves in the Jewish public, no movements or parties. But very soon dramatic forces would propel these new ideas into the very center of practical politics.

## ANTI-SEMITISM, EMIGRATION, AND NEW POLITICAL PARTIES

These forces appeared almost simultaneously in the East and West although in different forms. In France and Germany various groups felt that they were losing out in the advance of the social, intellectual, and political revolutions: peasants unsuccessful in the transition to the new forms of agriculture or unhappy with their new lives in the cities; small shopkeepers or artisans unable to survive in the new competitive marketplace; gentry resentful of their loss of status and power; clergy offended by the attacks on established religion; artists edged out of the limelight by talented outsiders. These resentments were vague, undirected indictments of modernity; it was not clear who was to blame for the new set of circumstances, for all this dislocation and disruption.

One answer became increasingly appealing: the Jews were at fault, they had gained most from modernity, they had in fact been central in advancing the new forms of politics, economics, and art. These claims, like all "big lies," were based on a small degree of truth, exaggerated far out of proportion to reality. The Jews had indeed benefited from the social, economic, and cultural transformations of the last century, but they were obviously in no way responsible for the march of modernity. They were only bit players in a global drama. But the irrational singling out of the Jews became very serious when it was combined with two potent forces: traditional Christian hostility, stripped of its theological axes, and a new pseudo-science, racism.

Christian hostility to the Jews, present in all ages, was based on the belief that the Jews had rejected Jesus' claim to be the messiah and were moreover responsible for his death. The Church taught that the Jews must therefore always be inferior to Christians and be encouraged to repent and accept Jesus Christ. In this view the Jews as a group had to be tolerated until they mended their ways, and any Jew who was baptized lost the stigma of Jewishness. In ways difficult to understand, many non-Jews who lost their faith in Christianity retained the hostility toward the Jews which they had learned at church, but without the limitations that were imposed on that hostility by the religious teachings. A secularized hatred of Jews was more dangerous than its religious antecedent.

At the same time, this secularized hatred of Jews was buttressed by the claims of pseudo-scientists who jumbled together current notions of social science and natural science and propounded hypotheses about the biological differences of races. Mankind, they argued, was composed of a large number of separate races unequal in nature and ability. The Jews were held to be a race, and one that was inferior to the Aryan race that made up the Christian population of northern Europe. On the basis of these specious lessons, it was only natural to argue for the separation of the Jews from the rest of European society and the dangers of mixing Jews and gentiles.

Cunning politicians in the late 1870's and early 1880's in France and Germany manipulated this combination of attacks on the Jews into a potent political force. A word was coined for this new kind of hatred of Jews: anti-Semitism (based on the supposed existence of a separate Semitic race).

The Jews of Western Europe regarded the new anti-Semitic parties and movements as a minor irritant, a temporary relapse of medieval prejudice that would easily be vanquished along the road to progress. At most, Jews and their friends would have to sharpen their defenses, but no significant change in strategy or beliefs was called for. More confusing and problematic was the attraction of some representatives of socialism to the new anti-Semitic ideas. Socialists had historically supported the Jews and fought against national and religious stereotypes and oppression. Some socialists, however, saw in anti-Semitism a useful tool for harnessing support among the lower classes; others recast their hatred of capitalism into opposition to Jewish capitalists. The emergence of socialist anti-Semitism only accentuated and reinforced the firm commitment of most Western European Jews to liberal politics and parties.

This belief in the efficacy of liberalism and emancipation was dealt a severe blow in the last two decades of the nineteenth century. In the spring of 1881 Tsar Alexander II was assassinated in the streets of St. Petersburg by a group of revolutionaries. Many people, and particularly arch-conservative newspaper editors, blamed the Jews for this shocking act. Rumors began to spread that the government would look with favor upon any attacks on the Jews. This dangerous situation was aggravated by a terrible famine that year in Russia, which left hundreds of thousands of seasonal agricultural workers out of work, furious about the state of their lives, and angry at all changes in Russia. Around Easter of 1881 groups of these workers in the Ukraine began to attack Jews, sack their stores, and steal their property. As these acts of barbarism became known, the Russian word for massacre, pogrom, came into international usage. The pogroms continued through the spring and summer of 1881, abated for a while, and broke out again the next year. Hundreds of Russian Jews were maimed and left homeless; millions of others reacted with shock. They were certain that the Russian authorities had either planned these attacks or approved of them, and had instructed the army and police not to intervene. At the very least the government could no longer be trusted to protect the Jews, much less to improve their lot. (**See Reading 6-19.**)

The profound outrage that gripped the Jewish community in Russia, as well as Jews around the world, was exacerbated by shocking developments in the West. In 1894 Alfred Dreyfus, a Jew who was a captain in the French army and a member of the General Staff, was accused of spying for Germany. The evidence against Dreyfus was forged, but the fact that he was a Jew seemed to be sufficient to convict him, and he was sent to Devil's Island. Reactionary forces in France whipped up a campaign of anti-Semitism that threatened to reverse all the gains of the previous century. Crowds shouting "Death to the Jews!" appeared throughout the birthplace of Jewish emancipation. Soon evidence that proved Dreyfus's innocence was made public, but the French courts refused to cast aspersions on the honor of their military. The famous writer Emile Zola then lashed out against the government and led the growing pro-Dreyfus camp, which quickly came to include all those interested in preserving the Republic against its monarchist, militarist, and anti-Semitic enemies. By the end of the century, the "Dreyfus Affair" became the most controversial issue in French politics. In 1899 the highest court of appeal in France set aside Dreyfus's conviction and called for a court martial to reexamine the case. That resulted in a finding of guilty with extenuating circumstances, which was followed by a presidential pardon. Still, Dreyfus's supporters persisted, determined to establish his full innocence and to punish the true culprits. In 1906 another court of appeal set aside the ruling of the court-martial and declared the judgments against Dreyfus erroneous and wrongful. Dreyfus was decorated by the government and raised to the rank of major. (**See Reading 6-20.**)

In the end French justice triumphed. Most Jews in France and other Western countries breathed a heavy sigh of relief, grateful that their faith in emancipation had survived intact. Jewish leaders dedicated themselves to a renewed struggle against anti-Semitism in the name of liberty and justice for all. Organizations aimed at defending the Jews against attacks were established or fortified, and life returned to normal. But grave doubts began to gnaw at the facade of confidence: if anti-Semitism could explode with such frenzy in France, the birthplace of emancipation, what lessons could be drawn about the fate of the Jews in the East, or for that matter, in the modern world as a whole?

These doubts bore their first fruits in Russia. Here they combined with the search for a new kind of Jewish national self-identity that had emerged in the previous decade to issue a radically innovative hybrid: modern Jewish nationalism. University students and young intellectuals rejected the optimistic liberalism of their teachers in Eastern Europe or the West. Emancipation and enlightenment were not sufficient solutions to the plight of the Jews: anti-Semitism had rendered the previous answers sterile. What was needed, they declared, was auto-emancipation—Jews taking their future into their own hands and liberating themselves—and the creation of a new Jewish culture, a new Jewish personality: in short, a new kind of Jew.

The first, and ultimately most popular, version of auto-emancipation was Zionism, the belief that the liberation of the Jews is possible only in their ancestral homeland, the Land of Israel. Immediately after the first pogroms in Russia, pamphlets appeared arguing that anti-Semitism was an eternal problem that could only be resolved if Jews would leave non-Jewish countries and build their own society where they could best nourish and protect themselves. Only in their own land could the Jews implement the prescription laid out for them by the Enlightenment—a return to agriculture, a reform of the communal structure, a secularized culture. Groups of young Jews preaching this new gospel began to gather throughout the Russian Empire and other East European communities, and some brave adventurers even made their way to Turkish-controlled Palestine where they established settlements based on these new principles. Societies called "Love of Zion" attracted large numbers of Jews but lacked organizational coherence and effective leadership.

That coherence and leadership were soon to be provided by a remarkable personality, Theodor Herzl. Born in Budapest and raised in Vienna, Herzl was a successful journalist and playwright who was deeply troubled by the problems facing the Jews in the modern age. He concluded that the only answer was a Jewish state where the Jews could build the liberal society that they had hoped and worked for in the West. Herzl began to organize Jews who agreed with him and soon discovered that similar ideas had arisen in Russia. Applying his considerable literary, conceptual, and political talents to the task, Herzl created the Zionist movement. In 1897 in the city of Basle, Switzerland, the first Zionist Congress was held, gathering together Jews from around the world, who pledged themselves to build a Jewish homeland in the Land of Israel. Over the next few years the Zionist movement grew by leaps and bounds, attracting Jews mostly in Russia but also in the West. Soon the movement was split into a large number of subgroups, which argued with one another about the extent of cultural versus diplomatic activity that their cause required, whether the new Jewish society should be socialistic or capitalistic, secular or religious, how best to deal with the Arab population of Palestine and the empires that ruled the region. All these disagreements, however, were secondary to the basic premise shared by all Zionists—that the Jews' only hope was to leave Europe for the Land of Israel. (**See Readings 6-21 and 6-22.**)

Other modern Jewish nationalists disagreed. A group of intellectuals led by the prominent Jewish historian Simon Dubnov—who along with his political work succeeded in transplanting to Eastern Europe the methods and teaching of the German Science of Judaism—argued that the Zionist idea was attractive but hopelessly impractical. Instead, the Jews should strive to create enclaves of cultural and national autonomy for themselves in the countries in which they already lived. Nationalism, they declared, had progressed to the point at which territory was superfluous. The Jews, especially in Eastern and Central Europe, should retain their trust in Western civilization and ally themselves with liberal forces that supported national rights for all oppressed groups. (**See Reading 6-23.**)

This "Diaspora nationalism" was modified by a growing number of Jewish socialists in Russia, who argued that national autonomy for the Jews and freedom for all oppressed peoples could only come about by means of a socialist revolution. Identifying themselves with the emerging Jewish working class of Eastern Europe, they left the Russian Social Democratic Party and established the Jewish Workers' Bund—the Jewish socialist party—in 1897. The Bund fought at one and the same time for Jewish national rights, the creation of a proletarian Jewish culture in Yiddish—the language of the Jewish masses—and the victory of socialism throughout the world.

Other socialists, Jewish and non-Jewish, condemned the Bund's amalgam of socialism and nationalism as reactionary; one prominent Russian theorist labeled the Bundists "Zionists afraid of sea-sickness." Indeed, many Jews continued to flock to the wide variety of other revolutionary parties in Eastern and Central Europe and often assumed leadership roles within these organizations. In Russia Julius Martov led the Mensheviks, and Leon Trotsky became a potent force within the Bolshevik party. In Poland, Rosa Luxembourg rose from head of one of the local revolutionary parties to a prominent position in international socialism; in Germany and Austria Eduard Bernstein and Victor Adler played critical roles in the evolution of socialist theory and practice.

To be sure, the importance of the Jews in these revolutionary parties was but a part of the growing role Jews were playing in the political world of turn-of-the-century Europe. In England and France, and to a lesser extent in other countries as well, Jews were assuming cabinet posts in governments and influential positions in oppositional, but nonrevolutionary, parties. This new-found political prominence of individual Jews was itself only a small part of the overall increased participation of large numbers of Jews in the cultural and economic life of Europe. To list the names of famous writers, poets, composers, scientists, actors, inventors, lawyers, physicians, bankers, and musicians who were Jews would in some way misrepresent the phenomenon. What is important is not simply that a handful of world-renowned people were Jews, but that the vast creative abilities of millions of Jews throughout Europe were allowed to be unleashed and to play a mighty role in the development of modern culture, art, science, and business.

At the same time as these Jews were furthering the advance of European society, other Jews were dedicating themselves to the creation of a modern Jewish culture. German, French, Italian, English, Hungarian, Polish, Russian, and many other languages became instruments of Jewish scholarship, literature, and religious thought. In Eastern Europe Yiddish was transformed into a vehicle of modern sensibility by extraordinarily talented writers such as Sholem Aleichem, Y. L. Peretz, and Mendele Mokher Seforim. Hebrew was recreated as a thriving tongue by these writers and others, and most of all by the great poet Hayyim Nahman Bialik. In the last years of the nineteenth century and throughout the beginning of the twentieth, the Jewish population of Russia and Poland climbed to a zenith of cultural, religious, and ideological creativity. (See Reading 6-24.)

This same period, however, marked a sharp decline in the political and economic status of the Jews in Eastern Europe. The Russian government, under the reactionary tsars Alexander III and Nicholas II, increasingly blamed the Jews for the problems of the empire and further restricted their mobility, social advance, and economic opportunities. Thus, beginning in 1882, laws were passed forbidding the Jews from settling in villages and rural areas even within the Pale; quotas were set on the number of Jewish students in schools and universities; Jews were excluded from the Bar and other professions; and the livelihood of hundreds of thousands of poor Jews was compromised by added restrictions and regulations. New and bloodier pogroms erupted in 1903 and continued sporadically thereafter. Even the Russian Revolution of 1905, which instituted a constitution that guaranteed basic freedoms to all subjects of the tsar, including the Jews, and a parliament in which Jewish political parties were represented, did not mitigate the intensified poverty and desperation of the Jewish masses. On the contrary, the reactionary forces in Russian society blamed the Jews for the Revolution, and their feelings erupted in even more pogroms and vicious anti-Semitism.

The Jews in Eastern Europe struggled valiantly to resist the evils that had befallen them and renewed their determination not only to survive but also to improve their lives physically, morally, and culturally. One way to do so was to move away from home, to seek one's fortune in a bigger city. In the last decades of the nineteenth century the tendency toward urbanization, noticeable among East European—as well as Western—Jews throughout the modern period, increased even more sharply as Jews flocked to the great cities of the Russian Empire. From 1870 on large numbers of Russian Jews began to go even farther: to America. After the pogroms of 1881–82, the option of emigrating to other, safer shores became more and more attractive. Between 1881 and 1914 approximately three million Jews, roughly a third of the Jewish population of Eastern and Central Europe, joined millions of others who were emigrating to the West. Some of these migrating Jews settled in the large cities of Western Europe—Berlin, Paris, London—where they transformed the local Jewish communities. Others followed their Zionist hopes to Palestine, creating a network of agricultural settlements based on communal ownership of land and property. But the overwhelming majority of Jewish emigrants flocked to the major target of the global migration of these years: the United States of America. Here they helped create an entirely new kind of Jewish community, unique in the annals of Jewish history.

When World War I broke out in August 1914 the Jews were not conscious of the fact that the long chapter of their history that began in the mid-eighteenth century was over. From a small minority, isolated politically and socially, the Jews had been thrust into the vortex of modern European society. Propelled by the intellectual, political, and social revolutions that created the modern world, the Jews faced unprecedented opportunities and disturbing new challenges. They responded by inventing new forms and patterns of Jewish life and by participating wholeheartedly in the creation of the modern world. Perhaps they were fortunate not to know what awaited them around the bend.

*Editor's Questions*
AFTER VIEWING AND READING

- What did Moses Mendelssohn counsel Jews who were unsure of how to approach the promises of Enlightenment and emancipation?
- What was the process whereby all the Jews of France were emancipated? Did Napoleon attempt to rescind the grant of equal rights to the Jews?
- How did Napoleon's defeat affect the Jews of Central Europe? Why did the Jews in 1848 believe that emancipation was finally at hand?
- How did the Reform movement attempt to refashion Judaism? How did other Jewish groups respond to the process of emancipation?
- Describe Jewish enlightenment efforts in Russia. How were these attempts greeted by the majority of the Russian Jews? Why was the situation so different from that in Western Europe?
- Define anti-Semitism. What were some of the major points of anti-Semitic ideology? How did the Dreyfus affair become a referendum on the status of Jews in France? How did it affect Theodor Herzl?
- Why did anti-Semitism in Eastern Europe erupt in physical attacks against the Jews? How did the Bundists and Zionists respond to this challenge?

SUGGESTED READINGS

Salo W. Baron, "The Modern Age," in Leo W. Schwarz, ed., *Great Ages and Ideas of the Jewish People* (Modern Library, 1956)

Lucy Dawidowicz, *The Golden Tradition* (Beacon, 1967)

Jacob Katz, *Out of the Ghetto* (Harvard University Press, 1973)

# 7

# The Golden Land
# (1654 to 1932)

## Michael Stanislawski

*Editor's Suggestions*
BEFORE VIEWING THE SHOW

Examine Chart 1 found in this chapter of the *Study Guide*.

*Overview of the TV Program*

The show opens with scenes of Russian Jews emigrating to the United States in the late nineteenth century. These Jews, however, were not the first to come to this country. Earlier refugees from the Spanish and Portuguese Inquisitions had come to South America and the Caribbean, and in 1654 twenty-three individuals had arrived in New Amsterdam, site of present-day New York. Peter Stuyvesant, the Dutch governor, wished to deport the Jews but the Dutch West India Company refused his request.

Some Jews lived in the colonies on the eve of the Revolution, were involved in the fighting, and helped in the financial backing of the rebel cause. According to the Founding Fathers, all people were to possess liberty, and as George Washington indicated in his speech to the Newport Jews, this statement clearly included the Jews.

An influx of German Jews burst upon these shores in the 1840's, and these immigrants participated in the American movement westward. Jews were pioneers and took up the roles of peddlers, shopkeepers, and, later, entrepreneurs helping fuel industrial expansion. Despite the Jews' successful integration into America, there were instances of anti-Semitism during the Civil War even as the Jews fought alongside their neighbors on both sides of the conflict.

Due to the economic strangulation and physical oppression suffered by Russian Jews in the late nineteenth century, America

193

witnessed a large-scale Jewish migration from tsarist lands. The immigrants worked mainly in the New York garment trade, often in unsanitary and dangerous conditions. The Triangle Shirtwaist Company fire galvanized the immigrants to band together to alleviate their harsh working situations. Thus the seed was planted for the growth of labor unions.

The Jewish immigrants wished to acculturate into American society and pursued education as a means to achieve full integration. The uptown German Jews helped their poorer brethren, but this assistance often caused friction with their downtown coreligionists. The immigrants founded mutual aid societies and helped each other to adjust to the new country and to overcome the hard economic times.

As the Jews emerged from their original immigrant settlements, they turned to other neighborhoods within the cities or moved to new areas across the nation. They attended American universities and pursued careers in high-risk industries such as moviemaking and show business.

Social anti-Semitism in the 1920's was fueled in part by the activities of Henry Ford, who published the infamous anti-Semitic pamphlet, "The Protocols of the Elders of Zion." These nativist sentiments were translated into political realities when the Congress of the United States passed immigrant quota laws which effectively shut down the Jewish migration to this country.

*Watch for . . . and Think about*

Observe the pictures of houses of shipping families, artifacts of the sea trade, and the synagogues of the Colonial Era. How did the early American Jews earn their livelihood?

Note the German Jewish peddlers and then the factories and department stores owned by these immigrants in the mid-nineteenth century. How did this wave of immigrants achieve prosperity?

At the beginning of the show you will see photographs of the ships that brought the Russian Jewish immigrants to this country. Observe the immigrants themselves. Later in the show you will glimpse the tenements in which they lived, the factories where they worked, and the machines they used. Reflect on the life of the turn-of-the-century Jewish refugees.

WHILE READING THE *STUDY GUIDE* AND *SOURCE READER*

Look for the following:

- Why the first Jews came to North America and how they were greeted. During the Revolution, did the Jews have to struggle for religious freedom?
- Why the German Jewish immigrants moved away from the old centers of population. Did this move affect their religious life?
- What drove Russian Jews to these shores in the late nineteenth and early twentieth centuries. How did they earn a living upon their arrival? Did they maintain a Jewish culture in their adopted land?
- How the rise of anti-Semitism in America affected American Jewry.

---

# THE BEGINNINGS OF AMERICAN JEWRY

The millions of Jews who flocked to America in the years from 1881 to the start of World War I found in their new home a vibrant Jewish community that dated back over two hundred years. In September 1654 twenty-three Jews arrived in New Amsterdam from the Brazilian colony of Recife, which had recently been recovered by Portugal after a brief Dutch occupation. These Jews had come to Recife, as well as to countless other colonies in Latin America and the Caribbean, as part of the great Sephardic migration that followed the expulsion of the Jews from Spain in 1492 and Portugal in 1497. In the New World, communities were established by Jews of Iberian origin who came from Amsterdam, London, and other centers of the Sephardic Diaspora, as well as by New Christians who decided to return to their ancestral faith in these islands of religious and economic experimentation. Sometimes Old World prejudices and problems were visible in the new colonies as well: when Portugal recaptured Recife, for example, it brought with its flag a prohibition on Jewish settlement. The Jews once more were forced to seek a place of refuge.

Those who found their way to New Amsterdam were not welcomed with open arms by Peter Stuyvesant, its Dutch governor.

Stuyvesant appealed to his superiors in the Dutch West India Company for permission to deport these representatives of what he called the "deceitful race." His request was denied. The Dutch West India Company was indebted to Jewish investors in Amsterdam and recognized that the Jews from Brazil had suffered enough and would serve the new enterprise in North America well. The Jews were therefore allowed to remain in New Amsterdam but were forbidden to practice their faith publicly. (**See Reading 7-1.**)

This inauspicious beginning of what was to become the largest and freest Jewish community in the world was quickly overcome by the forces of progress and liberty. While Stuyvesant's protest was being debated, more Jews arrived in the city. Within a few years the rights of Jews to settle, to own property, to conduct retail and wholesale trade, and even to serve in the militia was established in practice and by law. In 1666 New Amsterdam was taken by Britain and renamed New York. As British rule was extended from Maine to Georgia, Jewish communities gradually began to crop up throughout the colonies: Newport in 1677, Philadelphia in 1745, Charleston in 1750, Montreal in 1760, Savannah in 1773.

The most prominent members of these communities were rich Sephardic merchants, and the synagogues they established consequently followed the Spanish and Portuguese rite. Often the houses of worship were supported by contributions from prominent Sephardic communities in the Caribbean and Europe. But almost from the beginning these congregations and communities had an Ashkenazic majority. From London, Amsterdam, and other western ports, local Jews as well as German, Bohemian, and even some East European immigrants set sail for the new territories. There they readily adjusted both to the general character of colonial America and to the Sephardic dominance of Jewish life.

After all, the Sephardim were wealthier and more successful, and hence more American. Moreover, the Spanish and Portuguese Jews looked and acted more like the other colonists, and the new Jewish immigrants set out to emulate that cultural and religious adaptation. For the Ashkenazic Jews, rather unconcerned with religious formalities—or how could they have come in the first place?—appearing to be Sephardic meant seeming to be more American. And so the first synagogue in Philadelphia, Mikveh Israel, followed the Spanish and Portuguese customs although all of its founders were Ashkenazim. Even in the most famous shrine of Sephardic America in Newport, Rhode Island, two of the three trustees of the synagogue were of Ashkenazic families.

But the very point of being in America was that such Old World distinctions and sensibilities were irrelevant. The colonies nurtured newness and separation from the ways of Europe particularly in matters of faith. Religious tolerance was as natural to America as was its climate. Many, if not most, of the Christian colonists had come to these wild shores in the first place in order to seek a haven from religious persecution. How could an established church be imposed on this motley crew of Puritans, Quakers, Pietists, Catholics, Lutherans, Presbyterians, and Anglicans? Even if members of a certain denomination were dominant in one particular area—as were Puritan Congregationalists in New England and Quakers in Pennsylvania, for example—they were outsiders in others and thus were predisposed to tolerance as a means of survival, if not salvation. In colonial days, and after Independence as well, the common sentiment in America was that any religion was welcome so long as it advanced good deeds, moral behavior, and ethical precepts.

The Jews were therefore considered just another religious group among many. Their previous history of persecution and flight was hardly unique in these parts. On the contrary, many of the dissident sects cast themselves in biblical images as the Children of Israel struggling against Pharoah, Goliath, and even Rome. Some of these groups, in line with the Reformation's Hebraism, took very seriously the cultivation of the Hebrew language (Harvard College's commencement addresses in Hebrew as well as Latin and Greek were only the most public example of the study of Hebrew in America). Sometimes this affection for Hebrew was extended to the contemporary "Hebrews." For the Puritans in New England, just as for their forebears in the mother country, the reunion of the old Israel with the new Israel was an important aspect of the dream of redemption.

This religious egalitarianism intertwined with ideological, economic, social, and political factors to produce a society uniquely receptive to the Jews. The basic Enlightenment precept of the essential equality of all mankind found widespread acceptance, as did the corollary belief in the separation of church and state. Although the bulk of the colonists were farmers, trade was regarded as a valued and noble enterprise, and absolutely no stigma was attached to being a businessman. Finally, the absence of any social hierarchy worthy of notice—no native aristocracy, gentry, or privileged clergy—made it possible for newcomers to rise to positions of comfort and even power without hurdling the barriers of inherited class and privilege. This radical departure from the English model was even confirmed by the Parliament in London, which in 1740 granted dissident Protestants and Jews in the Colonies rights which were withheld from them at home: after seven years of residence, they could be naturalized as equal to native-born subjects, and they were exempted from taking oaths "on the true faith of a Christian." As the decades progressed, the few minor religious restrictions found in local law codes were increasingly ignored. By 1776 the Jews in the Thirteen Colonies, for all practical purposes, enjoyed the same political status as all American subjects of the Crown.

Still, most American Jews were avid supporters of independence. They shared the rebels' economic grievances, antagonism to European authority, and fundamental commitment to the "self-evident truth" that "all men are created equal, that they are endowed by their Creator with certain inalienable rights, that among these are life, liberty, and the pursuit of happiness." Jews enthusiastically embraced Thomas Jefferson's bill for establishing absolute freedom of religion (first legislated in Virginia in 1785) and then enshrined as the first amendment of the U.S. Constitution. By these acts, the emancipation of the Jews in the United States was certified without any special legislation—indeed, without even any mention of the Jews. (See Readings 7-2 and 7-3.)

As a symbol of their unique status in world Jewry, the Jews of Newport in August 1790, greeted their guest, George Washington, with a message of welcome that thanked God for "a government which to bigotry gives no sanction, to persecution no assistance." The first President responded with a reaffirmation of the principles of religious and political liberty and a prayer that "the children of the stock of Abraham" continue to live in peace and harmony in the new republic. (See Readings 7-4, 7-5, and 7-6.)

Washington's prayer was an apt description of the contemporary circumstances of American Jewry. As the power and prestige of the federal government grew, the few limitations on complete Jewish participation in political life that persisted in several state constitutions, at least on paper, fell to the wayside. By 1826, when the last archaic restrictions were rescinded in Maryland, the Jews were beyond question a secure and integral part of American society. (See Reading 7-7.)

Chart 1    Jewish Population of the United States, 1776–1967

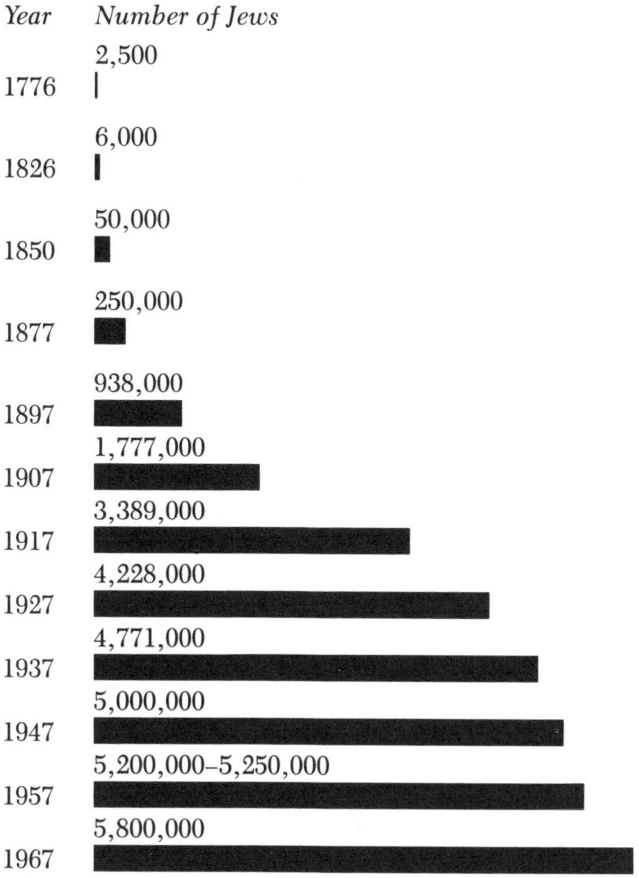

| Year | Number of Jews |
|------|----------------|
| 1776 | 2,500 |
| 1826 | 6,000 |
| 1850 | 50,000 |
| 1877 | 250,000 |
| 1897 | 938,000 |
| 1907 | 1,777,000 |
| 1917 | 3,389,000 |
| 1927 | 4,228,000 |
| 1937 | 4,771,000 |
| 1947 | 5,000,000 |
| 1957 | 5,200,000–5,250,000 |
| 1967 | 5,800,000 |

But on the world Jewish canvas, the U.S. community was a tiny, marginal landscape at the very edge of the civilized world. In 1776 there were probably about two thousand Jews in America; fifty years later their numbers had only increased to six thousand. Perhaps more Jews came than were represented in the congregational tallies—in the United States as nowhere else, affiliating with the Jewish community was entirely a matter of choice. Jews who wanted to have no connections with other Jews did not have to sever any formal link or become Christians. They could simply blend into the limitless melange of immigrants that was America.

The crucial fact about American Jews at this or any other time was that the vast majority *did* voluntarily organize themselves into communities; they built synagogues and imparted their heritage to their children. At the beginning of the nineteenth century these acts were particularly problematic not only because of the small size of American Jewry, but also because the Jewish communities were not exactly overflowing with cultural riches and traditional Jewish learning. Most of the native Jews, as well as the immigrants who continued to arrive in small numbers from Central and Western Europe, probably knew, observed, and transmitted the rudiments of their religion, but not much more than that.

## THE GERMAN IMMIGRATION

This situation changed most dramatically in the decades between 1820 and 1870 during which 150,000 Jews arrived in the United States from Germany. They came to escape narrowing economic opportunities and disappointing political conditions, as well as to share in the glorious age of expansion and reform that characterized the Jacksonian era and its aftermath. Unlike previous Central European Jews who came to the States, the new immigrants were entrepreneurial, German-speaking, and defiantly proud of their culture and heritage. When they settled in the established Jewish communities of the eastern seaboard, they founded their own congregations and practiced Ashkenazic customs. Thus, for example, in 1825 a group of German Jews in New York broke away from Shearith Israel, the Spanish and Portuguese synagogue, to found B'nai Jeshurun, the first German-Jewish house of worship in the city, and also to separate themselves from the rather casual attitude toward observance that marked the members of the older establishment.

But the remarkable fact about the German immigrants was their reluctance to remain in the old centers of Jewish population. On the contrary, they eagerly and rapidly spread across the continent, joining in the settlement of the territories up and down the Mississippi and Ohio rivers, on the shores of the Great Lakes, and even westward to California. The Jewish community in San Francisco, founded in 1849 in the heat of the Gold Rush, grew by leaps and bounds as business boomed for dry goods, mining equipment, and other provisions. (Among the peddlers was Levi Strauss, who sold cloth overalls to the miners.) By the outbreak of the Civil War in 1861, there were one hundred and sixty Jewish communities throughout the length and breadth of the United States, most spearheaded by the new immigrants from Germany.

The legendary pattern of German-Jewish success in America began with a son sent out from home with a bit of capital which was soon transformed into the basic pack of a peddler and carried to a new territory where competition was scarce and demand high. After accumulating enough funds to support a family, a wife—or a relative deemed suitable to be a wife—was sent for, and perhaps brothers and cousins as well. The peddler soon turned into a small shopkeeper or cotton broker and then into a comfortable merchant, a pillar of the commercial establishment of Memphis, Minneapolis, Cleveland, Des Moines, or Seattle. In many of these places the German Jews were active in German cultural and educational institutions and were not easily distinguishable as a group by outsiders. At the same time, however, the German Jews were enthusiastically American—and more: they took on the regional coloration of the areas in which they lived. There were now self-identified southern Jews and northern Jews, mid-westerners and Californians, Bostonians (if not quite Yankees!), Chicagoans, and New Yorkers. (**See Reading 7-8.**) Indeed, when the Confederacy seceded from the Union in the spring of 1861, Jews were identified with both causes in the struggle, fought under both flags, and many died on both sides. (**See Reading 7-9.**)

The fragmentation within the Jewish community by now was not simply geographic and cultural but religious as well. Along with the peddlers and brides from Germany came rabbis, who imported the spiritual and ideological ferment that was transforming Jewish life in Berlin, Frankfurt, Hamburg, and Fürth. From the start the demand for religious reform was joined with the call for the Americanization of Judaism—the creation of a mode of Jewish worship and self-expression appropriate in a pluralistic and progressive environment. At first the changes were modest and primarily aesthetic in nature. But soon Reform in America became much more radical than its European parent, both in practice and in theory. In regard to observance, for example, only in the States did the separation of the sexes cease in the synagogue with the introduction of mixed seating and family pews. Ideologically, Reform rabbis in America went much further than their German colleagues in arguing for the denationalization of Judaism and the identification of its mission with political liberalism. A few American rabbis even went so far in harmonizing

Judaism with the American ideal that the difference between their beliefs and Unitarianism was difficult to discern. One of the most famous of these radicals, Felix Adler, took the next logical step and created, on the centenary of the Revolution, a new religion called Ethical Culture, which was meant to provide a uniquely American distillation of the common faith of Christians and Jews.

The mainstream of the Reform movement rejected such extremism and met with great success, gradually capturing the allegiance of the majority of synagogues in America. In 1873 the newly triumphant Reform temples banded together in the Union of American Hebrew Congregations, the first such association in the land; their predominance was capped by the establishment of the first American rabbinical seminary, Hebrew Union College, in the important Jewish community of Cincinnati in 1875.

Alongside the growing number of temples and synagogues was an impressive number of social organizations and charitable institutions, serving the internal needs of the Jewish community as well as society at large. Philanthropy became a hallmark of American Jewry in this period, demonstrating a productive compatibility of social conscience and economic advance. American Jews were now as a group financially secure and upwardly mobile. There were, of course, still some peddlers, tailors, and skilled workers, but they constituted only a small fraction of the community as a whole. Most Jews were well entrenched in the middle- and upper-middle classes: retail merchants, wholesale brokers, salesmen, professionals, bankers, commercial agents. At the top of the community were the most famous members of the German-Jewish elite, men who stood at the forefront of important sectors of the American economy. Investment banking was transformed by the Schiffs, Warburgs, Loebs, and Seligmans. Merchandising was revolutionized by the Gimbels, Altmans, Bloomingdales, Sakses, Filenes, Magnins, Neimanns, and Marcuses, as well as the Strauses, who bought out the Macys, and the Rosenwalds, who took over a mail order firm called Sears, Roebuck and Co.

These business leaders dominated a Jewish community which had grown to 280,000 by 1877 but was still socially, religiously, and culturally homogeneous. Since 1870, however, a new phenomenon had appeared within American Jewry that would in a matter of a few years radically reshape its demographic, political, and social profile. East European Jews began arriving en masse in the United States.

# MASS MIGRATION FROM EASTERN EUROPE

From 1870 to 1880 approximately 30,000 Jews fled the economic hardships of Russia, Poland, Galicia, and Rumania to seek opportunity in America. They were the harbingers of a spectacular migration that would turn American Jewry into the largest Jewish community in the world. This immigration has been almost universally misunderstood as a direct response to the political repression of the Jews in Russia and especially to the pogroms. But it is easily demonstrated that pogroms and legalized anti-Semitism were not the decisive causes of this move. First, the large-scale emigration of East European Jews began in the decade before the pogroms; second, Jews left Galicia, where they were emancipated and where there were no pogroms at the same rate as they left Russia and Poland; third, Jews left Eastern Europe at the same time and in roughly the same proportions as non-Jewish Eastern Europeans—Russians, Lithuanians, Ukrainians, and others—all headed for a better life in the United States; and finally, the Jews were but a tiny part of the massive immigration to America by millions upon millions of Europeans in the latter part of the nineteenth and early years of the twentieth century—the timing and patterns of Greek and Italian migrations, for example, bore striking resemblance to that of the Jews.

In short, the emigration of millions of Jews from Eastern Europe was not caused by pogroms and political repression but by the biological and economic dynamics of Jewish life in Russia, Poland, and Galicia. The Jewish populations of these lands had grown at a remarkable pace throughout the nineteenth century, far outstripping the rate of the non-Jewish population. As a result, there were simply too many Jews to feed in the limited environment of these backward lands. An outlet had to be found. Political and legal restrictions limited the possibilities of change in Eastern Europe—and the United States was accessible and accepting. When the pogroms erupted, they served only as the last straw, a further incentive to continue what had already become a critical turn in the history of the Jews in Eastern Europe.

Over two million Eastern European Jews came to America in this vast migration. Most were from Russia and Poland, about a fifth from Galicia, and some four percent from Rumania. What began as an impressive but still modest flow in the early 1880's grew into a huge movement in the early 1890's, and snowballed into a massive exodus during the first decade of the new century. In the twenty years from 1880 to 1900 the Jewish population of the United States quadrupled, reaching the one million mark. In the five years of heaviest immigration, 1904–08, almost 650,000 East European Jews arrived in the United States. In 1880 East European Jews constituted about one-sixth of American Jewry; by the end of the era of mass migrations, five out of every six American Jews were of East European origin. (See Reading 7-10.)

Unfortunately, exactly who the East European immigrants were cannot be documented in any satisfactory way. American immigration officials were inundated by millions of foreigners, speaking hundreds of tongues, and desperately eager to answer any question put to them in what they guessed was the most acceptable fashion, regardless of its relation to reality. The records and statistics that do exist, therefore, are both very spotty and difficult to take at their word. But a few generalizations are possible. The other immigrant groups that came to America in these years included large numbers of workers who came to find temporary succor and employment, and then returned home to their families with their profits. The Jews came to stay; only a minuscule number ever left. In line with these intentions, the Jewish immigration was much more a family affair than that of any other group. Although, like all other migrants at all times, the typical East European Jewish immigrant to America was a young male of working age, women comprised a far larger percentage of the total than usual, as did young children and older parents. Not all the Jews who arrived in America, of course, had their wives, children, or parents in tow. Very often a man would come by himself and then save up enough money to send for his family.

It appears, in addition, that the Jewish immigrants included a greater proportion of skilled workers than either the other immigrants or the Jews who stayed behind. It also seems likely that most East European Jews came to America from larger cities and towns, and that many had gone through a previous urbanization in Russia itself. It can be assumed—although it is impossible to prove—that those Jews who came were more adventurous and less bound by religious and familial inhibitions than those who stayed behind. Certainly the rabbis and other spiritual authorities in Eastern Europe consistently discouraged pious Jews from immigrating to the States— which had become renowned as a place of religious laxity, if not outright sin.

Despite their presumed adventurousness and unlike their German-Jewish predecessors, the East European immigrants flocked to the big cities and especially to New York. The tiny Lower East Side of Manhattan soon sheltered a staggering number of Russian and Polish Jews—over half a million by World War I—and became a Yiddish-speaking enclave in the New World. Smaller neighborhoods in Chicago, Philadelphia, and Boston exhibited the same characteristics. The Jews called America the *goldene medine*—the golden land, and although almost none took literally the cliché that money flowed in the streets, most expected their lives here to be easy. Few were prepared for the horrors that awaited them.

The immigrants lived in tenement houses that were ugly when new and soon became decrepit and filthy. They huddled in crowded rooms and shared wretched kitchen and bathroom facilities in cold-water flats. At work, which usually meant the garment trade, conditions were hardly better. The infamous "sweatshops" were dens of dank, airless, unrelieved exploitation. But the Jews knew in their bones that these conditions were temporary. They believed wholeheartedly that life would improve if they worked hard enough, stuck together, and persevered. Even when objective reality was far less amenable than it had been in the Old Country, the immigrants gloried in the air of freedom and kept their eyes fixed on the light of prosperity that flickered at the end of the long, dark tunnel.

Along the way they helped one another, primarily through mutual-aid societies that were organized by town or region of origin: *landsmanshaft* societies, as they were called, lent money without interest, garnered information on jobs and apartments, organized cultural and social events, built small synagogues, dressed brides, buried the dead, and in general provided a sense of belonging that was missing in the bewildering new city. In time, many of these societies became politicized, as the internal controversies of East European Jewish life crossed the ocean—Zionism, socialism, Yiddishism, Enlightenment, anarchism, in innumerable hues whose distinctions were often exceedingly subtle. (**See Reading 7-12.**)

Many of these ideologies had little effect on the community at large, but one succeeded in mobilizing hundreds of thousands of Jews to take their lives into their own hands and improve the conditions they encountered in their new home. The socialist movement made such headway in this largely working-class, literate, and highly political population that, in 1914, one socialist leader, Meyer London, was elected to Congress from the Lower East Side, and in 1917, another of its stars, Morris Hillquit, gained twenty-two percent of the mayoralty vote in New York City.

But the major arena of success of socialist organizing among the immigrants was not in the ballot box but at the sweatshop. Jewish trade unions became the dominant political and social network among the East European Jews in America and a crucial force in the growth and consolidation of the labor movement in the country as a whole. Jewish men and women employed in the garment industry in New York and other major industrial centers, whether committed to socialism or not, brought with them from Eastern Europe ingrained habits of self-help, artisan cooperation, and a fundamental belief that America would brook no oppression, no unfair treatment of workers or of any other part of society. These Jews were a perfect breeding ground for working-class organizations. The beginnings of the Jewish unions were, however, slow and chaotic, immensely complicated by the multitude of conflicting ideologies pulling the workers in different directions. Political controversies continued, but after the turn of the century the sheer numbers of Jewish needleworkers seeking protection and change propelled the union movement into solidarity and cooperation. In 1900 the International Ladies' Garment Workers' Union was formed, galvanizing many disparate threads in the Jewish laboring class. After the depression of 1907-08 a series of major strikes broke out in the Jewish industries and continued for the next several years. In 1911 a fire in one of the largest garment shops in New York, the Triangle Shirtwaist Company, caused the death of one hundred and forty-six workers, mostly young women, and highlighted the desperate conditions in the factories and sweatshops. Throngs of strikes broke out in New York, Chicago, and other major manufacturing centers; their successful settlement further consolidated the rising trade union movement. By World War I the ILGWU (International Ladies' Garment Workers' Union), the Amalgamated Clothing Workers of America, and other large laborers' organizations spearheaded by East European Jews became a potent force in American life and politics. (See **Reading 7-11**.)

The intense political and organizational life in the immigrant community was matched by and often inspired a cultural efflorescence that for the first time put the United States on the map as a primary locus of Jewish creativity. New York became a center of Yiddish literature that rivaled Warsaw, Odessa, and Vilna, as writers exposed to the American literary scene began to experiment with novel techniques and innovative genres. Even more popular was the flourishing Yiddish theatre in New York, which reached unprecedented heights in mass entertainment as well as highbrow art, and had a lasting influence on American musical theatre and comedy.

But the most important medium in the Yiddish language was the press, which blossomed in the open political climate of America, where censorship, the scourge of East European Jewish journalism, was entirely absent. At the turn of the century every major immigrant Jewish community in America either had or would soon produce its own Yiddish newspaper. In New York alone there were already twelve Yiddish dailies. The most successful of these, the *Jewish Daily Forward*, climbed to a daily circulation of 200,000 and became a fountain of news and political information from the trade-union perspective. The *Forward* published pulp novels and serious literature, marriage offers and advice to the lovelorn. Equally important, the *Forward* and other newspapers served as a peerless conduit of American ideas to the immigrant community. Ironically, these purveyors of the Yiddish word also helped teach English to the newcomers, not in formal language lessons but through the repetition of terms and concepts ranging from subway to income tax to San Juan Hill.

The Americanization of the East European immigrants was not a simple matter, however. To begin with, there was no consensus on exactly what Americanization meant: just how much of their native culture, their customs, their heritage should the immigrants lose? The religious life of the Jews in Eastern Europe was governed by strict social controls and rhythms that were absent from, and sometimes profoundly alien to, the American context. Abstaining from work on the Sabbath, for example, resulted in a tremendous financial sacrifice that could not be sustained by most immigrants; at the very least, it demanded a boundless devotion to faith that most of the immigrants lacked or left behind in Russia. More critically, educating the young was the primary goal of Jewish parents through the centuries; this dedication had reached its peak in Eastern Europe. In the United States the East European Jews found a free, nonsectarian public school system that eagerly enrolled their children, taught them English, and prepared them for life in their new home. But the public school provided an unprecedented challenge, as well as an opportunity, to the age-old Jewish dedication to learning: how would the traditional Jewish curriculum—the Bible, Hebrew prayers, the *Talmud*—be transmitted to the next generation? Synagogues and traditional learning were increasingly associated with the life left behind, and masses of children channelled their zeal and intelligence to secular studies, remaining ignorant of even the basics of Jewish learning.

For a long while American Jews had improvised a solution to this quandary—a Hebrew school that would hold classes after regular school hours and on Sunday mornings to impart the basics of Judaism and the Hebrew language. But the existing institutions of this kind were inaccessible to the East European immigrants for a variety of reasons, not least of which was the schools' almost universal affiliation with the Reform movement, which was utterly foreign to the newcomers' perception of Judaism. On the Lower East Side and in similar Jewish neighborhoods elsewhere in America, attempts were made to create a Yiddish version of such after-hours schools, but the pressures of poverty and the attractions of the street took their toll. German-Jewish leaders sought to bridge the gap between immigrant life and Judaism by creating new institutions that would appeal to the Eastern Europeans; thus, for example, the Jewish Theological Seminary of America, established in 1887 as a traditional school for rabbis, was reorganized in 1902 as the home of the nascent Conservative movement, self-consciously aimed at the new immigrants. But it would take some time for this new amalgam to take hold among the masses of East European Jews.

This educational dilemma was but one of the many aspects of immigrant life that disturbed the German-Jewish establishment. Even more upsetting were the political radicalism of the newcomers and their general lack of middle-class gentility and culture. Undoubtedly many well-heeled, "proper" German Jews who felt themselves entirely integrated into American life and society feared that their status and achievements would be compromised by implicit association with the East Europeans. Relations between the old and new communities were at first both tense and tenuous. Many charitable and educational institutions were founded, but a deep chasm separated the givers and the receivers. (See Reading 7-13.)

## A UNITED COMMUNITY

This inner split was slowly healed in the wake of external problems that emerged both in Europe and in the United States. The Kishinev pogrom of 1903 and the subsequent deteriorating political situation of the Jews in Russia evoked outrage throughout all parts of American Jewry. Protest rallies were called, which brought together immigrant politicians, uptown leaders, and prominent American public figures. Talented and enlightened Establishment rabbis such as Judah Magnes and Stephen Wise recognized the integrity, authenticity, and magnanimity of the immigrant community and preached trust and concerted action to both old and new communities. In 1906 the German-Jewish elite founded the American Jewish Committee, dedicated to defending the civil and religious rights of all Jews at home and abroad. While social intercourse between the German elite and the newcomers remained limited, their political and communal—and increasingly, even their cultural—goals coalesced.

To some extent this meeting of the two communities was a response to an ugly new phenomenon that had grown in the United States in the last years of the nineteenth century: an American variety of anti-Semitism. Following the Depression of 1890 and the Panic of 1893, fear that the age of unlimited expansion was over—and that farmers would forever be poorer and currency unstable—combined with the natural striving for a definable identity on the part of a heterogeneous population. Fed by the new racial theories popularized in France and Germany at the time, the idea was born that the "real" American—white, Anglo-Saxon, Protestant, agricultural—was being overrun by hordes of swarthy East and South Europeans—Jews and Italians. These dangerous foreigners were not only threatening the "racial purity" of America, but were importing anarchism, communism, and other enemies of Christianity to the pristine New World.

These preposterous fantasies never developed into a serious movement; most Americans knew only too well that they, too, were the children of immigrants who had faced persecution or starvation at home, and that these industrious and productive newcomers added a great deal to America's bounty, as well as its civilization. Xenophobia, however, was given a strong boost by the isolationist forces that opposed American intervention in World War I, and anti-Semitism and a suspicion of immigrants as radicals were intensified after the

Russian Revolution. The most noxious effect of this rejection of the traditions of American pluralism and hospitality was the growing demand for closing the doors of the United States to further immigration from Eastern and Southern Europe.

After a vituperative debate, the United States Congress succumbed to the call for exclusion: in 1921 an immigration act was passed that limited immigrants from a given country to three percent of the total number of its nationals resident in the United States in 1910. Three years later an even more restrictive bill lowered the proportion to two percent of residents in 1890 and set a maximum of 150,000 immigrants annually from the whole world. Jews were not totally forbidden from coming to America—as were, for example, the Japanese—but it was clear that only an insubstantial number could get through the new quota system. As its enemies hoped, Jewish immigration trickled and then almost dried up entirely, just as the state of European Jewry was becoming more and more precarious. (See Reading 7-14.)

American Jews were naturally outraged by this development. But even at the height of the controversy anti-Semitism never seriously threatened the stability and security of American Jewish life. Social discrimination, never absent even in the best of times, may have increased in this period, as did restrictions on Jews in some parts of the business community such as commercial banking and insurance, but Jewish mobility and integration proceeded apace. Indeed, the years of declining immigration from 1914 on corresponded with a period of unmitigated economic advance and social improvement for the recent arrivals from Eastern Europe. One estimate has it that the average annual income of garment workers tripled in the years 1914–19. In general, economic recovery and the war boom created more jobs and better opportunities, and the new immigrants marched headlong into the middle class.

From the Lower East Side of New York and its counterparts in other cities, East European Jews moved in vast numbers to newer, cleaner, prettier neighborhoods and suburbs. Though still heavily concentrated in light industry and manufacturing, Jews entered into countless new fields of commerce and trade, as well as the professions. Jewish students streamed into colleges and graduate schools in numbers way out of proportion to their percentage in the overall population. In time, some of the top universities attempted to stem the tide of Jewish students by instituting an informal quota, which they cynically claimed was meant to prevent anti-Jewish feelings on their campuses. But other schools freely admitted all talented students, and the remarkable educational advance of second-generation American Jews continued without disruption. So thorough was the integration of these Jews into the American middle class that by the mid-1920's they had even acquired the ultimate characteristic of comfortable urban populations: a low birthrate. The Jewish population, estimated at 2,400,000 in 1924, now began to grow at a rate lower than that of the population as a whole.

These economic and social gains were matched by the cultural transformation of American Jewry. In their new neighborhoods and suburbs, second-generation Jews quickly disposed of the trappings of Eastern Europe that their parents had brought to America. Yiddish was forgotten or repressed, except for pockets of humor. Socialism gave way to liberalism, *landsmanshaft* societies to Jewish community centers, trade unions to professional and philanthropic organizations. Both Old World religious orthodoxy and the recently rampant secularism were rejected by the new middle-class community, which was increasingly attracted by the Conservative movement's moderate mélange of Judaism and Americanism. Those more traditionally inclined fashioned a "Modern Orthodoxy" based at Yeshiva College in New York, which saw itself as an American continuation of the school of Samson Raphael Hirsch. Even the Reform movement was reshaped by the children of the East European immigrants, abandoning its more radical stances and ultimately making its peace with Jewish nationalism, which it previously abhorred. In short, by the late 1920's the differences between the old German-Jewish elite and the East Europeans were progressively effaced as a new American-Jewish culture was born.

That culture was unique in the annals of Jewish history, but not because of its distinctive contributions to Jewish thought and behavior. There were, to be sure, some outstanding intellectual, religious, and literary Jewish figures in America, but they took a clear back seat to their contemporaries abroad. What was remarkable and revolutionary about American-Jewish culture was the fact that it was so much an integral part of American life as a whole. The most famous and public arena of this integration was the most American of all arts, the new motion-picture industry, which was created and developed almost exclusively by East European Jewish immigrants and their children. On a more serious level, American Jewry had succeeded, more so than any other Jewish community, in matching political emancipation with social, economic, and cultural integration. And it had done so without sacrificing its commitment to Judaism and the Jewish people around the world. On the contrary, in the aftermath of World War I, representatives of the American-Jewish community played a major role in securing Jewish objectives at the Versailles Congress and rose to positions of prominence in the international Jewish political world. In a short time American Jewry would assume the dominant position in world Jewry which it occupies to this day.

The preeminence of American Jewry, however, was only partially a result of its internal growth, its rapid maturing from an insignificant outpost of Jewish life to the largest and most secure Jewish community in the world. Tragically, the rise of American Jewry was paralleled by the decline and fall of its parent communities in Europe.

---

*Editor's Questions*
AFTER VIEWING AND READING

- How did the nature of colonial society influence the acceptance of the Jews in eighteenth-century North America?
- Trace the gradual rise of the German Jewish immigrants from "rags to riches." How did their economic success lead to the growth of the Reform movement?
- How did Eastern European Jews in this country combat the poor working conditions extant in the garment trade? How was their traditional religious life transformed? With what was it replaced?
- What were the results of the economic success of some of the immigrant Jews by the 1920's?

---

SUGGESTED READINGS

Nathan Glazer, *American Judaism* (University of Chicago, 1972)

Irving Howe, *World of Our Fathers* (Simon and Schuster, 1976)

# 8

## Out of the Ashes
## (1914 to 1945)

Michael Stanislawski

*Editor's Suggestions*
BEFORE VIEWING THE SHOW

Examine Chart 2 on world Jewish population found in this chapter of the *Study Guide*.

*Overview of the TV Program*

In the 1920's in Western Europe much progress was achieved in the sciences and the arts. But with these advances many people felt insecure and attempted to turn back the clock. The Jews were considered to be the major reason for their feelings of dislocation, since some Jews were at the center of politics and culture. Shocking to the minds of some, the Jews were indistinguishable from their fellow citizens.

In Eastern Europe Jewish culture was thriving as Yiddishists, Zionists, and Bundists competed with each other for the affection of the Jewish masses. In the Soviet Union Jews were emancipated but limited in the practice of their faith.

It was difficult for the well-integrated German Jews to react to the rise of anti-Semitism in Germany in the 1920's. When Hitler came to power, he first sought to eliminate his opposition. He disliked randomness in anti-Semitic attacks and sought greater efficiency in discriminating against the Jews. Through legislation the Jews were gradually removed from German life and isolated. The 1936 Olympic games staged in Berlin were used by the Nazis to show the respectability of their state.

As Germany intervened in neighboring countries to protect German-speaking communities, many of the Jews came under Nazi control and they suffered. Germans maintained that the Jews were being protected, but in November 1938 on "the night of broken glass," synagogues were set ablaze, Jewish businesses were wrecked, and many Jews were killed.

Where could the Jews go? Some went to Palestine to help build a new Jewish society, but Britain, which controlled Palestine, clamped down on immigration into that country. Some were allowed into the United States, England, Latin America, and the port of Shanghai. But, mostly, the countries of the world did not welcome them, as seen in the tragic story of the ship, the St. Louis. When World War II broke out millions of additional Jews came under Nazi rule. In the western areas of the Soviet Union mobile killing groups traveled with Nazi armies and murdered one and a half million Jews. Other Jews were crowded into ghettos, forced to work in labor camps, and endured indescribable deprivation.

Hitler and his advisers decided eventually on a "final solution" to the Jewish question: the Jews were to be transported in cattle-cars to camps where they would be killed in gas chambers. In this fashion Jews, Gypsies, Jehovah's Witnesses, homosexuals, the physically handicapped, and the mentally insane were eliminated.

The Jews were often not aware of the Nazi plans. Still, they resisted their Nazi captors in their daily lives in the ghettos and concentration camps. They organized schools and prayer groups, supported other cultural activities, and attempted to carry on some form of normal existence. Some of the Jews physically attacked the Nazis, as seen in the famous Warsaw ghetto uprising.

A few countries like Denmark protected their Jews. So did the Dutch people, but the Jews were rounded up anyway, including the young child Anne Frank. When the Allies entered the war, they did not bomb the concentration and death camps but devoted all their energy to ending the general war as soon as possible.

*Watch for . . . and Think about*

Note the portraits and photographs of Chagall, Kafka, Schoenberg, and Einstein. What does the existence of these famous people tell of the relationship of the Jews to twentieth-century European culture?

Street signs warning Jews to keep out of public and private establishments, photographs of book burnings, and location shots of Dachau will help you experience what it was like to be an outsider in Nazi culture during the 1930's. How did the Jews perceive their future in Germany at this time?

When viewing the wrenching scenes of Nazi cruelty to Jews, of degradation and mass extermination, reflect on how the Germans could wantonly destroy Jewish lives.

Pictures of daily existence in the Jewish ghettos, their cultural activities, and the Warsaw ghetto uprising show how human beings respond in the face of adversity.

WHILE READING THE *STUDY GUIDE* AND *SOURCE READER*

Look for the following:

- How the German Jews fared in the aftermath of World War I and how the Russian Jews were affected by the Bolshevik revolution.
- The cultural activities pursued by the Jews of East Central Europe.
- How Weimar Germany disintegrated and Hitler gradually rose to power.
- The tactics whereby Hitler eliminated the Jews from German life. Identify Nuremburg Laws, *Kristallnacht*.
- The stages in the destruction of European Jewry. How did the Jews respond? Identify and be able to describe the *Judenrat*, final solution, and Nazi-controlled ghettos.

---

## WAR AND REVOLUTION

In the dark shadow of World War II it is difficult to remember the utter shock and horror inflicted on Europe by the war of 1914–18. But the "war to end all wars" caused untold suffering and pain—and more: it shook European society from its belief in unending progress, and alerted the world that the twentieth century could be the most violent yet. In many ways the nineteenth century ended in 1914; the life, culture, even the national borders that millions of people had known and cherished were to be no more.

The Jews of Europe, fully participating in that continent's dreams, squabbles, and illusions, experienced the trauma of the Great War both as nationals of the combatting states and, uniquely, as Jews. Emancipation had made them citizens of their respective lands; from the beginning, civil rights meant civil obligations, includ-

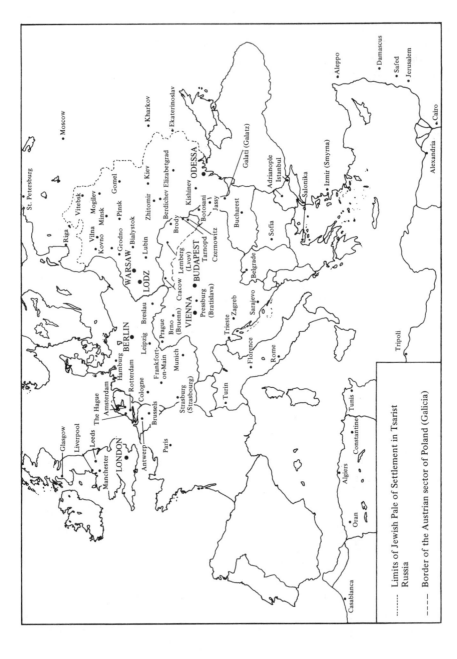

**Map 8  Jewish Population Centers at the Beginning of the Twentieth Century**

Limits of Jewish Pale of Settlement in Tsarist Russia

Border of the Austrian sector of Poland (Galicia)

216

ing military service, and Jews fought in all the battles of nineteenth-century Europe. But in the period from 1914 to 1918, when hundreds of thousands of Jews, dressed in different colors, were facing each other across battle lines, firing cannons at one another, perhaps killing distant cousins in the name of the kaiser, the king, the emperor, or the tsar—this involvement took on a new dimension. In the first place, the staggering size of the forces in arms and, therefore, the number of Jews involved, cast the dilemma in a new light. Secondly, and more difficult to pinpoint, the turns in Jewish history in the previous decades—the rise of anti-Semitism, the Dreyfus Affair, the Russian pogroms, the emergence of Jewish national politics—had raised the level of Jewish consciousness among even the most devoted partisans of integration.

Concern for fellow Jews, however, did not in the least temper devotion to one's native country. German and Austrian Jews sincerely swore fidelity to their nations' cause, just as French and English Jews devoted themselves wholeheartedly to the Allies' fight. On both sides of the trenches Jewish soldiers believed that victory for their side was in the best interest of the Jews as a whole. Even the Zionist parties, which in theory rejected the idea of emancipation as illusory, rallied to their respective flags in much the same way as the Social Democratic parties, ostensibly committed to the solidarity of the international working class, discovered a wellspring of patriotism in the hour of crisis. Only in Russia were the Jewish nationalists and socialists not overcome by dedication to the honor of the empire, but many still supported the Allies' side. Even here, hundreds of thousands of Jewish boys and men proudly donned the colors of the Russian Army, dedicated not so much to the person of the tsar as to the Russian nation and to the principle that they, too, could be responsible and brave soldiers.

For the masses of Jews in Eastern Europe, however, loyalty was not the burning question of the day. Concentrated in the western parts of the Russian empire and the eastern parts of the Austrian empire, they were caught from the beginning in the very center of the conflagration. In the first few months of the war Lithuania, Galicia, and central Poland went up in flames; by the end of 1915 the rest of Eastern Europe was decimated. The Russian forces were routed, having lost almost one million men, and beat a hasty retreat. In the chaos that ensued, as many as six hundred thousand Jews were forced out of their homes and took to the road as refugees. Some were evacuated behind the front along with other civilians; others simply fled as their towns and villages were destroyed and their homes burned; many more were expelled by the Russian army, which was obsessed with fear of Jewish support of the Germans.

The Russian civil authorities protested against the military's expulsions of the Jews—not out of humanitarian concern for the victims, but out of a combined outrage that precious railroad cars were being diverted for this ludicrous purpose and a genuine, albeit irrational, fear of admitting all of these Jews into the interior of Russia. But there was no choice: the Pale of Settlement was abolished, as a temporary war measure, in August 1915. It was never reinstated since the state that invented it collapsed and went out of existence.

By the winter of 1917 the war had devastated Russia morally, physically, and militarily. Nicholas II was incompetent in most realms of life and government and was especially disastrous as chief of an army at war. He succeeded only in alienating his most loyal ministers, generals, and supporters. There was virtually no government left in Russia, no guns for the soldiers, no food for the population. On March 12, 1917, a Provisional Government took power in St. Petersburg, and three days later, Nicholas II abdicated for himself and his son. The Tsarist Empire was no more.

The new government set about to create in Russia a constitutional republic based on civil rights and dignity for all. One of its first measures, on April 2, was to abolish all existing restrictions based on religion and nationality: all Russian citizens were now equal. In one stroke the millions of Russian Jews were emancipated, without any special legislation in their regard.

Exhausted by the war, uprooted from their homes and way of life, pining for relatives killed or missing, the Jews in Russia were still exhilarated by their liberation. They rushed forth in a frenzy of freedom—creating legal political parties, school systems, newspapers, journals, social organizations, clubs. The pitch of creativity was unbelievable; nothing like it had even been seen before.

Their optimism and excitement was further peaked by developments beyond the Russian border. On November 2, 1917, the British government, seeking support among Jews the world over, issued the Balfour Declaration, which announced that His Majesty's Government "looks with favor upon the establishment in Palestine of a national home for the Jewish people." It seemed that a new age of wonderment and promise had dawned. (See Reading 8-1.)

Five days later, however, these dreams and hopes were shaken as revolution overtook Russia once more. In the previous eight months the Provisional Government was debilitated by internal strife, its commitment to winning the war, and the difficulties of transforming a massive, beaten land into a Western state. On November 6, the Bolsheviks, led by Lenin and Trotsky, seized power. Swiftly they arrested their opponents, ignored the results of elections which yielded the Bolsheviks a distinct minority, abolished private property, and sued for peace. In March 1918, the new communist state signed a treaty with Germany surrendering Poland, the Ukraine, the Baltic provinces, Finland, and the Caucasus; eight months later the war was over throughout Europe.

But all was not quiet on the eastern front. From the beginning of 1918 the Russian forces—now renamed the Red Army—were embroiled in a bitter battle with the opponents of Bolshevism. A long, bloody, and devastating civil war began.

The little that was left of traditional Jewish life in the towns and cities of Eastern Europe was destroyed in the course of the civil war. At first most Jews bitterly opposed the Bolsheviks and prayed for the restoration of the Provisional Government. But soon the counterrevolutionary forces betrayed the trust of the Jews: increasingly dominated by reactionaries and chauvinists who blamed the Jews for the Revolution, the White Armies perpetrated countless pogroms against the Jewish population. At the same time the struggle over the future of the Ukraine resulted in extremely brutal pogroms against the Jews by various local groups. The only forces to defend the Jews against outlaw attacks on them was the Red Army, which pledged itself to combat anti-Semitism in its ranks to the greatest extent possible. Despite the lack of sympathy for communism on the part of the Jewish population, the Red Army and its leaders came to be seen by most Jews as the guarantors of their protection and survival.

When the dust settled in the early 1920's, the Jews found themselves in the perplexing environment of the new Soviet Union. Here was a society which pledged to eradicate the very forms of economic activity that had fed Jews for centuries and which sought to expunge thoroughly from its midst all religious life and non-communist political activity. As part of the overall cultural and social transformation orchestrated by the regime, synagogues, Hebrew schools, Jewish cultural institutions, and Zionist and Bundist parties were deemed to be counterrevolutionary and were forcibly destroyed. Yet at the same time the Soviet government was the only one in the world to declare anti-Semitism a serious crime and to act on that resolve by punishing acts of violence and discrimination against Jews. In the context of the 1920's and early 1930's, when a new form of vicious anti-Semitism erupted throughout Europe, the stance of the Soviet government earned it a great deal of support among Jews both within and outside its borders. In the late 1920's there even seemed to be an upsurge of officially sponsored Jewish culture in the Soviet Union: Yiddish authors and scholars were invited to well-paying positions in academies and writers' societies, and a part of the Soviet Far East was designated as a Jewish Autonomous Region where a new "proletarian Jewish culture" could thrive. At the same time the revolutionary recasting of Soviet society that accompanied the collectivization of agriculture and massive industrialization opened up countless opportunities for Jews to be employed in new white-collar, managerial, and bureaucratic positions. In the "construction of Soviet socialism" (as the local jargon would put it), Jewish scientists, economists, writers, musicians, Party functionaries, and soldiers played a fundamental role and rose to positions of eminence, fame, and even power. (See Reading 8-5.)

Through the devastating years of the 1930's the social and economic status of the Jews continued to climb, establishing them as perhaps the most educated, professionally successful, and economically secure minority in the country. In sharp contrast to this social advance, however, there was now cultural devastation under Stalin: all attempts at creating a Soviet Yiddish culture, a Jewish Autonomous Region, or a "Leninist Jewish scholarship" succumbed to the general obliteration of artistic and intellectual creativity and autonomy. Jews, too, suffered substantial political setbacks in the massive purges of the Communist Party, government bureaucracy, and Red Army. But the Jewish victims of the purges were not persecuted because they were Jews; they were arrested, deported to prison camps, and executed because they, along with millions of other Soviet citizens of all nationalities, were condemned by Stalin as enemies of the state. The vast majority of the Jews were still well-integrated and successful members of Soviet society. Moreover, in the same way as the Red Army gained the support of Russian Jews during the civil war by protecting them from pogroms, so too the leading role played by the Soviet Union in opposition to Nazism and Fascism around the world strengthened the loyalty of most Soviet Jews to their government. A paradox was at work which recalled in a strange and entirely unpredicted way the implicit contract of Jewish emancipation: for Jews as a collective religious, national, and cultural entity, the policies and practices of the Soviet Union were disastrous; for Jews as individuals, however, Soviet society provided extraordinary opportunities for social, economic, and even political integration.

## THE JEWS OF EAST CENTRAL EUROPE

Nearly the opposite situation prevailed for the Jews of the other states of Eastern and East Central Europe. In independent Poland, Lithuania, Latvia, Hungary, Rumania, and even in the more liberal Czechoslovakia, Jewish religious and national culture thrived, but Jews as individuals faced frustrating and at times insuperable obstacles. The Treaty of Versailles had made Jewish national as well as civil rights a condition of the independence of many of these countries, but in a few years the signed guarantees were worthless. The major problem facing the Jews in these parts was twofold: the rise of a native middle class challenging traditional Jewish economic activities, and the concomitant rise of anti-Semitism. Following the devastation of World War I, the Jewish population was already desperately poor and in need of serious economic and social rehabilitation—indeed, the Jews were faced with ever greater restrictions and unfair competition. Poverty became a problem of epidemic proportions for millions of Jews. The old solution to this plight, immigration to America, became impossible, as the doors of the United States were closed tighter in 1921 and 1924. At the same time, British support for the creation of a Jewish homeland in Palestine had waned since 1917 in the face of Arab opposition, and only a very small number of Jews from Eastern Europe were permitted to join the existing Jewish society being built in the Land of Israel.

The spirit of the Jews of Eastern Europe, however, was not crushed. They never succumbed to despair. On the contrary, they responded by rededicating themselves to the belief that education, social mobility, and progress would solve their problems and those of the world as a whole. They founded more and more schools, newspapers, theater troupes, religious institutions, literary salons, and political parties, all searching for a means of fashioning a new Jewish life in the bewildering reality of the twentieth century. (See Reading 8-4.) Despite the British policy on immigration to Palestine, the Zionist movement gained a new attractiveness and potency, and hundreds of thousands of Jews studied and prepared for an eventual move to the Jewish homeland. In Poland the strength of the Zionists was challenged by the Bund, which grew from year to year into a proud Jewish national party with support beyond the working class. Other parties, too numerous to list, sprouted as well—Orthodox and agnostic, social democratic and conservative, espousing all the languages and national cultures of this multiethnic territory. A small number of Jews continued to flourish economically and to rise in the ranks of the upper middle class. Industrialists, bankers, writers, musicians, painters, professors, and physicians felt, and often were, fully integrated in the top ranks of society and culture around them. In Budapest, Bucharest, Prague, Warsaw, and other big cities, however, the Jewish elite lived a life cut off and alienated from the Jewish masses. But even the most successful and acculturated Jews in these lands acknowledged the fact that sinister new forces shut off the possibilities of complete assimilation and integration for most of the Jews.

## WESTERN EUROPE

In Western Europe, however, assimilation and integration reached new heights in the years after the war. In France, England, and Germany, the Jews assumed positions of power and prominence in government, law, medicine, education, business, journalism, and the arts. Not only were all these endeavors open to the Jews, but Jews—as well as persons "of Jewish origin" who no longer identified with the Jewish people or religion—were essential to the countries' development. (See Reading 8-3.) The Jews, most of whom remained proud and committed members of their communities, felt supremely confident that they had adapted successfully to the demands and opportunities of the new century. There were problems, to be sure. Anti-Semitic parties continued to exist and even to grow, but these were vestiges of an unfortunate past which would disappear in time; to take them too seriously would be to succumb to their insults. Whatever social discrimination still existed could be attributed to the ever-growing presence of East European Jewish immigrants in Berlin,

Paris, London, or Vienna. The "native" Jews believed that the East Europeans refused to accommodate themselves to the mores and culture of their new homes; they persisted in speaking Yiddish and preaching distasteful radical politics. To some extent they brought on the hostility they encountered. They would either have to change or to leave: Zionism was perhaps not a bad solution for them and the millions of unfortunate Jews still in Eastern Europe, but it was obviously irrelevant to the "native" Jews of Western Europe.

The most fascinating of the Western Jewries was that of Weimar Germany, which became the quintessential laboratory for Jewish assimilation and integration in the 1920's. The new German Republic, born in the wake of World War I and an unsuccessful Soviet-style revolution (led, not coincidentally, by Jewish communists), included Jews in every stage of its genesis and growth, from the jurist who wrote its constitution to Walther Rathenau, the first minister of reconstruction and later foreign minister, who was assassinated in 1922. With the old imperial customs and hierarchies disbanded, opportunities abounded in all realms which previously were largely closed to the Jews—government, civil service, academic life—as well as those in which the Jews had already enjoyed enormous success—business, commerce, the arts, medicine. Jewish communal and philanthropic organizations flourished, as did youth groups, social welfare institutions, and cultural clubs. Although the precise degree of social interaction between German Jews and German Christians still remains a matter of controversy, in the Weimar Republic the German-Jewish community felt itself to be as integrated and at home in Germany as anyone else was.

Still, small pockets of dissent and discomfort were visible and increasingly vocal in the young generation of German Jews. These critics were opposed not so much to the ideology of their parents as to their way of life, their complacent embrace of upper-middle-class values and culture. This criticism was in a very complex way intermingled with political and literary currents popular among non-Jewish Germans as well; it also extended beyond the boundaries of Weimar Germany. Perhaps the most eloquent spokesman for this confusion and malaise was the great writer Franz Kafka, who lived in Prague but wrote in German. His brilliant and frightening fantasies earned him fame not only among readers of his time but to this day as well, as a symbol of the humane spirit struggling with the arcane mysteries of the modern age.

But Kafka also serves as a symbol of the specific Jewish component involved in this critical movement. Many young acculturated Jews, particularly in Weimar Germany, began to rethink their Jewish commitments and identity. The result was a numerically limited but intellectually impressive group of young Jewish artists and intellectuals who wrestled with the meaning of being Jewish in the midst of seemingly boundless cultivation and tolerance. This renaissance in German-Jewish culture revolved around the work of two important religious and cultural figures, Martin Buber and Franz Rosenzweig, who created new philosophies of Judaism based on a return to Jewish texts and Jewish learning in the search for meaning in life. Buber was a Zionist, Rosenzweig was not, but they agreed that the fundamental problem facing German Jews—and modern Jews everywhere—was the spiritual void which remained when traditional religious faith disappeared. (**See Reading 8-2.**)

Though these religious and cultural stirrings were poignant and profound, they could not possibly have responded to what was in fact the greatest problem facing German Jews—and European Jewry as a whole: the rise of the Nazi Party. The National Socialist Party, founded by Adolf Hitler and a small number of equally unimpressive and uneducated louts in 1919–20, was dismissed by most Germans of any faith as an insignificant band of boorish thugs. After trying to overthrow the Bavarian government in 1923, Hitler was arrested and imprisoned and seemed to be consigned to utter oblivion. But he was released after less than a year and began to spread his confused venom against the Jews—compiled during his prison term into a book, *Mein Kampf* (My Struggle)—to more and more sympathetic ears. Apparently a great number of Germans were still smarting from defeat in World War I and what they considered to be the humiliations of the Versailles pact. They combined this anger with a general hatred of the Weimar government and its liberal economic and social policies and a genuine fear of the growing communist movement in Germany. This type of anti-Western, antimodern, reactionary sensibility had fed the anti-Semitic parties in Germany and Austria for decades, but Hitler manipulated these resentments and fears into a unique amalgam whose attraction still baffles historians and psychologists. (**See Reading 8-6.**)

The Nazis were still a tiny minority in German political life when the Great Depression of the late 1920's led in Germany, as elsewhere, to massive unemployment and a subsequent rise in the popularity of extreme solutions. In the 1930 elections to the Reichstag (the German parliament), the Nazis spurted from twelve seats to 107. The moderate parties were increasingly unable to control the government, and the Left was unable to gain a majority. The pendulum of power swung heavily to the Right, reinforced by the presidential election of March 1932, in which the conservative candidate received eighteen million votes, Hitler eleven million, and the communist leader five million. In the Reichstag elections four months later, the Nazis won the largest number of seats, but not enough to form a majority. After a complicated series of fruitless attempts at organizing the center and left wing, Hitler was named Chancellor of Germany on January 30, 1933. A month later the new election campaign was disrupted by a fire in the Reichstag building, which Hitler claimed to be a communist plot but was actually set by one of his henchmen. The ploy was successful: the Nazis captured 288 seats and their nationalist allies 52; the Socialist Party received 120, the Communists 81, the Center Party 74, and other non-Nazi parties 23. This electoral power enabled the Nazis to pass a bill establishing a dictatorship in Germany on March 23, with Adolf Hitler as Fuehrer. Incredibly, Hitler came to power legally, using the letter of the law to subvert its spirit and moral basis.

## NAZI GERMANY

Hitler immediately set about implementing his radical programs for restructuring Germany, which from the first moment included far-reaching attacks against the Jews. He began with a boycott of Jewish businesses on April 1, marked by brutal violence, insults smeared on the windows of Jewish firms, defaced further with yellow Stars of David and the Nazi swastika, and the like. Public opinion in Germany and abroad, roused in indignation, convinced Hitler to abandon this boycott—especially since he feared a counterboycott of German goods in the West. But soon he found other, more potent, weapons against the Jews and felt himself secure enough to ignore protests from the outside world and to stifle all opposition within Germany. The latter was achieved by outlawing all opposing political groups, secretly executing their leaders, and establishing concentration camps in which anti-Nazis were detained without trial and tortured. Soon Hitler introduced the concepts of racist pseudo-science into German law: persons were divided into non-Aryans (Jews) and

Aryans (Christians), and a host of disabilities were heaped on the former. Supporters and critics of these measures described them as "medieval" but, in truth, the Middle Ages had never witnessed such brutal, senseless, and degrading acts against the Jews.

First, "non-Aryans" were dismissed from the civil service, denied entry to the Bar, and excluded from practicing law. Next, the "Law Against the Overcrowding of German Schools and Institutions of Higher Learning" set strict quotas on the number of Jews in educational facilities, and decrees banned Jews from artistic and literary work and from the press. Other laws outlawed Jewish religious rituals. The term "non-Aryan" began to be applied to anyone who had even one Jewish grandparent. This definition was an ominous indication of a radical shift in anti-Semitic theory and practice under the Nazis. Until this time, the Jews who converted to Christianity had ceased to be the object of hatred and scorn; at the very least their children were fully accepted as Christians. But the basis of the hatred was now moved from the religious realm to the genetic. Jewishness was implicitly likened to an inherited disease which had no cure.

The German Jews and hundreds of thousands of liberal and leftist non-Jews vociferously condemned these outrages, but their voices were lost in the din of hatred and madness. A large-scale emigration began as the Jews, their non-Jewish spouses, and anti-Nazi politicians and cultural figures repudiated their former home. But for most of the Jews in Germany, leaving was both impractical and regarded as surrendering to the enemy. Surely the forces of justice and honor, which had characterized Germany for centuries and had established it as the leading home of literature and art, would ultimately triumph and this disgusting nightmare would recede into the past as an ugly interlude. The appropriate response, most Jews felt, was to stay and resist.

This noble dedication to morality and faith soon encountered new and insurmountable obstacles. In September 1935, the infamous Nuremburg Laws were passed, formalizing the racist definition of degrees of "non-Aryanness." A Jew was defined as anyone having three Jewish grandparents; those with two Jewish grandparents were designated as "mixed type, first degree" and those with one Jewish grandparent, "mixed type, second degree." Decrees appeared forbidding intermarriage between Jews and non-Jews and establishing strict laws for dealing with already existing mixed couples. Severe penalties were enacted for any cases of sexual intercourse between

Jews and non-Jews, and "Aryan" women under the age of forty-five were forbidden to work as domestics in Jewish homes. The Nuremburg Laws were completed with the passing of the Reich Citizenship Law which formally distinguished between German citizens, who had "German or cognate blood," and subjects of the German Reich, who had no civil or political rights. The emancipation of German Jewry, won in stages between the 1790's and 1871, was now rescinded. A new era of rightlessness and powerlessness had descended on the Jews in a mad ruthless frenzy that no one could have predicted. (**See Readings 8-7 and 8-8.**)

After depriving the Jews of their status, the next step was to deprive them of their livelihood. A new term was added to the lexicon of infamy—Aryanization, i.e., confiscating businesses or property owned by Jews and handing them over to non-Jews. In typical Nazi fashion, these thefts masqueraded under the cloak of legality, disguised as purchase and sale agreements. But the Jews received little or no compensation.

Still, the incessantly optimistic German-Jewish community struggled to believe that the insanity was temporary and that true legality would prevail in the end. The number of emigrants rose, and almost all Jews began actively to consider leaving. But most remained and struggled to keep on going, to find new ways of earning their keep and retaining their dignity. Retrospective judgments are too easy; asking "why didn't they leave before it was too late?" assumes that the end of the macabre tale was predictable from the middle. The Jews had trained themselves over the past two thousand years to believe that concerted, united action was the best remedy to external threats. They believed with all their hearts that the world proceeded along a rational plan leading to ultimate justice and that the forces of evil could be overwhelmed if one remained calm and avoided rash judgments. Added to this historical consciousness, deeply etched in the minds of even the most assimilated Jews, was the profound love that the Jews felt for Germany, their indelible faith that the Germany of Goethe, Lessing, and Schiller would imminently reassert itself and undo all these horrors. In the interim they banded together as they never had before, helping their friends, relatives, and neighbors financially, morally, spiritually. Jewish educational, cultural, and social organizations were strengthened; youth groups were reinforced to gird children against the pain they were facing, welfare and emigration committees were expanded. The religious and intellectual return to Jewish roots and sources, begun under the leadership of Buber and Rosenzweig in the Weimar years, took on an added importance, as hundreds of thousands of Jews who had never before thought about their tradition and identity attempted to sort out what it meant to be Jewish.

Meanwhile, Hitler was carrying on his ceaseless surge for dominance over Europe. In the early years of his dictatorship he withdrew Germany from the League of Nations and the Disarmament Conference, concluded a treaty of nonaggression with the increasingly right-wing rulers of Poland, established close ties with Italy's fascist dictator, Mussolini, and renounced the clauses of the Versailles pact providing for the disarmament of Germany. In 1936 Hitler moved his forces into the Rhineland, sided with the Franco government in the Spanish Civil War, formalized an alliance—termed the "Axis"—with Italy, and concluded a pact with Japan. Still the Western powers believed that Hitler could be contained: the British Lord Halifax, sent to Berlin in November 1937 to ascertain Germany's intentions, returned to London convinced that Hitler wanted peace. Less than four months later the German army invaded Austria and annexed it. Another 190,000 Jews thus were added to the 350,000 German Jews under direct Nazi control. The prohibitions on Jewish life were applied in Austria as well, and new restrictions were added throughout the Reich.

In September 1938 British Prime Minister Neville Chamberlain's two visits with Hitler culminated in the Munich Agreement, which carved up the proud, independent state of Czechoslovakia and handed over its western territories to Hitler. Chamberlain was convinced that his policy of appeasement had assured "peace in our time."

A few weeks later Hitler ordered that some 15,000 Jews who had been living in Germany for a long time with Polish passports be deported to Poland. But the semi-fascist, anti-Semitic Polish government refused to accept them, and they were left to freeze and starve in a no-man's-land between the two countries. Finally some were admitted to Poland, others were returned to Germany, and many were sent to concentration camps. The son of one Jewish couple who had been deported avenged the atrocities committed against his parents by assassinating an official at the German Embassy in Paris.

Hitler retaliated by imposing a one-billion-mark fine on the entire Jewish community of Germany and used the attack on the diplomat as a pretext to launch a reign of terror against the Jews, one which had clearly been planned long in advance. On November 9–10, 1938, well-orchestrated mobs descended on the Jews and Jewish institutions throughout Germany: ninety Jews were killed, thousands were injured, hundreds of synagogues were burned, some 7,500 stores and businesses were destroyed. The shattering of the glass of windows, homes, and synagogues lent this pogrom its gruesome name "Kristallnacht"—the night of crystal. Immediately thereafter, over 25,000 Jews were arrested and sent to concentration camps. On November 15, 1938, all Jewish children were expelled from German schools (see **Reading 8-9**); two weeks later Jews were barred from attending public events, and Jewish publications and autonomous organizations were disbanded, replaced by a Nazi-controlled Federal Union of the Jews in Germany. The government set up an office, controlled by Adolf Eichmann, that encouraged the Jews to emigrate from Germany and began investigating the possibilities of extorting money from world Jewry in exchange for the lives of their fellow Jews in Germany.

By now the German Jews had lost all hope. They tried every means of escaping from the prison that had once been their beloved home. But finding a place to go to was not easy. An international conference on refugees, called under pressure from President Franklin Roosevelt, met in Evian, France, in July 1938 to discuss means of dealing with the Jews fleeing Nazi-occupied Europe, but only one government, the Dominican Republic, was willing to welcome the Jews. Nonetheless, the Jews persevered, and many managed to escape. In May 1939, however, there were still some 225,000 Jews in Germany and another 175,000 in the other territories annexed by the Reich. At the very same time the last remaining option for the Jews was dashed: the British government, anxious about oil supplies in a potential war and seeking Arab support, issued a White Paper—a policy statement—on Palestine that totally reversed the promises of the Balfour Declaration. Britain now opposed the establishment of a Jewish homeland in the Land of Israel and would permit Jewish immigration only at the acquiescence of the Arabs. In response to the plight of the Jews in Germany, over the next five years a total of 75,000 Jewish immigrants would be admitted to Palestine. German Jews desperately sought any means of escape, but their primary attention was drawn once more to the arena of global politics.

## DESTRUCTION

In the summer of 1939 international tensions reached a peak over the question of Hitler's next target: Poland. Everyone feared that war was imminent, but people of good faith still hoped that hostilities could be avoided. Britain, France, and the Soviet Union attempted to negotiate a "peace front" to block further Nazi expansion. This last chance dissipated, and the fate of the world as a whole hung in the balance. On August 23, 1939 the West was shocked by an announcement from Moscow: the Soviet Union and Nazi Germany had signed a pact of nonaggression; each side would abstain from attacking the other and would remain neutral if attacked by a third party.

With the Soviets out of the fight, the descent to war was inexorable. On September 1, 1939 Germany attacked Poland on land and in the air. Two days later, after their demands for German withdrawal were rebuffed, Britain and France declared war. World War II had begun.

The first battleground was Poland, which the German mechanized divisions, protected by overwhelming air support, swept through with amazing rapidity. The poorly equipped, antiquated Polish army was crushed almost immediately. Alarmed by this unexpected German success, Stalin sent his troops into Poland in mid-September, and by the end of the month Nazi Germany and the Soviet Union divided Poland in what many have called the Fourth Polish Partition: Germany annexed the city of Danzig and areas of Poland that belonged to Prussia before World War I; a huge section of central and southern Poland was termed a German protectorate; and the eastern provinces of Poland were ceded to the Soviet Union.

Poland's enormous Jewish population, which had seen its political and legal status deteriorate rapidly through the 1930's and had suffered serious pogroms in the last years before the war, was now divided into two groups. Approximately two million Polish Jews came under Hitler's direct control. Another million and a half were under Soviet occupation.

In the German-controlled regions the fury of Nazi anti-Semitism was unleashed as never before. The non-Jewish population suffered horribly under Nazi occupation, but from the beginning it was clear that the Jews were to receive special treatment of an inordinately cruel kind. To Hitler and his followers, East Europeans in general were inferior to Germans. But the Jews occupied the lowest rungs of all, and East European Jews were the epitome of all that was hateful and despicable in the world. Immediately, therefore, brutal acts of violence erupted against the Jews—random shootings, senseless beatings, bestial attacks. Jewish businesses were looted and destroyed, Jewish property seized and demolished, often with no purpose other than terror and intimidation. Old Jews were paraded in the middle of streets, where their beards and sidelocks—signs of piety and devotion to the Lord—were shorn, and they were defaced before the sadistic hilarity of the assembled German soldiers and their collaborators. Beyond these individual depravities, legal restrictions followed closely one after another: all the laws that had been implemented in Germany were enforced here, and more. The Jews were forced out of small towns and villages and required to move to cities, which quickly became overcrowded dens of poverty, disease, and hunger. Jewish men were required to present themselves for forced labor, often in special camps set up outside major Polish cities. All Jews were forced to don yellow Stars of David to distinguish them from the rest of the population; they were forbidden to own radios, attend schools, appear in public parks and performances, own stores, or practice their professions. Most synagogues were razed to the ground in Kristallnacht-like fires. Jewish institutions were shut down, and communal organizations replaced by an agency appointed by the Nazis to run Jewish affairs. In each city with a substantial Jewish population, such a council—called in German, a *Judenrat*—was forced to carry out the orders of the Nazis: to round up fellow Jews for labor brigades, enforce restrictions on religious and social life, and ensure obedience to the Nazi overlords. Many Jewish leaders refused to take on such onerous and distasteful tasks; a large number committed suicide rather than bear the burden of implementing these savage orders. In many places the councils were manned by the least savory elements in the Jewish population. But a good number of honorable and responsible men and women felt that it was their holy duty to try to represent their communities in the best possible way, to make sure that the horrors were not added to by corruption and dishonesty. To say the very least these leaders had no notion of where the Nazis' mania would lead; on the contrary they could not easily rid themselves of the idea that Germany was a rational, Western nation that could be dealt with rationally. There was no choice but to try to maintain dignity and order, to cope as well as they possibly could with a horrible dilemma. By the time the unthinkable ultimate goal of the Nazis—the murder of all the Jews—became known, the old strategies were irrelevant.

The Nazis' next move was to concentrate the Jews into a restricted number of sealed-off areas in major cities: Jewish ghettos. The first ghetto was set up in Lodz in the winter of 1940, and the Warsaw ghetto was established later that year. By November almost a half million Jews, rounded up from hundreds of surrounding localities, were locked up in the Warsaw ghetto. Soon there were ghettos all over Poland.

It is important to understand that although the establishment of ghettos was described as a reimposition of a medieval practice, there was no historical precedent for the Nazi ghetto. In the first place the common notion that throughout medieval Europe the Jews lived in ghettos is seriously wrong; the old-style ghetto was an invention of the early modern period and never applied to most Jews. There were never any ghettos, properly understood, in pre-1940 Eastern Europe. In many places the Jews lived in separate quarters, sometimes voluntarily, sometimes not. But these Jewish streets, neighborhoods, or sections were typically not surrounded by walls and locked up at night. Even when they were, the Jews' mobility was not compromised: they could work outside the ghetto and only had to return there to sleep. Their essential rights were not affected by ghettoization; their religious, social, economic, and communal life could continue in its normal ways.

The Nazi ghetto was unique, entirely different in purpose and organization from its namesake. The Jews were stripped of all their rights; they were forbidden to leave the ghetto at any time; any Jew caught without permission outside the ghetto—the term was "on the Aryan side"—was shot on sight. Inside the walls of the ghetto, the Jews were crowded in indescribable squalor. Starvation and epidemics were rampant; bodies dropped like flies. The most remarkable feature of ghetto life was that somehow the Jews were able to carve out for themselves a semblance of dignity. They organized schools, political parties, orchestras, theatre troupes, literary events, religious services, all in a desperate attempt at salvaging some vestiges of normal human activity in the midst of the incomprehensible inhumanity which they confronted at every turn. (**See Reading 8-11.**)

As the ghettos were erected throughout Poland, the Nazi army swept through country after country in northern and western Europe: Denmark and Norway in April 1940, the Netherlands, Belgium, and Luxemburg in May. In June the most dramatic defeat occurred: France fell to the Nazis. Almost half a million Jews in these lands, including many refugees from Germany, now came under Nazi rule, and (with the exception of those in Denmark and Norway) were subjected to the same treatment as the Jews in Germany. In the unoccupied part of France, ruled by the Vichy government, Jews were restricted by laws and racist measures invented by local French anti-Semites. Resistance against the Nazis and their collaborators appeared in small measure in all these countries but had little effect; protests against the treatment of the Jews—most vocal in the Netherlands—were of no avail.

Similar problems affected the very substantial Jewish populations of Germany's allies. Under pressure from the Nazis and the Soviet Union, in September 1940 Rumania ceded one-third of its territory and population to the Soviet Union, Hungary, and Bulgaria. The approximately 300,000 Jews who remained in Rumania were stripped, for the most part, of their citizenship and subjected to a reign of terror led by the Iron Guard, the local version of the Nazis. On January 21, 1941, a pogrom was launched in Bucharest that resulted in the death of 120 Jews, much looting, and the desecration of many synagogues. In Hungary, the Jewish population of over half a million was subjected to stringent discriminatory legislation, as was the case with the smaller Jewish communities of the other Nazi allies, Slovakia, Bulgaria, and Yugoslavia. In Italy, where anti-Jewish laws had been on the books since 1938, the government consistently resisted Nazi pressure to deport the Jews. In general, even at this early stage a pattern emerged that was literally to have life-and-death implications for the Jews: their fate was determined to a large extent by the degree of direct Nazi control in their country. Where the Nazis worked through allies, degrading and debilitating measures, informed by traditional anti-Semitic prejudices, were taken against the Jews. But in these lands the Jews had a far better chance to survive than those in places directly occupied by the Nazis, where the new, virulent, racist anti-Semitism resulted in virtually total extermination.

The mass murder of Jews began after Hitler's surprise attack on the Soviet Union on June 22, 1941. Within a few months the German forces controlled all the territory of former Poland and Lithuania and most of the Ukraine. By the end of October the siege on Moscow began. From the very beginning of the Russian campaign the Nazis incited the local populations to conduct attacks against the Jews. Soon the Germans did their own killing: special murder squads were sent to shoot Jews in a systematic fashion. Official German records proudly claimed that by November 1941 one-quarter of a million Jews were massacred in this fashion. The most infamous case of such slaughter occurred on the Day of Atonement in Babi Yar, a suburb of Kiev, where over 33,000 Jews were mowed down.

It seems clear that these mass killings were the first stage of what Hitler and his major advisers called "the final solution to the Jewish problem in Europe"—the annihilation of every Jewish man, woman, and child. It is impossible to know for certain exactly when the actual decision to implement this incredible plan was taken; historians continue to debate the precise date and to search for more evidence. The mechanisms for the extermination began to be available at the end of 1941: death camps were built either adjacent to already existing concentration camps or at separate sites. The names of these places have come to symbolize the absolute incarnation of evil—Auschwitz, Birkenau, Dachau, Maidanek, Treblinka. From evidence submitted to the Nuremburg Trials of Nazi war criminals after the war, the following gruesome chronology emerges. The Nazi leadership scheduled a top-level secret meeting to take place on December 7, 1941 to finalize the plans for the murder of all the Jews in Europe. The meeting had to be postponed because of the entry of the United States into the war after the bombing of Pearl Harbor on December 7. On January 20, 1942 representatives of the S.S., the Gestapo, and other agencies of the Third Reich gathered at a villa in a suburb of Berlin named Wannsee and laid out in detail the plans for the Final Solution: Jews in all parts of Europe would be transported from west to east, gathered in ghettos, brought to Poland and, in Poland, exterminated in the death camps. (See Reading 8-10.)

Deportations from Western and Southern Europe to Poland and within Poland from ghettos to death camps followed in relentless succession. In the ghettos of Warsaw, Vilna, Bialystok, Kovno, and Minsk, and even in several death camps, Jewish resistance groups rose up and bravely fought the Nazi murderers, knowing full well that there was no chance of winning. The uprisings were quelled, but nevertheless succeeded in symbolizing to the Jews and to the rest of the world the noble spirit of the Jewish victims of Nazism throughout Europe. Other Jews formed partisan bands or joined any resistance movement that allowed them to participate. But the Nazis' mania could not be stemmed. Murder of the Jews enjoyed top priority in Hitler's Nazi war plan even after the tide of fortune turned against the Axis. (See Readings 8-12 and 8-13.)

By the time the Allied forces landed at Normandy on June 6, 1944, most of the Jews of Europe had been killed. While the crucial last battles were still being waged, the Nazis diverted critical railroad cars from the front to transport Jews to their deaths. The last major Jewish community to fall prey to what was now the Nazis' self-defeating obsession with murdering Jews was the proud Jewry of Hungary, deported in the summer and fall of 1944. On January 17, 1945 the Red Army liberated Warsaw, and by the end of February was within thirty miles of Berlin. (See Reading 8-14.) At the beginning of March the United States First Army crossed the Rhine. On April 20 the Russians reached Berlin; five days later the Soviet and American armies met at the Elbe River. On May 1 a German radio report from Berlin announced the news the Western world was awaiting with bated breath: Adolf Hitler had died during the Battle of Berlin. Six days later, German army leaders surrendered to the Allies. May 8, 1945, was proclaimed Victory in Europe Day (V-Day) by President Truman and Prime Minister Churchill; the war against the Nazis was over.

Sixty-seven percent of European Jewry, six million innocent men, women, and children had been devoured by the Nazi beast. Only three Jewish communities remained intact on the Continent. In Denmark the entire population had joined in a remarkable rescue mission that secretly ferried 8,000 Jews to Sweden, a neutral country. The two Nazi-allied states which never succumbed to German occupation, Rumania and Bulgaria, managed to spare the Jews considered to be native to their realms. The ancient Jewish communities of Poland, Lithuania, Latvia, Germany, Hungary, Czechoslovakia, and Greece were almost totally eliminated; only a tiny remnant remained alive. Between two-thirds and three-quarters of the Jews of Holland, Belorussia, and the Ukraine were killed. Belgium, Yugoslavia, and Norway lost half their Jewish populations. Murdered as well were a quarter of French Jewry and a fifth of Italian Jewry, representatives of the first Jewish communities to be emancipated at the beginning of the modern era—an era which promised unending progress and yielded unimaginable evil. (See Reading 8-15.)

# Chart 2  World Jewish Population, 1939, 1948, 1967 (in thousands)

| Europe | 1939 | | 1948 | 1967 |
|---|---|---|---|---|
| Russia (including Congress Poland) | | | | (1959) |
| U.S.S.R. (including Asiatic parts) | 2,825 | U.S.S.R. (including Asiatic parts) | 2,000 | 2,650 |
| Poland (including Galicia, Posen, etc.) | 3,250 | Poland | 88 | 21 |
| Rumania (enlarged after 1918) | 850 | Rumania | 380 | 100 |
| Austria (1934) | 191 | Austria | 31 | 12.5 |
| Czechoslovakia (1930) | 357 | Czechoslovakia | 42 | 15 |
| Hungary (1930) | 445 | Hungary | 174 | 80 |
| Yugoslavia (1931) | 68 | Yugoslavia | 10 | 7 |
| Bulgaria | 64 | Bulgaria | 45 | 7 |
| Greece (1928) | 73 | Greece | 8.5 | 6.5 |
| Turkey (European 1935) | 80 | Turkey (including Asiatic provinces) | 80 | 39 |
| Germany (1933) | 504 | Germany (West and East) | 153[1] | 30 |
| Switzerland (1930) | 18 | Switzerland | 35 | 20 |
| Italy (1936) | 48 | Italy | 53[1] | 35 |
| Great Britain and Northern Ireland (1931) | 300 | Great Britain | 345 | 410 |
| | | Ireland | 4.5 | 5.4 |
| France (including Alsace-Lorraine) (1936) | 260 | France | 235 | 535 |
| Netherlands (1930) | 112 | Netherlands | 28 | 30 |
| Belgium (1930) | 60 | Belgium | 45 | 40.5 |
| **The Americas** | | | | |
| United States (1940) | 4,975 | United States | 5,000 | 5,870 |
| Canada (1931) | 1,557 | Canada | 180 | 280 |
| Mexico (1930) | 9 | Mexico | 25 | 30 |
| Argentina (1935) | 275 | Argentina | 360 | 500 |
| Brazil (1930) | 35 | Brazil | 111 | 140 |
| Uruguay (1931) | 12 | Uruguay | 37 | 54 |
| **Asia** | | | | |
| Palestine | 475 | Israel (Palestine) | 750 | 2,436 |
| Iraq (1935) | 91 | Iraq | 90 | 2.5 |
| Syria and Lebanon (1935) | 26 | Syria | 20 | 4 |
| | | Lebanon | | 3 |
| Yemen and Arabia (1935) | 50 | Yemen | 45 | — |
| Iran (1935) | 50 | Iran | 50 | 30 |
| India (1931) | 24 | India | 30 | 15 |
| China (1936) | 10 | China (Mainland) | 15 | — |
| | | Taiwan | | |
| Japan | 2 | Japan | 2 | 1 |
| **Africa** | | | | |
| Egypt (1937) | 70 | Egypt (U.A.R.) | 75 | 1 |
| Morocco (1936) | 162 | Morocco | 286 | 50 |
| Algeria (1931) | 110 | Algeria | 130 | 1.5 |
| Tunisia (1936) | 59.5 | Tunisia (1946) | 71.5 | 10 |
| Ethiopia (1935) | 51 | Ethiopia | 51 | 12 |
| Union of South Africa (1936) | 90.7 | South Africa | 100 | 115 |
| **Oceania** | | | | |
| Australia (1933) | 23.6 | Australia | 37 | 70 |
| New Zealand (1936) | 2.7 | New Zealand | 3.5 | 5 |
| **World Total** | 16,724 | **World Total** | 11,373 | 13,837.5 |

[1]Including displaced persons

236

World Jewry was never to be the same again. The first immediate effects of the destruction was a radical shift in the geography and demography of the Jewish people. Reconstruction began in all the devastated communities, but it was clear that except for the Soviet Union, which still contained a substantial Jewish population, Europe would no longer be a dominant center in the Jewish world. Poland and Germany, the two mainstays of Jewish life in Europe for half a millennium, were so stained with Jewish blood that most of the few survivors who returned from death camps, hiding, and partisan units could not bear to remain in their former homes. Refugees gathered together in displaced-persons camps, desperately yearning to leave the scene of the murder of their families, their children, their entire civilization. As soon as they were granted visas, they rushed to new parts of the world to make new homes, to try to begin new lives. Most wanted to go to Palestine, to join in the building of a Jewish homeland where they would no longer have to rely on non-Jews for their lives or their culture. Others simply sought respite wherever they could find it. The Jewish communities of North and South America, Palestine, Great Britain, North Africa, and Asia, spared direct encounter with the catastrophe, were now the major bearers of the torch of Jewish continuity.

The biological results of the Holocaust are too easily summarized. It is too easy to forget that the macabre statistics are truly unfathomable. But the slaughter of European Jewry resulted in other wounds to the Jewish people as well, wounds that are more difficult to describe: a psychological and spiritual trauma that has yet to be healed. How could it have happened? How could the rest of the world have let it happen? How could God have let it happen? What possible meaning can be found for Jewish existence, for human existence, in the face of such evil, of so much suffering? Many of the questions are as old as the Book of Job, but the events of World War II brought them to the consciousness of the world and especially of the Jewish people in ways previously unimaginable.

As Jewish history continued in the wake of the Holocaust, comprising an essential chapter in the story of human civilization, the search for answers combined with a determination that never again would Jews—or any other human beings—meet a similar fate.

*Editor's Questions*
AFTER VIEWING AND READING

- How would you compare the state of Jewish culture among the Jews of the Soviet Union with those living in East Central Europe?
- Give examples of Jewish integration into Weimar Germany. Did some Jews seek out their Jewish roots?
- How did the Nuremburg Laws serve to separate the Jews from Germans?
- From which countries, in what years, and under what conditions, do you find Jews traveling to Palestine and helping build the Jewish homeland?
- How did the Jews attempt to survive in the ghettos? Were they successful? What were their options?
- How would you sum up the effect of the Nazi destruction on Jewish life in Europe? On the Jews? On world civilization?

---

SUGGESTED READINGS

Nahum Glatzer, *Franz Rosenzweig: His Life and Thought* (Jewish Publication Society of America, 1953)

Raul Hilberg, *Destruction of European Jews* (Quadrangle, 1961)

Isaiah Trunk, *Judenrat* (Stein and Day, 1972)

# 9

## Into the Future
## (1945 to 1967)

_____ Michael Stanislawski _____

*Editor's Suggestions*
BEFORE VIEWING THE SHOW

Reexamine Chart 2 on the world Jewish population.

*Overview of the TV Program*

This program surveys the state of contemporary Jewry through-out the world, focusing mainly on the Jews of Israel, the United States, and the Soviet Union.

After World War II in Europe many Jews were in Displaced Persons' [DP] camps. Those who wished to immigrate to Palestine were prevented from doing so by British authorities. Still, some were able to immigrate illegally. Tiring of the strife between Arabs and Jews, Britain decided to end its mandate over Palestine and leave the country. After a tumultuous debate in the United Nations, the world body voted for the partition of the land into Jewish and Arab states.

The Jewish areas of Palestine had been laboriously improved by years of hard work. Swamps had been drained, stony areas reclaimed for agriculture, and desert land brought under cultivation. When the British left Palestine, the Jews declared all the areas they controlled to be the new independent state of Israel. Arab armies immediately attacked and the war for Israeli independence began. After the hostilities, Jews from many countries flocked to Israel to join in the building of the new Jewish state.

The six million Jews residing in the United States constituted the largest concentration of Jews in the world. These Jews, living in a free society, were able to integrate successfully into America. This, however, was often at the expense of their Jewish identity. Intermarriage and assimilation threatened to undermine the Jewish community. However, as the TV interviews indicate, there has been a renaissance of Jewish identification among those who are pursuing new forms of Jewish communal and religious expression.

Some of the nearly three million Jews who live in the Soviet Union suffered persecution in the years immediately prior to Stalin's death. Some have requested to emigrate to Israel and a few have been allowed to leave. Public expressions of Judaism and Jewish peoplehood are frowned upon, causing hardship for many Jews. Those who wish to emigrate, but have not been granted permission, often endure constant harassment by the Soviet authorities.

The show ends with a wide-ranging discussion of the possibilities for Jewish identity and expression in the contemporary world. While answers are not provided, the eloquent opinions of a number of Jews are presented.

*Watch for . . . and Think about*

Note the vociferous quality of the U.N. debates on Palestine and the enthusiastic Jewish response to the vote on partition. How do you explain these strong reactions?

Observe the footage of contemporary American Jewish life. How would you characterize this largest Jewish community in the world? Are they successful? What is the nature of their Jewish commitments?

Listen to the interviews and glimpse the photographs of Jewish life in the Soviet Union. How do the majority of Jews fare in Russia?

Listen carefully to the variety of individuals who voice their opinion on what it means to be Jewish in the contemporary world. Evaluate their responses.

## WHILE READING THE *STUDY GUIDE* AND *SOURCE READER*

Look for the following:

- Where Jews left from to settle in the state of Israel. Why did most of them come? What was the Israelis' vision of the new society they wished to create? Identify *yishuv, kibbutz.*
- How native and immigrant Jews in Russia in the 1940's viewed the Soviet government and its policies toward the Jews. Identify Stalin.

- How fully the Jews were integrated into American society in the years following World War II.
- The wars that were fought by the state of Israel between 1948 and 1967. What were the causes of these wars?

## THE STATE OF ISRAEL

The most immediate goal of world Jewry after World War II was to find a home for the survivors of Nazism stranded in Europe. (See **Reading 9-1.**) This mission was intricately connected with the struggle for the establishment of a Jewish state in the Land of Israel.

By 1939 the Jewish population of Palestine had grown to 449,500. Almost half of this number had arrived since Hitler's assumption of power in Germany. For the first time not all immigrants to the new Jewish homeland had been dedicated Zionists before fleeing their former places of residence; most were convinced of the Zionist message by the grim realities of life. They learned in a most shocking way that anti-Semitism was not an unimportant vestige of medieval prejudice but a hateful part of the modern world. The Zionist experiment was not a wild idea of rebellious youths but the only hope for Jews rejected and expelled from what for centuries had been their home. The immigration to Palestine of these Jews, mostly from Germany and Poland, drastically changed not only their own self-perception, but also the nature of the *Yishuv*—the Hebrew term for the Jewish community in the Land of Israel.

Until this time the overwhelming majority of Jews who came to Palestine had been young idealists bent on creating in the ancestral home of the Jewish people a new kind of Jewish society, a new kind of Jewish culture, in short, a new kind of Jew. In line with the basic Zionist premise that the point of creating a Jewish homeland was to "normalize" the Jewish people, the early immigrants attempted to rid themselves of what they considered to be "abnormal" or unhealthy traits that resulted from perpetual minority status. The new type of Jewish society created in the Land of Israel would be based not on commerce or trade but on the most natural of all human activities, agriculture. It would therefore not have to rely on other people's production of food and other basics essential to life. Jewish farmers created communal agricultural settlements known as the *kibbutz*, a collective farm in which all property—land, equipment, homes, produce, even members' clothes and personal goods—was owned in common. On a kibbutz, absolute equality reigned supreme: work was distributed equally and by joint decision; women and men bore the same rights and obligations including physical labor; children were raised in a collective nursery, spending only a few hours a day with their parents. A network of such settlements, as well as other types of less extensive communal farms, was set up throughout the length and breadth of Jewish Palestine, reclaiming marshes and desert land. Stemming from this agricultural self-sufficiency, the pioneers believed, there would emerge a more general sense of autonomy and self-confidence and less fear of the effect of one's actions on one's neighbors. Physical labor and self-assertiveness would, in turn, be further developed in military service, which in the Jewish homeland was to be made universal for men and women. A Jewish soldier would not only defend the Land of Israel but also symbolize the determination of the Jewish people as a whole to take its defense into its own hands, and not have to rely on other nations or international guarantees. Beyond physical prowess and economic self-suffiency, the new Jew would also be the bearer of a proud new culture, based on the renewal of the Hebrew language and the teachings of the Hebrew Bible.

Within a few short decades, and despite increasing hostility from the Arabs and the British authorities, the pioneering groups had indeed successfully planted in the Land of Israel the seeds of a productive and fruitful Jewish homeland based on these principles. The Hebrew language, basically unspoken for two thousand years, became the mother tongue of hundreds of thousands of Jews. In addition to prayers and religious commentaries and poetry, there was now a secular literature in Hebrew describing plows and fertilizers and sex; babies cried out to their mothers in the language of Isaiah and Amos.

The crises of the 1930's and the mass immigration to Palestine of middle-class Jews not committed to Zionism, farming, or the Hebrew language forced the *Yishuv* to expand its ways of life. Cities such as Tel Aviv and Haifa, previously disdained by the pioneers, now grew into large centers of business in which trade was conducted in German, Polish, and Yiddish—most offensive to the early pioneers as symbolic of the life of the Jews in exile. Religious Orthodoxy, abandoned by the majority of early immigrants in favor of an unrelenting secularism and dedication to principles of socialism, established itself more strongly in the urban communities. The labor movement was still the backbone of Jewish society and provided almost all its political leaders, but there was now competition from other quarters.

Of course, none of the pioneers regretted the arrival of these different kinds of Jewish settlers. All agreed that the primary purpose of the Jewish homeland was to provide a refuge for every Jew threatened around the world. In fact, the *Yishuv* as a whole was outraged by the sharp reduction in immigration resulting from implementation of the British White Paper of May 1939. In the months that followed that drastic measure, the leadership of the *Yishuv* determined to continue saving Jews from the European horrors. The problem, of course, was not only how to conduct illegal immigration during a world war, but also how to do so without disturbing the British fight against the Nazis. Indeed, the overriding consideration of the Jewish people as a whole was to defeat Hitler, and Jews in the *Yishuv*, just like their brethren in the Allied lands, volunteered in large numbers for the fight. The basic policy of the Zionist movement and its supporters throughout the Jewish world was articulated by the head of the *Yishuv*, David Ben-Gurion: "We must fight Hitler as if there were no White Paper, and the White Paper as if there were no Hitler."

During the war, this policy yielded satisfactory results on all fronts. Palestinian Jews served bravely in the British army, while the *Haganah*, the illegal Jewish underground army, struggled valiantly to save as many European Jews as possible. At the same time the world Zionist leadership consolidated itself sufficiently to make a critical decision at a meeting held at the Biltmore Hotel in New York City in May 1942: as soon as the war ended an independent Jewish state must be established in Palestine. All previous debates about possible alternatives such as autonomy without independence or binationalism, disintegrated in the face of the realities of recent history.

After the end of World War II the relations between the *Yishuv* and the British authorities took a sharp turn for the worse. The British remained adamantly opposed to the creation of an independent Jewish commonwealth and even to the immigration to Palestine of large numbers of the survivors of Nazism. The *Haganah* and the more radical resistance forces of the *Yishuv*, furious at what they considered to be the incomprehensible inhumanity of British policy, compounded by anti-Semitism, organized large-scale illegal immigration operations as well as attacks against British forces in Palestine. The tension mounted when British ships seized boats carrying Jewish refugees from Europe and sent the Jews to still another form of imprisonment—detention camps in Cyprus. The Jewish forces responded with more violence against the British; the British retaliated with arrests, imprisonments, and stronger measures against the illegal migration. Finally, the British government realized that the problem could not be solved without international mediation and turned over the question of the future of Palestine to the newly formed United Nations. On November 29, 1947, after much study and vociferous debate, the General Assembly of the United Nations voted more than two to one in favor of partitioning Palestine into two states, one Jewish, the other Arab. The Zionist movement, although unhappy with some of the details of the resolution (Jerusalem, for example, was not included in the Jewish portion), accepted the partition and set about planning the creation of a small but independent Jewish state. (**See Reading 9-2.**)

The leaders of the Palestinian Arabs, on the other hand, were outraged by the very notion of a Jewish state in what they considered to be their land and vociferously opposed the partition plan. Supported by Arab states, they began to launch attacks against the Jewish settlements from the day after the United Nations' vote. During the fighting that ensued, an exodus of much of the Arab population from Palestine took place. The Jews claimed that the Arabs fled; the Arabs claimed that they were expelled. Undoubtedly, as in many similar situations, flight and expulsion went hand-in-hand and sometimes were indistinguishable.

While the violence mounted into full-scale war, the resolution of the United Nations was implemented at least in part. On May 14, 1948 the leaders of the Yishuv gathered at the Tel Aviv Museum and declared the independence of the first Jewish commonwealth in two thousand years: the State of Israel. The figurehead president of the new state was Chaim Weizmann, the elderly leader of the Zionist movement who had negotiated the Balfour Declaration. Both the American and the Soviet governments quickly recognized the new Jewish state. (**See Reading 9-3.**)

This international support was vital to Israel, because on the night after its independence was declared, five Arab armies invaded the tiny country. A bitter war raged for over a year and finally resulted in a surprising massive victory for Israel. After armistice agreements with its enemies but no peace treaties, Israel gained more territory than it had been awarded in the partition plan, including half of the city of Jerusalem.

Jews around the world rejoiced in unbridled celebration of the establishment of the State of Israel. Much of the opposition to Zionism that had existed in the Jewish community in the previous decades stemmed from the belief that the hope to restore the Land of Israel to the Jews was a beautiful but impracticable dream. Now the dream was a reality, and it seemed possible that the Jewish people, which had suffered so grievously in the recent past, was on its way to rejuvenation.

The first step on the road to recovery was the transplantation of Jews to their new homeland. The State of Israel opened its doors to all Jews, promising immediate citizenship and help in resettlement. In the first year of Israel's existence, 203,000 Jews from forty-two countries arrived in the Jewish state; by the end of 1951 the total of new immigrants was an astounding 684,201. Almost half of these immigrants were refugees, but some were voluntary migrants. There were even several cases in which virtually entire Jewish communities transferred themselves to Israel: Bulgarian Jewry, spared in the Holocaust, elected to join the new Jewish enterprise en masse. Such a communal immigration was more common among the Jews of the Middle East. In North Africa and the Arab countries the status of ancient Jewish communities, unemancipated and largely impoverished, deteriorated rapidly as a result of the reaction of their Islamic governments to the creation of Israel. Almost all the Jews of Yemen, Iraq, and Libya were transplanted to Israel, as was the case later with large numbers of Moroccan, Tunisian, and Algerian Jews. In many cases, the upper classes of these communities emigrated to the West, particularly to France, while the lower classes came to Israel. Only in Morocco and Iran did substantial Jewish communities remain in Islamic lands. (**See Reading 9-10.**)

Despite both the state of war that persisted as a result of the steadfast refusal of the Arab states to recognize Israel and the tensions occasioned by continued Palestinian Arab raids on Israeli territory, the young state was able to turn most of its attention to its internal affairs.

The inner life of Israel was determined first and foremost by its continuous absorption of new immigrants. Although the frantic pace of immigration slowed down after huge flows from North Africa,

Poland, and Rumania in the mid-1950's, significant numbers of Jews from around the world arrived in Israel every year. They and those who came before them had to be housed, fed, and employed in a country with few natural resources and less accumulated capital. Some help was, of course, afforded by world Jewry through generous philanthropic funds, as well as by the United States and other countries and international agencies. Perhaps the most dramatic—and controversial—financial assistance came from the Federal Republic of Germany, which began to pay retribution to survivors around the world as well as to the Jewish state for losses to life and property suffered under the Nazis. Various right-wing forces in Israel opposed accepting any assistance from Germany, or establishing diplomatic relations with the new German state, but Prime Minister David Ben-Gurion successfully argued that the German government's apology should be honored and that Jewish life must continue.

The absorption of Israel's millions of immigrants produced problems beyond the financial sphere. Extremely troublesome was the ethnic tension that had arisen in Israel between the Ashkenazic Jews, who for the most part had come earlier and controlled the political parties and positions of influence, and the Oriental Jews, who had come later and thus had less access to power and money. The gulf between the two communities was widened by the fact that the Oriental Jews were slowly becoming the majority in the country, due both to immigration and to the higher birthrate characteristic of a more traditional group. Intermarriage between the two communities grew from year to year, as did the absorption of non-European Jews into influential and lucrative professions, but there still existed a dramatic economic, social, and political gap between the two groups. A significant role in bridging that gap was played by the campaign to produce in Israel a new kind of Jew, regardless of origin: a Jew sensitive to his tradition and heritage but dedicated to forging a new Israeli consciousness and culture. (See Reading 9-11.)

The vision of the new kind of Jewish community that was implemented by the government was still that of the early pioneers. A coalition of social democratic parties ruled Israel from its inception. Dominated by David Ben-Gurion, who served as prime minister from 1948 to 1953 and from 1955 to 1963, the government of Israel achieved remarkable success in fulfilling most of its hopes. Its ideology was not shared, however, by the plethora of other parties that competed for seats in the Israeli parliament. The major opposition party was the right-wing *Herut* (Freedom) party, led by Menachem Begin, which strenuously opposed socialism at home and concessions abroad. Significant, too, were the parties that tried to combine Zionism with modern Orthodox Judaism—an attempt that met the support of a small minority in predominantly secular Israeli society. Smaller groups of Israelis created parties that preached views ranging from liberalism to non-Zionist Orthodoxy to communism. The latter group, as well as some of the more left-wing elements of the social democratic coalition, were profoundly affected by developments in the Soviet Union and Eastern Europe in the postwar period and especially by the fate of the Jews in those countries.

## JEWS IN THE SOVIET UNION

The situation of Soviet Jews was most complex and can only be understood through a retrospective review. The territorial expansion of the U.S.S.R. at the beginning of the war in Europe resulted in a substantial increase in the Soviet-Jewish population. First, the annexation of eastern Poland brought over one million Jews under Soviet rule; in addition, about another 300,000 Polish Jews who found themselves under Nazi control in central Poland fled to the Soviet-occupied zone. Second, in the summer of 1940 another half million Jews were brought into the Soviet Union after the Red Army occupied the Baltic states of Lithuania, Latvia, and Estonia, and when Rumania ceded parts of its territory to the Soviets. The Soviet Union was left with the largest Jewish population in the world.

But that population now included millions of Polish, Lithuanian, Latvian, and Rumanian Jews who had never been subjected to the cultural ravages of Sovietization; these were Jews who still actively practiced and studied their religion and who belonged to the gamut of Jewish nationalist and socialist parties banned in the Soviet Union proper since the early 1920's. All of these religious, political, and cultural activities were outlawed by the new Soviet masters (and many activists were imprisoned); nonetheless this group was bound to influence the native Soviet-Jewish population.

This demographic stimulus to Jewish national self-perception was augmented by another important phenomenon that emerged in the course of World War II. As already noted, the majority of the Jewish population of the western provinces of the Soviet Union was murdered in the Nazi Holocaust. But for those Jews who survived the occupation and the much larger number who remained alive in parts of the country never conquered by the Nazis, the Soviet Union loomed large as the protector and defender of Jewish lives. To be sure, the Soviet government steadfastly refused to publicize the atrocities against the Jews, to acknowledge the specific sacrifices of Jewish victims of the Nazis—even to commemorate the Jewishness of those murdered at Babi Yar. But this acknowledgment was hardly of primary consideration to those who felt their lives had been saved. Moreover, during the war Stalin had in a small way encouraged Jewish national and cultural self-awareness and expression: just as he relaxed restrictions on the Russian Orthodox Church and stimulated Russian nationalism, he permitted a renewal of Jewish cultural activity and migration to the Jewish Autonomous Region. In addition, he appointed Jewish writers, poets, and artists to a Jewish Anti-Fascist Committee that condemned Nazi policy toward the Jews and called on world Jewry to rally together in the struggle against Hitler. In retrospect it is clear that this campaign was meant primarily for external consumption, aimed specifically at encouraging American Jewry to support the United States' entry into the war. But the activities of the Anti-Fascist Committee continued after the Americans joined the war and had a significant impact on Jews inside the Soviet Union. Through the Jewish Anti-Fascist Committee the Soviet government acknowledged what it had previously denied and strenuously repressed: the common ties and mutual interests uniting Jews around the world. Through literary creativity, cultural events, and mass media, the Anti-Fascist Committee supported the notion that Jewish specificity and solidarity were not unacceptable to the Soviet leadership.

After the war this perception was stimulated by the support given by the Soviet government to the establishment of the State of Israel. The Soviets publicly argued the Zionist cause in a variety of international forums; they and the East European countries they controlled voted in favor of the partition of Palestine. The U.S.S.R. was the first country formally to recognize the new Jewish state after its independence. The Israeli victory in the battles that followed was aided enormously by Czech arms sent to the Jews with Soviet approval. Again, it is now clear that the Soviet support for Zionism and Israel was not ideologically motivated but was based on opposition to Britain and the hope of gaining influence in the strategically vital Middle East. The effect of this pro-Zionist activity at the time, however, was to ally the Soviet Union with Jewish interests around the world and thus to strengthen the loyalty and gratitude, as well as the sensibilities, of Soviet Jews.

This Jewish pride was most graphically exhibited by Soviet Jewry when Israel's first minister to the U.S.S.R., Golda Meir (then called Meyerson), arrived in Moscow for the High Holy Days of 1948. Tens of thousands of Soviet Jews received her enthusiastically at the synagogue. The excitement of the Jews was absolutely genuine, spontaneous, and innocent; they did not know that the Soviet government would disapprove of what they were doing. (See Reading 9-4.)

This demonstration, however, marked a turning-point in Soviet-Jewish history. The government apparently began to realize the domestic implications of Jewish national solidarity. Support of the State of Israel among Soviet Jews raised the question of the success of the overall nationalities policy pursued by the regime for thirty years. That policy was in fact both two-faced and utterly unsuccessful— but so public an acknowledgment of its failure was unacceptable to the authorities. They therefore began a propaganda campaign against Jewish nationalism and separatism. This attack was immensely complicated by the personality of Josef Stalin, whose every whim dictated all aspects of Soviet life. As part of the madness that gripped him in the last years of his life, Stalin became uncontrollably anti-Semitic. He was convinced that the Jews were his main enemies, that they were all spies, that they were to blame for all the problems in Soviet society; they were "rootless cosmopolitans" not truly loyal to Russia, communism, or anything but themselves. Soon Zionism was added to the charges against the Jews—though diplomatic relations with Israel were not affected. The Anti-Fascist Committee was closed down, its newspaper outlawed; all other Jewish cultural institutions were disbanded. Jewish intellectuals, writers, and artists began to be arrested on a large scale, accused of being nationalist bourgeois Jews, agents of the international Zionist conspiracy and American imperialism.

On August 12, 1952 the elite of Soviet Jewish culture was executed in one fell swoop. The newspaper *Pravda* reported the following January that a plot on Stalin's life by a group of mostly Jewish doctors had been discovered. Rumors spread that all Soviet Jews would be rounded up and deported to Siberia; Jews were attacked in the streets and dismissed from jobs. The tension was unbearable and then, on March 5, 1953 the announcement came: Stalin was dead. Soviet Jews, along with the rest of the country, and indeed the world, were stunned. For so long and so completely had this one man dominated the life of the world's largest country that it was almost impossible to imagine the Soviet Union without him. Three weeks later the Soviet press reported that the doctors' plot had been a fabrication of the security police with absolutely no basis in fact. The doctors were released from prison. The Jewish population as a whole breathed a collective sigh of relief. (**See Reading 9-5.**)

The following period witnessed a lessening of the terror of the preceding years and, after Khrushchev's denunciation of Stalin's crimes, a general relaxation of the extreme measures of the Stalinist nightmare. But after the experience of Stalinist anti-Semitism, life was never the same for Soviet Jews. Jewish culture and self-confidence were never restored even to their pre-1948 level; the Jews knew that their dream of successful integration into Soviet society had been destroyed. Many, of course, wanted nothing more than a quiet, peaceful life with family and friends, a respite from the horrors of the war and the terror of Stalinism. Their Jewishness was an obstacle to a normal life; it was best to forget, hide, and pretend. But for other Soviet Jews, particularly those in the parts of the country occupied during World War II (as well as those in Soviet Georgia and the Asian republics), Jewish sensibilities and culture went underground, to reemerge at a later date in a different context. (**See Reading 9-12.**)

## THE SOVIET BLOC

Developments in the Soviet Union had an equally disruptive effect on the Jews in the rest of Eastern Europe, which had come under Soviet-controlled communist rule in the years after the end of the war. In all of these countries Jews had played a prominent role in the communist parties before and after the war and rose to positions of influence in the new communist governments. This led to resentment based both on anti-communism and anti-Semitism. During the anti-Jewish terror before Stalin's death, Jews in these countries were accused of disloyalty to him and his brand of communism; after Stalin's death, they were accused of being Stalinists. Thus in Czechoslovakia in 1952 a group of prominent Party and government officials of Jewish origin, led by Rudolf Slansky, was charged with forming a Zionist conspiracy against the interests of the state and the Party. Eight of the accused, including Slansky, were executed; three others were sentenced to life imprisonment. A commission of inquiry established during the short-lived "Prague Summer" of 1968 discovered that the show trials and their anti-Semitic charges were carefully orchestrated by the Soviet secret police. (**See Reading 9-6.**)

In Poland the years after Stalin's death witnessed an intense internal struggle within the Communist Party which resulted in severe attacks on the old-guard Stalinists, who were blamed for all of the very serious problems plaguing the country. There were innuendoes from the start that these Stalinists were mostly Jews, and that for this reason they were disloyal to Poland. The new government actively opposed any manifestations of overt anti-Semitism, however, and these charges did not lead to any measures against the small Jewish community of Poland. Indeed, the authorities attempted to convince Polish Jews not to leave the country and encouraged them to participate in the construction of a socialist Poland. But the seed was planted: a decade later, after the new Polish government failed to solve the economic woes of the country, the accusation that it was the Stalinist Jews who had ruined Poland reemerged and led to the final ousting of the Jews from Poland. (**See Reading 9-7.**)

## INTEGRATION IN WESTERN EUROPE AND THE UNITED STATES

The dismal failure of Jewish integration in the Soviet Union and the communist bloc yielded a crucial lesson about the very nature of modern Jewish history. The first advocates of emancipation had been willing to grant everything to the Jews as individuals but nothing to them as a group, but this distinction obscured many of the complexities of the dilemma of Jewish integration. Legal guarantees of the equality of individual Jews or even commitments to Jewish group rights were insufficient to ensure the successful emancipation of the Jews. Equally insufficient, it turned out, was a social integration of the Jews in which their right to choose how to define themselves—how to live their lives as Jews—was effaced. Emancipation could only succeed in societies which were based on both a firm commitment to the inviolable integrity of the individual and its corollary, to the right of individuals to exercise whatever group ties, loyalties, and characteristics they chose. In short, only in pluralistic democracies could the Jews experience the full fruits of emancipation.

In sharp contrast to the decline of Jewish life in Eastern Europe in the postwar era, therefore, stood the unprecedented flourishing of the Jewish communities of the West. In the 1950's and 1960's the Jews of North America, Western Europe, and, to a lesser extent, Latin America experienced an impressive cultural, economic, and demographic renewal. Immigration of Holocaust survivors and the Jews fleeing North African and Arab countries served to reinforce Jewish self-awareness and to revivify religious and cultural institutions in these communities. "Native" Jews as well responded to the horror of the destruction of European Jewry and to the excitement of the founding of the Jewish state by increasingly rejecting the option of assimilation and by identifying themselves with Jewish culture, religiosity, and peoplehood.

The most important center of the Jewish revival in the Western world was, of course, the United States. American Jewry was the largest Jewish community in the world with a population of over five and a half million. By far the majority of these Jews were third- and fourth-generation Americans who felt themselves—and indeed were—as much at home in America as anyone else. The postwar boom in American prosperity, self-confidence, culture, and even international influence affected Jews in exactly the same way as it did all other Americans. Just as the United States became the leading power in the world, so did American Jewry become the dominant Jewish community in the world. All the obstacles to the full integration of the Jews that had existed in American society up to World War II were now removed: Jews could and did enter all professions, universities, political organizations. While some measure of social discrimination still persisted, it was both on the decline and increasingly irrelevant to American Jews. They continued to rise to positions of influence and prominence in medicine, law, business, academic life, government, and the arts. But such a list almost misrepresents their accomplishment in America: the Jews not only benefited from the unique opportunities available to them in the United States, they were integral partners in the creation and development of American society. No realm of American life was closed to them and no aspect of American society was conceivable without them.

Parallel to this deeper penetration of Jews into the social fabric of America was their wider geographic dispersion throughout the country. The largest Jewish community in the United States—and indeed, the world—remained New York City, but other major metropolitan centers such as Los Angeles, Miami, Boston, and Philadelphia included Jewish communities that grew larger and more influential in American-Jewish life.

Naturally, part and parcel of this unqualified integration of Jews in the United States was the unparalleled possibility of assimilation in American life. Here as nowhere else in the world, or for that matter as never before in Jewish history, could a Jew cease to consider himself or herself part of the Jewish religion or the Jewish people. In America and other Western countries, affiliation with a Jewish community had always been voluntary. But as the United States increasingly became a remarkably secularized and pluralistic society, a person's religious or ethnic origins were more and more a private affair. Thus, in the States it became virtually impossible to know whether anyone was Jewish unless that person chose to identify himself or herself as such.

This freedom to disaffiliate or disappear had a significant impact on American Jewish life. In the first place there was no way of knowing how many Jews there were in America. More importantly, Jewish communal, cultural, and religious institutions obviously would be threatened by assimilation. Intermarriage between Jews and non-Jews rose dramatically: by the mid-1960's, approximately thirty percent of the Jews who married chose spouses who were not Jewish. This diminution of the Jewish family was especially important for an urban, mobile population that exhibited a very low birthrate.

But once more, the crucial fact about American Jewry was that by far most Jews did not stop thinking of themselves as Jewish and living as such. Despite the serious demographic danger signals, the Jewish community continued to grow. The ways in which Americans understood, exhibited, and expressed their Jewishness were new—and constantly changing. Critics and religious leaders worried about the implications of this behavior on the future of the community as a whole, but American Jews proceeded undaunted along their uncharted and creative way.

This creativity was channeled in part into the development of an indigenous American Jewish culture. Debates over whether Jewish literature, art, or music consist of anything written by Jews or only those creations on Jewish themes or meant for Jewish audiences are irresoluble, and largely pointless. In America in the 1950's and 1960's Jewish novelists, short story writers, playwrights, poets, actors, comedians, directors, painters, sculptors, composers, musicians, dancers, television and radio writers, and countless other varieties of creative artists produced and performed works that fit all definitions of Jewish art and artistry. Jewish writers from Saul Bellow to Phillip Roth to Lenny Bruce made explorations of the Jewish experience in America one of the dominant motifs of American literature. Jewish scholars and intellectuals investigated all aspects of the humanities, social sciences, and natural sciences, as well as Jewish history and thought. Indeed, the integration of Jewish studies into American intellectual life as a natural and necessary part of the work of the university, the literary journal, and learned discourse in general is at once a symbol and a measure of the degree of true integration of Jews into American civilization. (See Readings 9-8 and 9-9.)

Alongside the centrality of Jews in American culture was their increased importance in the political life of the country. In addition to the rise in the number of Jewish senators, congressmen, state and local legislators, judges, government officials, and party activists, Jews became increasingly vocal in expressing their beliefs about the nature of American society, as well as about issues of specific concern to the Jewish community. Once more, the radical novelty here was the American Jews' insistence that there was no distinction between the two realms: all Jewish concerns were American concerns, and vice versa. In line with this perception, Jews were active in the civil rights movement of the 1960's, manifesting their fundamental commitment to the principle of equality. Even the prominence of the Jews in the forces opposing the war in Vietnam and in the New Left—movements that rarely articulated a specific Jewish commitment or bent—can be regarded as a result of the unique role Jews played in American politics and American politics in Jewish life.

By the mid-1960's the subject that more and more dominated the intersection of Jewish and American politics was the State of Israel. The overwhelming majority of American Jews had become enthusiastic supporters of the Jewish state and firm believers that Israel, as a democratic, Western country, was a vital key to American interests and foreign policy in the Middle East. The American government and the American population as a whole strongly supported and admired the Jewish state.

## THE SIX DAY WAR

Israel was by this time an important member of the international community of nations. From a fragile, tiny outpost of dedicated pioneers facing relentless external threats and internal crises, the Jewish state had become a mature, cohesive, secure, and militarily powerful country. After the Suez campaign of 1956, in which Israel, at the urging of Britain and France, occupied and then withdrew from Egyptian territory, an extended period of relative external calm set in. Tensions and terrorist attacks persisted, but security reigned supreme. That security was shattered in the late spring and early summer of 1967. Skirmishes with the Syrians and continued terrorist attacks on Israeli settlements were followed by the decision of President Nasser of Egypt to send large numbers of his forces into the Sinai desert adjoining Israel. Nasser also demanded that the peace-keeping forces of the United Nations guarding the border between Egypt and Israel be removed. After the Secretary General of the United Nations hastily agreed to remove the troops, Nasser further upped the ante of international tension by declaring that Egypt would impose a sea blockade on Israel's southern ports, cutting the Jewish state off from its essential means of supply. Israel had long warned that any such action, directly violating international law, would be considered a cause of war. Nasser apparently believed that he could win a war with Israel. The last week of May 1967 left the entire world waiting in frightened suspense while negotiations to ease the crisis collapsed.

Jordanian, Saudi Arabian, Iraqi, Kuwaiti, and Algerian forces joined the Egyptians and Syrians in a state of alert. The Israeli government invited opposition party leaders to join a cabinet on national unity and debated between waiting for an Arab attack or launching a preemptive strike to gain the upper hand. On the morning of June 5, 1967 the second option was chosen: the Israeli army and air force moved in tandem against their enemies. Within a few hours, the air war ended in an astonishing Israeli military success. Fighting on the ground was harder, but in four days the Israelis had crossed the Suez Canal and were in control of the Sinai peninsula. At the beginning of the war, the Israelis had informed King Hussein of Jordan that they would not attack his country if he would keep his army out of the battle. Misled by Nasser, Hussein believed that the Israelis had been routed by the Egyptians and so sent his forces across the border. By the next day the Israeli army had reunited Jerusalem; three days later the West Bank of the Jordan River was in Israeli hands.

What became known as the "Six Day War" was over. Israel had won an astounding victory that surprised the entire world. For the Jewish state, the war led to far-reaching economic, cultural, and political changes that virtually transformed the essential fabric of the country's life and continue to dominate political debate today. (**See Reading 9-13.**) For Jews around the world, the effects of the June 1967 war were less tangible, but equally lasting. As Israel stood at the brink of destruction in the last weeks of May and first week of June of 1967, Jews everywhere—from Montreal to Moscow, from Teheran to Bucharest, from Buenos Aires to San Francisco—sat at the edge of their chairs in fearful disbelief that the events of 1939–45 might be repeated. It seemed possible that a major Jewish community, indeed the heart of the Jewish world, might be attacked and destroyed. In the course of the war, Jews who thought they had no connection with Judaism or Israel felt a curious, undefinable pull at their hearts, their minds, their souls. In the wake of the war, hundreds of thousands, if not millions, of Jews awoke to a new sense of solidarity with the State of Israel and the Jewish people. In American and other Western countries this increased identification resulted in a rise in philanthropy, affiliation with synagogues and Jewish community organizations, renewed interest in Jewish learning, and a newly assertive and self-conscious Jewish politics. In the Soviet Union and other parts of Eastern Europe the Six Day War galvanized the vague but profound Jewish sensibilities of millions of Jews and led to a resurgence of Jewish national feeling that continues to have dramatic effects and implications on Jewish, as well as international, affairs.

The years after 1967 cannot yet be viewed with the historical distance necessary for inclusion in this study. The future, of course, is impossible to predict: neither Jewish history nor any other yields clear lessons, not to speak of prophecies. Indeed, perhaps the only "lesson" of modern Jewish history is that the utterly unpredictable, even the impossible, may in fact occur.

But unless history itself changes in a way we cannot foresee, it is safe to assume that Jewish history will continue along its three-thousand-year course as the continuously evolving saga of a remarkable people, an integral part of civilization as a whole.

---

*Editor's Questions*
AFTER VIEWING AND READING

- Characterize the relations between the *Yishuv* and the British Mandate authorities between 1939 and 1945.

- Did the visit to the Soviet Union of Golda Meir, Israel's envoy to Moscow, force the Soviet government to rethink its policies toward the Jews?
- How did Stalinist policies affect the Jews both within the Soviet Union and in the Soviet Bloc countries?
- What role did the American Jews play in American culture in the post-World War II era?
- How did the Six Day War in 1967 affect the Jews in the United States and throughout the world? How did the Israelis perceive this conflict?

SUGGESTED READINGS

Lionel Kochan, *Jews in Soviet Russia since 1917* (Oxford University Press, 1978)

Nadav Safran, *Israel: The Embattled Ally* (Harvard University Press, 1981)

Marshall Sklare, *Conservative Judaism* (Schocken, 1972)

# Glossary

*aggadah*:  literally, telling or narration; generally, lore, theology, fable, biblical exegesis, or ethics.

**amphictyony**:  literally, league of those dwelling around; a coalition of tribes sharing in the maintenance of a common central sanctuary.

*Apocrypha*:  literally, hidden writings; a collection of books included with the Greek translation of the Hebrew Bible but not found in the Hebrew original.

**Ashkenazi(m)**:  northern European Jew(s), those who generally follow the customs originating in medieval German Judaism.

*Avot*:  literally, Fathers; a tractate of the *Mishnah* consisting of ethical statements of the rabbis.

*ba'alei tosafot*:  authors of the novellae on the *Talmud*, who generally added to the commentary of Rashi. They flourished in northern France in the twelfth and thirteenth centuries.

**B.C.E.**:  before the common era (equivalent of B.C.)

*beraitot*:  Palestinian rabbinic statements not included in the *Mishnah* of Judah the Prince.

**C.E.**:  common era (equivalent of A.D.)

**covenant**:  a formal treaty.

**cuneiform**:  literally, wedge-shaped; the writing system of ancient Mesopotamia and adjacent lands.

**Davidic dynasty**:  the successive rulers who trace their ancestry to King David.

**Decalogue**:  literally, ten words or sayings; the Ten Commandments thought to have been divinely ordained for Israel at Mount Sinai.

**Diaspora**:  dispersion, the exile of the Jews from the Land of Israel.

*dhimmis*:  a protected class in Muslim society made up of Christians, Zoroastrians, Jews, and a few other faiths.

*dina de-malkhuta dina*:  literally, the law of the state is the law; a rabbinic formulation originating in Babylonia that meant the civil law of the secular government was synonymous with the *Torah* law.

**dynasty**:  a succession of rulers belonging to the same royal house or family.

**Exodus**:  the dramatic deliverance of the Israelites from Egyptian oppression; their departure from Egypt.

*gaon/geonim* (plural):  literally, eminence, excellency; title of distinguished Talmudic scholars who headed Babylonian academies in the Middle Ages.

**garrison-cities**:  fortified cities where supplies were stored, chiefly for military purposes.

*Gemara*:  literally, completion; comments and discussions on the *Mishnah*. The *Mishnah* and the *Gemara* make up the *Talmud*.

259

*genizah*:   a burial chamber for old Jewish books; the most prominent one was discovered in Fustat, Egypt, at the end of the nineteenth century.

*goldene medine*:   literally, the golden land; figurative name for the United States among Eastern European Jewish immigrants.

*hadith*:   the oral traditions of Muslim law.

*halakhah*:   literally, the way things are done; from *halakh*; the prescriptive legal tradition of Judaism.

**Hapiru/Habiru:**   a social or ethnic group in the ancient Near East, possibly identical with the biblical Hebrews.

**Hasidism:**   a movement of pietistic revival originating in Eastern Europe in the eighteenth century founded by Israel ben Eliezer of Medzibozh, called the *Ba'al Shem Tov*.

*heder*:   literally, room; used as name for traditional Jewish elementary school.

**Hellenistic:**   pertaining to the Greek culture characteristic of Alexander the Great and his successors.

**hieroglyphic:**   literally, sacred carving; the principal writing system of ancient Egypt.

*hijra*:   the migration of the prophet Muḥammad from Mecca to Medina in 622 C.E.

*jizya:*   a poll tax paid by *dhimmis* to the Muslim government.

**Judaism:**   the religion and culture that emerged out of Israelite traditions beginning sometime during the Persian period.

**judges:**   temporary military leaders who ruled one or more of the tribes of Israel before the establishment of the monarchy.

*kabbalah*:   literally, tradition; generally refers to Jewish mystical tradition.

*Kalam:*   school of Muslim philosophy, especially in medieval Baghdad, which strove to harmonize Muslim faith and Greek philosophy.

**Karaites:**   Middle Eastern Jewish sect in Middle Ages which rejected the oral law of the rabbis.

**kibbutz:**   collective farm set up in the Land of Israel.

*Koran*:   the Muslim sacred scriptures.

*massekhtot/massekhet* (singular):   tractates, sub-sections of the *sedarim* of the *Mishnah*, and subsequently the *Talmud*.

**messiah:**   literally, the anointed one; originally any Israelite king daubed with oil by priest or prophet; later the Davidic king whose future restoration was, in Jewish belief, to usher in the kingship of God.

*Midrash/Midrashim* (plural):   rabbinic exegesis of scripture; also refers to collections of such exegeses.

*Midrash Rabbah*:   a major collection of rabbinic *midrashim* on the *Torah* and the *Five Scrolls* (Song of Songs, Ruth, Lamentations, Ecclesiastes, and Esther).

*Midreshei Aggadah*:   collections of homiletical exegeses on non-legal, narrative sections of scripture.

*Midreshei Halakhah*:   collections of exegeses on the legal sections of scripture.

*Mishnah*:   code of law edited by Judah the Prince organized in six orders (ca. 200 C.E.)

*mitnagdim/mitnaged* (singular):   opponents of the Hasidim of the eighteenth century led by the Talmudic authority Elijah the Gaon of Vilna.

*mizvah/mizvot* (plural):   commandments; scriptural or rabbinic injunctions, generally used in the sense of good deeds.

*nasi*:   prince.

**Palestine:**   that portion of the Holy Land first settled by the Philistines; later, the entire land.

**patriarchal:**   pertaining to the reputed ancestors of the tribes of Israel (Abraham, Isaac, and Jacob) or to their times.

**Pentateuch:**   literally, five-part book; the first five books of the Hebrew Bible, also known as the Five Books of Moses or in Hebrew as the *Torah.*

**pharaoh:**   the king in ancient Egypt.

**Pharisee:**   from Hebrew, *parush*, separate; party in ancient Judaism teaching the oral *Torah* revealed at Mount Sinai along with the written one; preserved and interpreted by the rabbis.

**pogrom:**   from Russian, violent attack on Jewish lives and property.

**pre-Socratic:**   pertaining to Greek thinkers who preceded the great Athenian philosopher Socrates (469–399 B.C.E.).

**prophet:**   literally, forth-speaker; a person inspired by the deity and speaking, or claiming to speak, in God's name.

**promulgate:**   proclaim, enact, or institute, especially with reference to a new law or laws.

**protohistory:**   a phase of national traditions reconstructed entirely from literary sources unsupported by documentary evidence.

*resh galuta*:   exilarch: literally, head of the exile; leader of the Jewish community in Babylonia in Talmudic and medieval times.

**Sanhedrin:**   Jewish legislative-judicial institution in ancient times.

*sedarim*:   the orders of the *Mishnah.*

*Sefer ha-Zohar*:   medieval kabbalist work, written in Spain in the thirteenth century.

**Semitic:**   a group of related Near Eastern languages including Hebrew, Arabic, Aramaic, and Akkadian, among others.

*Shulhan Arukh*:   literally, prepared table; authoritative code of Jewish law written by Joseph Caro in the sixteenth century.

**Temple:**   a monumental place of public worship, particularly in Jerusalem.

**theocracy:**   rule by God or by the priesthood.

*Tosefta*:   supplements to the *Mishnah.*

**yeshiva:**   advanced Talmudic academy.

*Yishuv*:   the Jewish community in the Land of Israel before 1948.

*zaddik*:   literally, righteous man, in Hasidism; the spiritual leader of the Hasidic community.

**ziggurat/ziqqurrat:**   a stepped Babylonian temple tower, typically in the form of successively smaller trapezoids.

# Index

## A

Aaron, 16, 70
Aaron family, 87, 88
Abbasids, 81, 86
Abd al-Raḥman III, Caliph, 95
Abraham, 10, 11, 12, 82, 106
Abraham Eliezer ha-Levi, 138–39, 142
Abraham of Saragossa, 90
Abravanel, Don Isaac, 122, 127–28
 commentary on Book of Kings, 127
academies of Tiberias, Caesarea, and Sepphoris, 77
Achemenes, 38
Adam, as first civilized man, 7
Adapa, 7
Adler, Felix, 202
*adversos Judaeos* ("testimonies against the Jews"), 68–69, 90
Aelia Capitolina (Jerusalem), 73
Agobard, archbishop of Lyons, 90
Agrippa, Cornelius, 135
Ahab, King, 31
Akiva bar Yosef, 73, 74
Akkad, empire of, 10
al-Andalusi, Said, 94–95
al-Ḥakam, Caliph, 95
Alemanno, Yohanan, 135
Alexander of Macedon, 43–44
Alexander II, Tsar, 182
Alexander III, Tsar, 189
Alexandria, Judaean settlement in, 44, 52, 54–55, 73
Alfasi, Isaac, 99

al-Ḥakim, Caliph, 83
Almohades, 83, 98, 99, 101
Almoravides, 83, 98, 99
alphabet, beginnings of modern, 21
Amalgamated Clothing Workers of America, 206
American Jewish Committee, 209
Ammonites, 23
Amos, 28, 31, 70
amphictyony, 22
Amsterdam: haven for *conversos*, 153, 154
 leading European commercial center, 154, 196
Amulu, 90
Anan ben David, 88
Anatolia (Turkey), 28
Andalusia, 95
Anti-Judaism in medieval northern Europe: Church vilification, 110–111, [aid from apostate Jews, 110–11, 119; discriminatory legislation, 111; special costumes, 111; *Talmud* burnings, 111]
 exclusion from commerce, turn to money-lending, 108–09
 by marauding crusaders, 103–07, [cultural and spiritual loss, 105; massacres and martyrdom, 105, 106–07, 119]
 reduced legal status, 107–08, [in England, 108; in Germany, 107–08]
 religious calumnies, 109–10, [diabolical image, 109–10]

responsibility for, 111–13, [deeper
social strains than merely
religion, 112–13] (see also
anti-Semitism)
Antioch (Syria), 52, 69
anti-Semitism, 185, 217
American variety, 209–10
Dreyfus Affair, 186, 217
in East Central Europe, 221
fighting, 186–89
of Hitler and Nazis, 224, 225–26,
230–32, 233 (see also mass
killings of Jews by Nazis)
opposition pledged by Red Army,
219, [supported by Soviet
government, 219–20]
war-time spread of, 233
in Western Europe, 222–23 (see
also anti-Judaism)
Antoninus Pius, 74
Aphrahat, 69–70
Apocrypha, 45
Aquinas, Thomas, 108
Aragon, 118–20, 121
Aramaic language, 40
Arameans, 16, 19, 25, 29, 39
Arba'ah Turim (Four Columns),
115, 142
Aristotle, 133, 135
ark, of the law, 22, 23
Aryanism, pseudo-science of,
225–26
Ashkenazim: French citizenship
granted as result of Revolution,
167–68
medieval German culture,
105–06, 113
migration of, to U.S., 200–01
self-martyrdom of, during
crusades, 105, 107, 119
spread of, to Eastern Europe, 149
Assembly of Jewish Notables, 170
Assyria, 21, 27–28, 29–30, 37

Augustine, St., 71–72, 90
Austrian Empire, 178, 179
Austria annexed by Germany
(1938), 228
Austria-Hungary, 178

B

ba'alei tosafot, 114–15
Ba'al Shem Tov, Besht (Israel ben
Eliezer), 151
Babel, tower of, 9
Babi Yar, massacre at, 234, 248
Babylonia, 9, 11, 15, 16, 21, 37, 52
capture of, by Hittites, 12
conquered by Persians, 39
Jewish cultural life in, growth of,
78–80
post-Kassite, 25–26
resurgence under
Nebuchadnezzar, 30
under the Seleucids, 44
Babylonian exile, 30, 37–38, 52
end of, 39
Baghdad, 81, 84, 86, 87, 88, 95
Balaam (ben Beor), 19
Balak, of Moab, 19
Balfour Declaration, 218, 244
reversal of, 229
Bar Kokhba, Simon, 73
Barcelona, 111, 118
Basle, Switzerland, 187
Bathsheba, 26, 31
Begin, Menachem, 247
Belgium, 233, 235
Bellow, Saul, 254
Belorussia, 179, 235
Ben-Gurion, David, 243, 246
beraitot, 75
Bernstein, Eduard, 189
Berr, Berr Isaac, 168
Bet Yosef (House of Joseph), 142
Betar, 73
Bialik, Hayyim Nahman, 189

Bible, Hebrew, 39, 74, 133
    correspondence to cuneiform and
        hieroglyphic sources, 7–8,
        10–11, 12, 15
    creation in, 7
    Daniel, 38, 44, 45
    Deuteronomy, 30, 40
    Ecclesiastes, 17
    end of biblical history, 45
    Esther, 41
    Exodus, 14, 15, 16–20
    Genesis, 6, 7–8, 9, 10, 11, 12, 13,
        14
    Greek translation (Septuagint),
        44
    Joshua, 20
    Judges, 21
    Noah and the flood, 8
    passion for monotheism spread to
        world by, 72
    Proverbs, 27
    Rashi's commentary on,
        113–14
    Song of Songs, 27, 117
birkat ha-minim, 67
Black Death, 109, 119
Blois, France, 109
blood libel against Jews, 109
B'nai Jeshurun, synagogue, 200
Boccaccio, 129
Bonaparte, Napoleon, 169–70,
    171
Book of Beliefs and Opinions, The,
    88–89
Book of the Covenant, 18
Book of the Khazars (Sefer
    ha-Kuzari), 99–101
Brahe, Tycho, 140
Bronze Age, 7, 19, 37
    Late, 14
Bruce, Lenny, 254
Buber, Martin, 224, 228
Buddha, 37

Bulgaria, 233, 235
Byzantium, 95


C

Caesarea, 48
Cairo, 141
Caligula, 49
Canaan, 12, 13
    Israelite conquest of, 20–21
Canaanites, 6
Caracalla, emperor, 55
Carchemish, Battle of, 30
Caro, R. Joseph, 141–42, 143
Castile, 118–20, 121
Castro, Isaac Orobio de, 154–55
Catherine the Great, 180–81
Charlemagne, 89
Christian offensives against Islam:
        crusades, 103–07, [cultural and
        spiritual losses of Jews, 105–06;
        dangers to Jews during,
        105–06; Jewish religious
        martyrdom, 106–07]
    in Spain, 98–99, 103
common or Christian era (C.E.),
    45
Christiani, Pablo, 111
Christian-Jewish estrangement,
    64–72
    adversos Judaeos, 68–70,
        [one-sided biblical
        interpretations, 69–70]
    Christianity as official religion of
        Rome, 70–71, [anti-Jewish
        prohibitions, 71]
    as found in Christian Gospels,
        67–68, [beginnings of Church's
        anti-Jewish attitudes, 67–68]
    and Jesus, 64–65
    little bloodshed for first
        millennium C.E., 70

Paul, teachings of, 65–66,
[opposed by rabbinic authority,
66–67]
St. Augustine, views of, 71–72
Christians, 50–51, 64
a separate religion, no longer a
sect, 51
Chrysostom, John, 69, 70, 72
Churchill, Prime Minister, 235
Cincinnati, 202
civilization: beginnings of, 6–8
consolidation of, 8–9
Claudius, emperor, 54, 55
Concerning Jews and Their Lies,
139
confraternities (hevrot), 137
Confucius, 37
Congress of Vienna (1815), 171
Consolation for the Tribulations of
Israel, A, 128, 129
Constantine, emperor, 70
Constantinople, 141
conversos, 120–21, 128, 130, 142,
143, 147
havens from Iberian persecution,
153–54, [other choices than
old-line Judaism, 155; return
to Judaism by, 154–55]
Cordova, 94, 95, 96, 98, 101
Cordovero, R. Moses, 142, 143
Costa, Uriel da, 155
Council of Four Lands, 149, 150
Counter-Reformation, 143
court bankers, 87
covenant, 11, 18
Cracow, 141
creation, 7
crusades, 103–07
cuneiform writings, 6, 7–8, 10–11,
12, 14, 21
Cyprus, 73
Cyrene, 73
Cyrus, 38–39
enlightened policies of, 39

Czechoslovakia, 221, 235, 250–51

D

Damascus, 81, 141
Daniel, 41
Danzig, 230
Darius, King, 41–42
David, 23–25, 26, 27, 29, 30, 31
David ben Zakkai, 88
Dead Sea, 20, 50
Deborah, 21
Decalogue, 18
Delmedigo, Elijah, 135
Denmark, 233, 235
Dialoghi d'amore (Dialogues of
Love), 136
Diaspora, 48, 79
civil rights and citizenship,
problems of, 54–55
clash with Hellenism, 54
distinctive pattern of the, 39
later Babylonian growth and
importance, 78–80
noteworthy communities of
(B.C.E.), 40–41, 52,
[Babylonia, 40, 52; Persia,
40–41; Syene (Egypt), 40]
reasons for growth of, 52
Sephardic, 195
Diaspora nationalism, 188
Disarmament Conference, 228
Disraeli, Benjamin, 173
disruptive forces of late nineteenth
century, 183–91
Alexander II, assassination of,
185, [Jews blamed, with
ensuing pogroms, 185–86]
Dreyfus Affair, 186, 217
fighting anti-Semitism, 186–89,
217, [auto-emancipation, 187;
Jewish Workers' Bund, 188;
national autonomy, enclaves
of, 188; revolutionary parties,

188–89; Zionism and Jewish nationalism, 187–88, 190]
Jews blamed in France and Germany, 183–85, [anti-Semitism, 185, 186; combined with secularized Christian hostility and racism, 184–85; Jewish commitment to liberal politics and parties, 185; turning of socialism against Jews, 185]
Dohm, Wilhelm Christian von, 158
Donin, Nicholas, 110
Donmeh, 148
Dov Baer of Mezeritch, Maggid, 152
Dreyfus, Alfred, 186, 217
Dubnov, Simon, 188
Dutch West India Company, 196

E

Early Dynastic Period (Mesopotamia), 8–9
East Central European Jews between World Wars, problems of, 221–22
Eastern Europe, Jewish life in:
    Cossack massacres (pogroms) in Ukraine and Poland, 147, 150
    decline of, in 17–18 centuries, 150
    Frankist movement in Poland, 148
    Hasidism, 151–53
    Poland-Lithuania, migrations to, 149, [functioning self-governments, 149]
    rabbinical scholarship, heights of, 149–50, [communication with other areas, 150]
    (see also Polish-Lithuanian Commonwealth; Russian Empire)
Eastern European immigrants to

America: Jews and non-Jews, 203
    reasons for migration, 203
    (see also Jewry in America)
Ebreo, Leone (Judah Abravanel), 135–36
Edward the Confessor, Laws of, 108
Egidio of Viterbo, 135
Egypt, 6, 12, 16, 21, 27, 29, 30, 86
    Diaspora community at Syene, 40
    expulsion of Hyksos, and expansion, 14
    invaded by Asiatic peoples, 12–13
    and State of Israel, 255
    Israelite exodus from, 16–17
    Israelite slavery in, 14
    New Kingdom, 14, 15
    origin of kingship in, 22
    Ptolemaic dynasty in, 44, [Judaean settlement in Alexandria, 44]
    Third Intermediate Period, 25
    vanished Jewish refugees in, 38, 40
Eichmann, Adolf, 229
Eldad of "the lost tribe of Dan," 97
Eleazar ben Yair, 59–60
Elijah, 28
Elijah, gaon of Vilna, 152
Elisha, 28
emancipation, Jewish, in West:
    culmination of, 178
    in England, 172–73
    in France, 166–68, 171
    in Germany, 174–77, [conversions and abandonment of Jewish community, 174–75; reconciling Judaism to modern era, 174, 177; Reform Judaism, 175–77]
    in other lands, 169, [rescinded after 1815, 171; struggles to renew, 171–72]
    social and intellectual changes,

173–74, [civil service and liberal professions, entry into, 174]

Emar, 12

England: changed status of Jews in, 108–09
fall of restrictions on Jews, 172–73
as haven for *conversos*, 154
Jewish political participation, 189
no Jews remaining in, 122

Enlightenment, 180, 181, 197
Jewish participation in, 164, 174, 178, 179, 181, 182, 183, 187
tenets of, 164

Enlightenment and modern secularism, inroads of, on traditional Jewish institutions:
definition of a Jew, 164
early encounter in Amsterdam, 153–56, [Spinoza, 155–56, 157]
German *Hofjuden* and financiers, 157, 158
problems concerning, 158–59
views of Locke and Toland in England, 157–58

Essenes, 50, 51

Estonia, 247

Ethical Culture, 202

Exodus, 16–17, 38

Expulsion from Spain, reflections on meaning of, 127–30

Ezekiel, 32, 38

Ezra, 42, 43, 44


F


Ferdinand and Isabella, 120, 121, 122

Ferrara, Italy, 128, 132

Fertile Crescent, 4

Ficino, Marsilio, 134

Figo, Azariah, 133

flood (or Deluge), 8

Florence, 132, 134

France: changed status of Jews in, 108, 109
edicts of universal suffrage (1790–91), 158, 167–68
Jewish political participation, growing, 189
no Jews remaining in, 122
northern, 103, 106
southern, 95, 154

Franco, Francisco, 228

Frank, Jacob, 148, 150, 151

Frankel, Rabbi Zecharias, 177

Frankfurt, 139

Frankists, 148, 150, 151

Frederick II, Holy Roman emperor, 108

French Revolution, 166–71, 180
Jews, emancipation of, 167–69, [early for Sephardim, 167; later for Ashkenazim, 167–68; necessary adjustments, 168–69; in other than France, 169]
Napoleon, rise of, 169–71, [changed relations with Jews, 170; modern Sanhedrin, 170]

Fustat (Old Cairo), Egypt, 84


G


Galicia, 179, 203, 217

Galilee, 45, 74

Gamaliel II, Rabban, 63, 66, 73

Gans, David, 139–40

*gaon* (pl. *geonim*), 86–87

"Garden of Eden," 7

Geiger, Abraham, 176

*Gemara*, 78, 114

*genizah*, 84–86, 87, 141

Gerizim, Mount, 42
rivalry with Jerusalem, 42–43

German pietism (*Ḥasidut Ashkenaz*), 115–16, 118
Germany, 103, 235, 237
  changed status of Jews in, 108, 109
  Jewish emancipation in, 178 (*see also* emancipation, Jewish, in West)
  only small Jewish community remaining in, 122
  post-World War I, 222–23, [excellent status of Jews, 222–24]
  rise of Nazis, 224–25 (*see also* Nazi Germany)
Gerona, 116–17
Gershom ben Judah, Rabbenu, 105
ghettos, 232
Gideon, 21, 22
*goldene medine* (golden land; America), 205
Goshen, land of, 13
Granada, 98, 121
Greece, 235
  conquests of Alexander, 43–44, [subsequent division of his realm, 44]
  similarity of early history to Israel's, 43
  Spanish refugees into Ottoman, 140–41
Gregory the Great, Pope, 90
*Guide of the Perplexed*, 102


H

Habiru (people), 14, 15
Hadadezer, 25
*Hadith*, 82
Hadrian, 73, 78
*Haganah*, 243
Haggai, 32, 41

Haifa, 242
*ḥakham kolel*, 133
*halakhah*, 74, 77, 102
Halifax, Lord, 228
Hamburg, 154
Hammurabi, Laws of, 11, 18
Harran, 12
Harvard College, 197
Hasidism (modern), 151–53
  Ḥabad, 153
Hasmoneans (*see* Maccabees)
Hebrew: as modern literary tongue, 189, 197
  as mother tongue of Land of Israel, 242
Hebrew Union College, 202
Heine, Heinrich, 175, 178
Hellenization, 47
Herod (the Great), 48
*Herut* (Freedom party; Israel), 247
Herzl, Theodor, 187
Hezekiah, King, 29–30
Hieroglyphic writings, 6, 12, 14, 15, 21
Hijaz region, 82
*hijra*, 81
Hillel, rabbi, 63–64
Hillquit, Morris, 206
Hippolytus of Rome, 68–69
Hiram of Tyre, King, 26
Hirsch, Rabbi Samson Raphael, 177, 211
Hitler, Adolf, 224, 225, 234, 235, 243
Hittites, 12
  empire in Turkey, 15, 16
*Hofjuden*, 157, 158
Holocaust, how explain it?, 237 (*see also* mass killings)
Holy Roman Empire, 95
Hungary, 178, 221, 233, 235
Hussein of Jordan, King, 255
Hyksos, 12, 13, 15
Hyrcanus, John, 47

I

ibn Daud, Abraham, 98
ibn Labrat, Dunash, 96
ibn Migash, Joseph, 99
ibn Naghrela, Samuel, 98 (see also
    Samuel ha-Nagid)
ibn Saruk, Menahem, 96, 97
ibn Shaprut, Ḥasdai, 94–98, 100,
    101, 122
ibn Verga, Solomon, 129–30
Idumaea, 45
Industrial Revolution, 165, 174
Inquisition, Spanish, 120–21, 143,
    148
International Ladies' Garment
    Workers Union, 206
interpower relationships B.C.E.,
    15–16, 17
Ionia, 37
Iron Age, 20, 21, 27, 37
Iron Guard, 233
Isaac, 10, 106
Isaiah, 30, 31–32
Isaiah, second, 32, 38
Islam: effects of Judaism on, 82–83
    effects on Jewish life, 82, 83–89
    and Greek thought, 87–88
    rise of, 79, 81
    significance of Hebrew Bible to,
        72
Israel (Jacob), 13
Israel, ancient: emergence as a
        nation, 22
    expansion under David, 23–25
    kingship, beginnings of, 22–25
    kingship experiment, end of, 31
    a major power under Solomon,
        26
    prophets, period of the, 28–29,
        [absorption of Israel by
        Assyria, 29; exile, 29]
    protohistory, 4–13, [Joseph, stor
        of, 12–13; patriarchal period.

10–12; primeval period, 6–10]
    rule of theocracy in, 22–23
    separation from Judah, 27 (see
        also Jewish history, early)
Israel, modern: government by
        coalition of parties, 246–47
    independence declared, 244,
        [Arab invasion and war,
        244–45; partial acquisition of
        Jerusalem, 245; U.S. and
        Soviet recognition, 244, 248]
    maturation of, 254–56, [capture
        of Jerusalem and West Bank,
        255; Six Day War, 255; Suez
        campaign, 255]
    open immigration to all Jews,
        245–46, [absorption, problems
        of, 245–46; Holocaust
        survivors, 245; from Islamic
        countries, 245]
    preindependence population
        growth, 241, [aid in defeat of
        Nazis, 243; independence,
        insistence on, 243; kibbutzim,
        241–42; land improvement,
        242; Yishuv, transformation of,
        242–43]
    retribution payments by West
        Germany, 246
    solidification of identity with,
        worldwide, 256
    United Nations partition of
        Palestine, 244, [Arab
        opposition and departure, 244]
    Zionism, beginnings of, 187–88
Israel under Ottoman Turks,
        Spanish refugees to, 141–42
Israelites, 14–27
    twelve tribes of, 21–22
Isserles, Moses, 150
Italy, 95, 97, 122, 228
    changed status of Jews in, 109
    emancipation of Jews in, 178
    growth of Jewish communities

during Renaissance, 132,
    [cultural exchanges with Jews
    in Turkish empire, 131]
Izmir, 141

J

Jacob, 10, 11, 13
Jacob ben Asher, 115, 142
Jannaeus, Alexander, 47
Japan, 228
Jefferson, Thomas, 198
Jehoiachin, 37, 40
Jehu ("son of Omri"), 28
Jephthah, 21
Jeremiah, 32, 38
Jericho, 20
Jeroboam II, 28
Jerusalem: building of the Temple,
    26
  captured by Babylonia, 30
  conquered by Pompey, 47
  establishment as capital of
    ancient Israel, 23
  partial acquisition by modern
    Israel, 245, [complete
    acquisition, 255]
  reconquered by Titus, 49, 59
  reconstruction of city and
    Temple, 42
  Spanish refugee settlements in,
    141
  spared by Sennacherib, 29
Jerusalem, 158
Jesus, 50–51, 64, 82
Jewish Anti-Fascist Committee,
    248, 249
Jewish civilization in Muslim Spain,
    94–103
  Christian offensive for control,
    beginning of, 98–99, 103,
    [greater hostility to Jews, 99]
  cultural creativity, greatest
    heights of, 99–103,

[controversy between views of
    the two, 103; Judah ha-Levi,
    99–101, 102, 103
  Moses Maimonides, 101–03]
  period of petty kingdoms, 98,
    [Samuel ibn Naghrela
    (ha-Nagid), elitism of, 98]
  shift of cultural dominance from
    Baghdad, 94–95, [a courtier
    class, 96, 97; Ḥasdai ibn
    Shaprut, role of, 94–98;
    literary flowering, 96–97]
Jewish creative abilities, unleashing
    of, throughout Europe, 189
Jewish culture, medieval, 113–18
  kabbalah, 115–18, [German
    pietism, 115–16, 118]
Jewish Daily Forward, 207
Jewish Era of Creation, 45
Jewish expulsions from medieval
    Christian Europe, 122
Jewish history, early: authority and
    oppression in Egypt, 13–15
  Book of the Covenant, 18
  Canaan, conquest of, 20–21
  correspondence with cuneiform
    sources, 7–8, 10–11, 12
  correspondence with hieroglyphic
    sources, 15
  David, rule of, 23–25
  Decalogue and covenant, 18
  a divided monarchy, 27
  divine aid for escape from Egypt,
    16–17
  expansion and reorganization
    under Solomon, 26–27
  Joseph, story of, 12–13
  judges, period of the, 21–22
  kingship, beginning of, 22–25
  movement of Semitic tribes, 6, 8,
    9, 11, 12, 13, 16, 19–20
  origins of, 4–6
  patriarchal period, 10–12
  primeval period, 6–10

prophets, period of the, 28–30,
[absorption of Israel by
Assyria, 29; Babylonian exile,
30; double capture of
Jerusalem, 30; exile to Assyria,
29; religious reforms in Judah,
29–30]
recognition of God, 17, 18
wanderings in the desert, 18–20
Jewish influence on Islam, 82–83
Jewish life, effects of Islam on, 82,
84, 86–89
academic practices, 86–87
commercial revolution, 84, 87
legal and political status, 83–84
Jewish life after Temple's
destruction, 59–64
synagogues, importance of, 63
views of Pharisees, 61–63,
[mizvot, system of, 62;
rabbinic authority, 61–64;
twofold law in Judaism, 61–62]
Yavneh community, 61, 63–64
Jewish life in late sixteenth century,
deterioration of: Church-
instigated in Italy, 136–38
islands of refuge, 139–40
Luther-and-Reformation-instigated
in Germany, 138–39
Jewish Theological Seminary of
America, 208
Jewish War, The, 59
Jewish Workers' Bund (socialist
party), 188, 222
Jewry in America: blend of
Sephardim and Ashkenazim,
196–97
in British colonies, 196, 197–98
from Eastern Europe, 203–08,
[Americanization, problems of,
207–08; big-city dwellers,
primarily, 205; cultural heights
reached by, 206–07;

demographics of, 204; friction
with German-Jewish
establishment, 208; living
conditions, 205; preponderance
of, 204; reasons for migration,
203; socialism and trade
unionism among, 205–06;
specific origins, 203]
German (Ashkenazic) immigration, 200–02, [cross-country
spread, 200–01; famous
families, 202; homogeneity of
total community, 202; regional
coloration, assumption of, 201;
religious fragmentation among,
201–02]
independence, avid supporters of,
198, [emancipation achieved
without legislation, 198]
integral part of American society,
198, [freedom of movement
and organization, 200]
New Amsterdam, 195–96
old and new form united
community, 209–10, [anger at
limitations on immigration,
210; combating anti-Semitism,
209–10; reaction to European
events, 209]
overall betterment after World
War I, 210–12, [economic,
social, cultural transformation,
210–11; an integral part of
American life, 211]
religious tolerance for, 197–98
Jews, relationship of, to major
revolutions of modern life,
163–66
intellectual (Enlightenment),
164
political, 164–65, [question of
citizenship, 165]
social and economic (Industrial

Revolution), 165–66, [competition in trade and commerce, 166; rise of middle class, 166]

Jews, Renaissance, in cultural dialogue in Italy, 130–36

Jews, Spanish, in Christian Spain, 118–22

  decline of community life, 118–19

  expulsion from Spain, 109, 121–22

  Inquisition, 120–21

  mass conversions to Christianity, 119–21

Jonathan, 23

Jordan River, 19, 20

Joseph, 13, 41

  motive and function of story of, 13

Joseph, Jacob, 151

Joseph, king of Khazars, 97

Joseph II of Austria, edict of tolerance of, 158

Josephus, Flavius: *The Jewish War*, 59–60

  writings of, 45

Joshua, 20, 61

Josiah, 30, 40

Judaea (former Judah): given to Ptolemy, 44

  Maccabean empire, 45–47, [conquered by Pompey, 47, 48, 52; fall from power, 47]

  opposition to Seleucids, 44–45, [Hannukkah, origin of, 44–45; Maccabean revolt, 44, 45]

  religious restoration in, 41–42, [cult at Mount Gerizim, rivalry with, 42–43; Judaism, emergence of, 42; true theocracy, 42]

  Roman control of, 48–50, [complete conquest, 49–50; social unrest, 49; under Herod, 48]

Judah (tribe and kingdom), 23, 27, 29–30

  Cyrus's restoration of, 38–39

Judah ha-Levi, 99–101, 102, 103, 128

Judah ha-Nasi, 74, 75, 77, 78

Judah he-Ḥasid (the pious), 115–16

Judah Loew ben Bezalel (Maharal), 140

judges, early Israelite leaders, 21–22

Justinian, 71

  code of, 111

**K**

*kabbalah*, 115–18, 130, 138, 142

  Christian, 134–35, 143

  Lurianic, 143–46, 147, 151

Kafka, Franz, 223–24

*Kalam*, 88, 89, 102

Kalonimides, 115–16

Karaites, 88, 89

*kelippot*, 144, 145, 147, 152

Khazars, 96, 97, 99, 100 (*see also Book of the Khazars*)

Khrushchev, Nikita, 250

*kibbutzim*, 241–42

*Koran*, 82, 83

**L**

labor movement and trade unionism in U.S., 206

Ladino, 173

*landsmanshaft* (mutual-aid) societies, 205, 211

Lao-Tse, 37

Lateran Council, fourth (1215), 111

Latvia, 221, 235, 247
League of Nations, 228
Leghorn, 154
Lenin, Nikolai, 219
Leon, Moses de, 117
Lessing, Gotthold Ephraim, 129, 158
literary prophecy, 31
Lithuania, 148, 150, 179, 217, 221, 234, 235, 247
Locke, John, 157
Lodz, 232
London, Meyer, 205–06
Louis XVI, King, 169, 180
Louis the Pious, 89
Luria, Isaac, 130, 143–46, 151
Luria, Solomon, 150
Luther, Martin, 138–39
  his writings, 138–39
Luxembourg, Rosa, 188–89
Lyra, Nicholas de, 114

**M**

Maccabee, Judah (Judas), 44, 47, 48
Maccabees, 45–47, 48
Magnes, Judah, 209
Maharal, 140
Maimonides, Moses, 101–03, 107, 115, 122, 156
Mainz, 105
Manasseh, 30
Manasseh ben Israel, 155
Mantua, 132, 138
Mari, 11
marranos, 120
Martinus, Raymond, 111
Martov, Julius, 188
Marx, Karl, 178
Masada, 48, 49, 59, 61
mass killings of Jews by Nazis, 233–35

Babi Yar, 234
death camps, 234
the Final Solution, 234–35
the toll, 235 (see also Holocaust)
massacres of Jews: by Cossacks in Ukraine and Poland, 147, 150
by marauding crusaders, 105–07
Matthias (king of Bohemia), 139
Mecca, 81, 82
Medes, 37, 38
Medina, 81, 82
Megiddo, 30
Mein Kampf (My Struggle), 224
Meir, Golda, 249
Meir, rabbi, 74
Memphis (Egypt) captured by Hyksos, 12
Mendelssohn, Felix, 178
Mendelssohn, Moses, 158, 164, 174, 178
Me'or Einayim (Enlightenment to the Eyes), 138
Merneptah, Pharaoh, 20
Mesopotamia, 4, 6, 7, 8, 10, 12, 22, 27, 37, 73
Early Dynastic Period in, 8–9
empires of Akkad and Ur, 10
Messer Leon, Judah, 132–33
Messianism, 41, 128–29, 142–48
paradoxical ideology of Shabbetai Zevi, 146–48
Midreshei Aggadah, 76–77
  Midrash Rabbah (the Great Midrash), 76
Midreshei Halakhah, 75
Mikveh Israel (Philadelphia), synagogue, 196
Mirandola, Giovanni Pico della, 134–35, 136
Miriam, 16
Song of, 17
Mishnah, 74–76, 77, 78, 79, 102, 114
parallel relationship to New

Testament, 75–76
six *sedarim* (orders), 75
*Mishnah Avot*, 61
*Mishneh Torah* (The Repetition
    of the Law; a.k.a. *Yad
    ha-Ḥazakah*, the Strong Hand),
    102
Mitanni kingdom in Syria, 15, 16
Mithridates, Flavius, 135, 136
*mitnagdim*, 152
*mizvot*, system of, 62
Modena, Leone, 133, 137, 138
Molkho, Solomon, 142–43
monotheism: Hebrew Bible's im-
    portance in spreading belief,
    72
  importance of, to rest of world,
    38
  Jewish mission to spread
    teachings, 41
  Jewish recognition and
    acceptance of, 17, 18, 38
  Maccabean preservation of, 47
Montefiore, Moses, 172
Mordecai, 41
Moscato, Judah, 133
Moscow, 180, 234
Moses, 16, 20, 31, 61, 82, 135
  Song of, 17
Moses b. Naḥman, Rabbi
    (Naḥmanides), 111, 116
Moslem Era, 45
motion-picture industry, an
    East-European-Jewish
    creation, 211
Muhammad, 81
Mussolini, Benito, 228
Mutazilites, 88, 89

N

Nabonidus, 38, 39
Naḥmanides, 111, 116

Naram-Sin, 10
*nasi*, 74, 78, 95
Nasser of Egypt, President, 255
Nathan, 31
Nathan of Gaza, 146
Nathan the Babylonian, 86
Navarre, 95
Nazi Germany, 224–35
  anti-Semitism, spread of, to all
    controlled lands, 233
  bans and decrees against Jews,
    225–27, [confiscation of
    property, 227; Nuremburg
    Laws, 226–27; Reich
    Citizenship Law, 227]
  degradation of Polish Jews,
    203–32, [ghettos, 232]
  the end of, 235
  greater terror against Jews,
    228–29, [concentration camps,
    228, 229; emigration
    encouraged, 229; Federal
    Union of Jews in Germany,
    Nazi-controlled, 229;
    *Kristallnacht*, 229; no place for
    Jews to escape, 229]
  mass killings of Jews, 233–35
  Soviet treaty and invasion of
    Poland, 230, [partition of
    Poland, 230]
  surge for European dominance,
    228, [Austria annexed, 228;
    treaties with Poland, Italy,
    Spain, Japan, 228]
  unwillingness of Jews to face
    reality, 227–28
Nebuchadnezzar, 30, 38
Neco, 30
Nehardea, academy at, 79
Nehemiah, 42
*Neḥmad ve Na'im* (Delightful and
    Pleasant), 140
Netherlands, 233, 235
Netira family, 87, 88

New Amsterdam, 195–96
New Testament, 75–76
New World: discovery and
    colonization of, 130
  as haven for *conversos*, 154, 195
New York City: as center of Jewish
    literature and theatre, 206–
    07
  earliest Jews in, 195–96
  East European immigrants to,
    205
  labor movement and trade
    unionism in, 206
  largest Jewish community, 252
  socialist politicians in, 205–06
  twelve Yiddish dailies in, 206
Nicholas II, Tsar, 189, 218
Nimrod, 10
Noah and his sons, 8
*Nofet Zufim* (Book of the
    Honeycomb's Flow), 132–33
Northern Europe, beginnings of
    Jewish settlements in, 89–91
  charters of imperial protection,
    89–90
  general opposition of Church,
    90
  resilience of Judaism in early
    Middle Ages, 91
Norway, 233, 235
Norwich, England, 109
Nuremburg Trials of Nazi war
    criminals, 234
Nuzi, 11


O


Old Babylonian Period, 11–12
  Laws of Hammurabi, 11
Ottoman Empire
  Jewish communities in, 130,
    140–47, [cultural exchanges
    with other areas, 141; Spanish
    refugees, large influx of,
    140–41]
  Jewish decline in, 149


P


Padua, 132
  University of, 138
Pale of Settlement, 180, 182, 189,
    218
Palestine, 19, 54, 73, 187
  Balfour Declaration and, 218
  British inability to handle
    immigration situation, 243–44,
    [matter turned over to United
    Nations, 244]
  growth of Jewish population in,
    241–43
  reversal of Balfour Declaration,
    229
  waning British support for Jewish
    homeland, 221, 222
Paris, 110
Parthians, 45, 73, 78, 79
patriarchal period (biblical), 10–12
Paul IV, Pope, 136, 137
Pella, 64
Pentateuch, 42, 75, 76, 117
Peretz, Y.L., 189
Persian Empire, 38–41, 43
  defeated by Alexander of
    Macedon, 43–44
Persians, 37, 38
Pharisees, 50, 51, 61–63, 76
Philistines, 19, 20, 21, 23, 29
Philo of Alexandria, 44, 54
Phoenicia (Lebanon), 28
Plato, 134, 136
pluralistic democracies needed for
    full Jewish emancipation,
    251
  flourishing of Jews in North
    America, Western Europe,

Latin America, 251–52
pogroms, 147, 150, 185, 190, 203, 217
  Kishinev (1903), 209
  Rumanian, 233
  White Army, 219
Poland, 217, 219, 221, 222, 228, 234, 235, 237, 251
  Cossack massacres in, 147, 150
  emigration to U.S. from, 203
  Frankist movement in, 148, 150
  mass migration to Israel, 245–46
  Nazi invasion of, 230, [ghettos, establishment of, 232; partition between Soviets and Germany, 230, 247; violent anti-Semitism evoked, 230–32] (*see also* Eastern Europe, Jewish life in)
Polish-Lithuanian Commonwealth, partition of, 179–80
Pompey, 47, 48
Portugal, 121–22, 142
  annexation by Spain, 153
  Inquisition in, 153
Positive Historical Judaism, 177
Prado, Juan de, 155
Prague, 139, 141
"Prague Summer" of 1968, 251
*Pravda*, 249
Promised Land, 6, 13, 14, 18, 19, 20
prophets, 28–29, 61
  decline of, 42
  literary prophecy, 31
  poor heed given to, 31–32
  role of, 31–32
Provence, 97, 103
  kabbalists in, 115, 116, 118
Prussia, 178, 179, 230
Ptolemy, 44, 52
*Pugio Fidei* (The Dagger of Faith), 111
Pumbedita, academy of, 79
*purim*, use of, 41

**Q**

Qumran, 50

**R**

rabbinic civilization, emergence of, 73–81
  Babylonia, 78–80
  Judah ha-Nasi, 74, 75, 77, 78
  *Mishnah* redaction, 74–76
  Roman-Jewish tensions relaxed, 73–74
  *Talmud*, Jerusalem or Palestinian, 77–78
Rachel, 13
Radanites, 84, 89
Ramses II, 15
Rashi (*see* Solomon b. Isaac, R.)
Rathenau, Walther, 223
Recife, 195
Reformation, 130, 138
Renaissance, 130, 132–36, 139
*responsa*, 86, 102, 114
Reuchlin, Johannes, 135, 139
Reuveni, David, 142–43
Revolutions of 1848, 171
rhetoric, Jews, and Italian humanism, 132–33
Rhineland, German, 105–06, 113, 228
Romans (Rome), ancient, 45, 47, 48–50
Rome, 132
Roosevelt, President Franklin, 229
Rosenzweig, Franz, 224, 228
Rossi, Azariah dei, 137–38
Rossi, Salomone de', 138
Roth, Phillip, 254
Rothschild, Lionel de, 172
Rudolph II (Bohemia), 139
rulership, concepts of, 22

Rumania, 203, 221, 233, 235, 247
  mass migration to Israel, 245–46
Russian Empire: Alexander II,
    assassination of, 185, [Jews
    blamed, with ensuing
    pogroms, 185–86]
  backward condition of Jews in,
    179–80, [aborted
    modernizations of Alexander
    II, 182; Catherine's efforts for
    betterment, 180; confusion as
    to whether religion or na-
    tionality, 183; government
    intervention into Jewish
    society, 181–82; no
    emancipation, 181; Pale of
    Settlement, 180, 182]
  emigration, Jewish, to Western
    Europe and America, 190,
    203
  further restrictions on Jews,
    189–90
  Jewish search for national
    self-identity, 187, [socialist
    revolution, 188–89; Zionism,
    187–88]
  Jews repressed by military in
    World War I, 217–18
  Revolution of 1905, Jews blamed
    for, 190
  tsar's abdication and end of
    empire, 218
  urbanization, increased Jewish,
    190
Russian Provisional Government,
    218, 219
  Bolshevik takeover, 219, [peace
    treaty with Germany, 219;
    protection of Jews by Red
    Army, 219; Red Army,
    opposition fought by, 219]
  emancipation of Jews by, 218

S

Saadia Gaon, 88–89, 96, 103
Sadducees, 50, 51
Safed, 141
  major religious center in, 141–42,
    143, 145
St. Petersburg, 180
Salonika, 141
Samaria, 28, 29, 42, 45
Samaritans, 42, 43
Samson and Delilah, 21
Samuel, 22–23, 31
Samuel ha-Nagid (Samuel ibn
    Naghrela), 99, 101, 122
Samuel the Small, 66
Sanhedrin, 63, 74, 95
  modern, in France, 170
Sardis, 54
Sassanian Persians, 79
Saul, 23
Science of Judaism, 176, 188
scribes, class of learned, 42
sea-peoples, invasions of, 16
sectarianism, ancient Jewish, 50–52
  democratization of Judaism, 51
Sefer Bahir (Book of Brightness),
    116
Sefer ha-Hasidim (Book of the
    Pious), 116
Sefer ha-Mizvot (Book of
    Commandments), 102
Sefer ha-Zohar (Book of Splendor),
    117
sefirot, 117, 144
Seforim, Mendele Mokher, 189
Seleucid Era, 45
Seleucid Greeks, 44–45
Semites, movements of early, 6, 8,
    9, 11, 12, 13, 16, 19–20
Sennacherib, 29
Sephardic Jews, 167, 195, 196

Severan emperors (Rome), 74
Shabbetai Zevi, 146–48, 151, 155
Shalmaneser III, 28
Shammai, Rabbi, 63
Shearith Israel, synagogue, 200
*Shevet Yehudah* (The Scepter of Judah), 129
*shevirat ha-kelim* (breaking of the vessels), 144–45
Sholem Aleichem, 189
*Shulhan Arukh* (Prepared Table), 142
Sicily, 95
Simeon bar Yohai, Rabbi, 117
Simeon ben Gamaliel, 74
Sinai, Mount, 18, 22, 61
Six Day War, 255–56
sixteenth-century millennial and messianic stirrings, 142–43
  among Christians, 143
  Luria's ideas, 143–46
  Reuveni and Molkho, 142–43
Slansky, Rudolf, 250
socialism: among Jewish immigrants to U.S., 205–06
  and anti-Semitism, 185
  in Russia, 188
Solomon, 25–27
Solomon b. Isaac, R. (Rashi), 106, 113–14
Soviet satellite states, Jewish repressions and anti-Semitism in, 250–51
Soviet Union, 237
  early opposition to anti-Semitism by, 220
  government's apparent role as protector of Jews, 247–48, [Stalin's appointment of Jewish Anti-Fascist Committee, 248]
  increased Jewish population brought by war, 247,
[influence of, on native Jews, 247–48]
  Jewish Autonomous Region designated, 220, 248
  Jewish nationalism and separatism, campaign against, 249, [only relaxed by Stalin's death, 249–50]
  nonaggression pact with Nazis, 230, [partition of Poland, 230; partition of Rumania, 233]
  paradox of Jewish life under Stalin, 220–21
  support for Israel with votes and arms, 248, [not ideological but anti-British, 248]
Spain: Christian, [expulsion of Jews from, 109, 121–22; Inquisition, 120–21; Jewish community life, decline of, 118–19; mass conversions to Christianity, 119–21; renewed *conversos* problem, 153]
  Civil War, 228
  Muslim, 94–103, [breakup into petty kingdoms, 98; Christian offensive for control, 98–99; Jewish civilization and culture in, 94–103; Jewish kabbalists in, 115, 116–17, 118]
Speyer, 105
Spinoza, Barukh, 155–56, 157
Stalin, Josef, 220, 248
  anti-Semitism of, 249
Strauss, Levi, 200
Stuyvesant, Peter, 195–96
Sura, academy of, 79, 86, 88
Susa (Shushan), 41
Sweden, 235
Syene (modern Aswan), 40
synagogues, 50, 63, 196–97, 200
Syria, 21, 25, 28, 44, 52, 54

**T**

*Talmud*, Babylonian, 77, 78, 79, 80
  Rashi's commentary on, 113, 114
*Talmud*, Jerusalem or Palestinian,
  77–78
Tam, Rabbenu, 114
Tel Aviv, 242
Temple in Jerusalem, the, 26, 30,
  50, 73
  completion and dedication of
    new, 42
  destroyed by Titus, 49, 59
  destruction of First (Solomonic),
    30
  rebuilt by Herod, 48
  recapture, cleansing,
    rededication of new, 44, 45
Ten Commandments (*see*
  Decalogue)
ten plagues in Egypt, 16
*That Jesus Christ Was Born a Jew*,
  138–39
Theobald V, count of Blois, 109
Theodosius II, code of, 71, 77,
  111
Tiglath-pileser III, 29
*tikkun* (restoration), 144, 145
Titus, 49
Toland, John, 157
Toledo (Spain), 99, 103
*Torah*, 61, 80, 82, 152
Torquemada, Tomas de, 120
Tortosa, 119–20
*Tosefta*, 75, 77
*Tractatus Theologico-Politicus*,
  155–56
Trajan, emperor, 73
Transjordan, 19–20, 45
Triangle Shirtwaist Company fire,
  206
Trotsky, Leon, 188, 219
Troyes, 106, 113
Truman, President, 235

Turkey, Donmeh movement in, 148
Two Rivers, Valley of the
  (Mesopotamia), 4, 7

**U**

Ukraine, 147, 150, 179, 185, 219,
  234, 235
Umayyad dynasty, 81, 95, 98
Union of American Hebrew
  Congregations, 202
United Nations, 244, 255
United States, center of Jewish
  revival in West, 252
  assimilation a threat to Jewish
    community, 253
  dispersal throughout country,
    252–53
  full integration into all phases of
    life, 252, 253–54
  Israel supported by Jews and
    nonJews alike, 254
  political life, importance to, 254
Ur, empire of, 10, 12
Usha, 74
Usque, Samuel, 128–29, 130, 140

**V**

Venice, 132, 138, 141, 154
Versailles, Treaty of, 221, 224
  German denunciation of, 228
Vespasian, 49
Vienna, 139
Vilna, 150
vineyard, parable of the, 65, 69
Vital, Ḥayyim, 143

**W**

Warsaw, 235
  ghetto, 232, 234

Washington, George, 198
Weimar Republic, Germany, 223–24
Weizmann, Chaim, 244
Western Europe, twentieth-century: excellent status of Jews in, 222, [little concern over anti-Semitism, 222–23; Weimar Republic example of, 223]
  religious and cultural stirrings in Germany, 223–24
  rise of Hitler and Nazi Party, 224–25 (*see also* Nazi Germany)
White Paper, British (May 1939), 243
Wise, Stephen, 209
*Wissenschaft des Judentums* (Science of Judaism), 176, 188
World Jewry, shift of, from Europe after World War II, 237 (*see also* Israel, modern)
World War I, 190
  Jewish participation in national forces, 215–17
Worms, 105, 139

X

Xerxes, 41

Y

Yaffe, Mordecai, 150
Yatrib (Medina), 81, 82
Yavneh, 61, 63–64, 73
Yemen, 82, 103, 245
Yeshiva College (New York), 211
Yiddish, 173, 180, 188, 189, 207
Yiddish theatre in New York, 207
*Yishuv*, 241, 242–43
Yoḥanan ben Zakkai, Rabban, 60, 61, 62, 63, 66, 74, 91
Yugoslavia, 233, 235

Z

*ẓaddik* (righteous one), 152
Zealots, 61, 73
Zechariah, 32, 41
*Ẓemah David* (offspring of David), 140
*ẓimẓum* (contraction), 144
Zionism, 187–88, 190, 223, 245
  contemporary, 241–42
  first Zionist Congress, 187
  growth of, between World Wars, 222
  Soviet Union and, 248–49
Zola, Emile, 186
Zoroaster, 37
  Zoroastrian religion, 79–80
Zunz, Leopold, 176

# Project Funders

Funding for this publication and other college materials created for *Heritage: Civilization and the Jews* was provided by the Charles H. Revson Foundation and the National Endowment for the Humanities. Additional educational funding was provided by The Brookdale Foundation, The Endowment Fund of the Greater Hartford Jewish Foundation, and The Jaffe Foundation.

Funding for the production of *Heritage: Civilization and the Jews* and for related activities was provided by the following generous contributors:

The Charles H. Revson Foundation, Milton Petrie, and the National Endowment for the Humanities.

The Frances and John L. Loeb Foundation, the Bank Leumi le-Israel Group and Israel Discount Bank of New York, the Nate B. and Frances Spingold Foundation, Inc., the Crown Family, and Joseph Meyerhoff.

The Columbia Foundation, the Corporation for Public Broadcasting, The Green Fund, Inc., and the Norman and Rosita Winston Foundation. The Ann L. Bronfman Foundation, Mr. and Mrs. Ludwig Jesselson, Carl Marks and Company, Inc., Public Television Stations, the Billy Rose Foundation, Inc., The Samuel and David Rose Foundation, John M. Schiff, and the Miriam and Ira D. Wallach Foundation. Irwin S. Chanin, Max M. Fisher, William S. and Selma Ellis Fishman, the Morris and Rose Goldman Foundation, Leonard E. Greenberg, The Isermann Family, The Ethel and Phillip M. Klutznick Charitable Trusts, The Louis B. Mayer Foundation, the Samuel I. Newhouse Foundation, Arthur Rubloff, The Swig Foundation, Laurence A. Tisch, and The Weiler-Arnow Family.

Nathan S. Ancell, The Goldstein Family Philanthropic Fund, Integrated Resources, Inc., the Morris L. and Barbara Levinson Philanthropic Fund, the Henry and Lucy Moses Fund, Inc., Louis Rogow,

# About the Authors

*William W. Hallo*, the author of the chapters on the ancient period, is an eminent scholar in the field of ancient Near East history. His area of specialization is Assyriology and he is the curator of the Babylonian Collection at the Sterling Library at Yale University. He graduated from Harvard College with a B.A. and received an M.A. and Ph.D. from the University of Chicago in Near Eastern Languages and Literature. Professor Hallo has written many articles and is the author of a widely used introductory text, *The Ancient Near East: A History.* He has received numerous honors including a Fulbright Fellowship, a Guggenheim Fellowship, and a National Endowment for the Humanities grant.

*David B. Ruderman*, the author of the chapters on the medieval period, is Professor of the History of Judaism, Department of Religious Studies, Yale University. His area of specialization is Italian Jewish history. He received his B.A. from the City College of New York, his M.A. from Columbia, his rabbinic degree from the Hebrew Union College—Jewish Institute of Religion, and his Ph.D. from Hebrew University. Professor Ruderman is the author of *The World of a Renaissance Jew: The Life and Thought of Abraham b. Mordechai Farissol*, for which he received the National Jewish Book Award in History in 1982. He is also the author of many articles and reviews on medieval and early modern Jewish history.

*Michael Stanislawski*, the author of the chapters on the modern period, is Assistant Professor of Jewish History on the Miller Foundation at Columbia University. His area of specialization is East European Jewish history. He received his A.B., A.M., and Ph.D. degrees from Harvard University. Professor Stanislawski is the author of *Tsar Nicholas I and the Jews: The Transformation of Jewish Society in Russia, 1825-1855*, for which he received the national Jewish Book Award in History in 1984. He is also the author of numerous articles on Jewish and Russian history.

*Benjamin R. Gampel*, editor and author of Directions to Students, is a visiting Assistant Professor of Jewish History at the University of Maryland. He has also taught at the Jewish Theological Seminary of America and Rockland Community College. A specialist in medieval Spanish Jewry, he received his doctorate from Columbia University, where he wrote his dissertation entitled *A Medieval Jewry on the Eve of Dissolution: The Last Years of Jewish Life in the Kingdom of Navarre.*